CKL

County Council

941·083

Libraries, books and more . . .

- 8 APR 2014		
1 4 MAY 2014		
- 7 MAY 2014		
2 1 NOV 2014		
- 9 DEC 2014		

Please return/renew this item by the last due date.
Library items may be renewed by phone on
030 33 33 1234 (24 hours) or via our website
www.cumbria.gov.uk/libraries

Cumbria Libraries
CLIC
Interactive Catalogue

Ask for a CLIC password

Peace and War:
Britain in 1914

"YOUR COUNTRY NEEDS **YOU**"

PEACE AND WAR: BRITAIN IN 1914

NIGEL JONES

First published in 2014 by Head of Zeus Ltd

1 3 5 7 9 10 8 6 4 2

A CIP catalogue record for this book is available from the
British Library.

ISBN (HB) 978-1-78185-253-8
ISBN (E) 978-1-78185-258-3

Designed by Nigel Soper

Printed in Italy

Head of Zeus Ltd
Clerkenwell House
45–47 Clerkenwell Green
London EC1R 0HT

www.headofzeus.com

PREVIOUS PAGE:
CALL TO ARMS: H. H.
Kitchener, legendary
soldier turned Secretary of
State for War, as portrayed
in the century's most
famous recruiting poster,
September 1914. Kitchener
saw it would be a long war
requiring millions of men
to fight it.

TO MY DAUGHTER MILENA,
IN HER OWN RIGHT

THERE MAY BE TROUBLES AHEAD: King George V and Queen Mary visiting Ireland, 1911 – the last British monarch to do so until his granddaughter Elizabeth II a century later.

CONTENTS

SITTING COMFORTABLY? Prince Victor Duleep Singh and Mrs Henry Coventry and friends rest during a pheasant shoot at Stonor Park near Henley-on-Thames, November 1911. India's upper crust were welcomed by their English counterparts.

INTRODUCTION

Introduction

W E HAVE LONG SINCE CEASED TO THINK of the Edwardian era –
which most historians now see as being bookended by the death
of Queen Victoria in 1901 and the outbreak of the First World
War in 1914, rather than merely the reign of the eponymous King Edward
himself – as an age of tranquillity, comfort and languid leisure; a period
typified by ladies with parasols in long white muslin skirts, green lawns
under endless summer skies, and chaps in boaters or cricket whites, shooting at nothing more offensive than a passing pheasant.

In his play *Look Back in Anger* (1956) John Osborne sneers at his alter
ego Jimmy Porter's disapproving father-in-law Colonel Redfern as 'one of
those sturdy old plants left over from the Edwardian wilderness who
just can't understand why the sun isn't shining any more'. Grudgingly,
though, he admits that in retrospect the Edwardians had made their world
look 'pretty appealing'. Two decades previously, the historian George
Dangerfield, in his seminal study *The Strange Death of Liberal England*
(1935), had exploded the myth of Edwardian stability and progress, reveal-
ing an England marked by three major upheavals: the rearguard battle
conducted by the Tory party and their Ulster Unionist allies against the
reforms, including Irish Home Rule and a rudimentary welfare state, introduced by Asquith's Liberal government; the struggle for votes for women
led by the Pankhurst family; and the strife and strikes racking industry led
by militant trade unionists. These convulsions had combined in a perfect
storm of unrest which had only been halted by the greater tempest of the
war in 1914.

In this book I have tried to present a picture of the nation as it was
on the eve of war, concentrating on the figures and developments which
historians – aided by the remarkable wisdom of hindsight – have deemed
to be outstanding. Like Dangerfield, I have given due weight to the major
political and social issues of the year – the Ulster crisis, the suffragettes and
the growing fears of European war – but I have also highlighted some of
the undercurrents that, little noticed at the time, have since come to char-
acterize our view of that year from the perspective of the past century. I
have looked in some detail at the artists of the age – the poets, painters and
sculptors – whose self-conscious modernism threatened to blow away the

CRUBBING UP: boys
cleaning coal at
Bargoed, South Wales,
where bitterly fought
strikes and labour disputes
had reached a violent
climax by 1914.

cosy certainties of an era already outmoded before the first guns of August
had spoken and whose work foreshadowed and prophesied the disasters
that lay in wait just around the corner.

What was it really like, the England of 1914? An orderly garden party
about to be interrupted by a devastating thunderclap and cloudburst, or a
seething mass of unresolved conflicts and contradictions racing towards
inevitable destruction? The evidence of cold, hard statistics suggests the
latter. Contrary to the sepia images of lazy country house weekends, out
of a population of just over forty-six million the vast majority of British

people belonged to the impoverished working class, living cheek by jowl in huddled poverty in the cities or eking out a bare existence on the sufferance of their landlords in a countryside where most land was privately owned and jealously guarded.

～

As summer came into full bloom at the beginning of August 1914, the last weekend of the old world was crowded with sporting fixtures. Fashionable race-goers gathered at Goodwood on the Sussex Downs; yachtsmen raced their craft on the Solent in preparation for the Cowes Regatta; at Canterbury and Hove, Kent and Sussex were playing at home.

Watching Sussex play Yorkshire at Sussex's hallowed County Ground in Hove was the future playwright and novelist Patrick Hamilton, whose prep school overlooked the ground. The home side were doing well. The previous day Joe Vine and Vallance Jupp had enjoyed an unbroken second-wicket partnership of 250 runs. Then, just after 3 p.m., the spectators heard the blare of martial music. A file of khaki-clad soldiers appeared, preceded by a marching band. Ignoring the match, the troops strode across the greensward and onto the pitch itself, where they turned and wheeled in formation to the bellowed commands of a regimental sergeant-major. The cricketers stood around gaping, unable to comprehend that the gentle activities of an England at peace were being brutally shoved aside. In his novel *The West Pier* (1952) Hamilton noted:

> This entirely unnecessary, gratuitous and largely bestial assault upon the players (curiously akin in atmosphere to the smashing up of a small store by the henchmen of a gangster) beyond doubt ended in the victory of the aggressor – though at the time of its happening very few people present were able vividly or exactly to understand what was taking place… [We] inhaled unconsciously the distant aroma of universal evil.

As the shadows lengthened across the County Ground and the umpires drew stumps, the crowd making its sheepish way home knew that the party really was over.

HAYMAKING near Ambleside, Westmorland, 1910. But the harvest scene was deceptive: such pastoral peace hid grinding rural poverty and squalor.

1. THE DARKENING SKY

1. The Darkening Sky

ON NEW YEAR'S DAY 1914, the strong man of Britain's Liberal government, Chancellor of the Exchequer David Lloyd George, gave his thoughts on the coming year to the *Daily Chronicle*, a top-selling popular newspaper that was effectively the house organ of Lloyd George's radical wing of Liberalism.

The chancellor's message was soothingly reassuring, his normal tone of aggressive eloquence muffled by the olive branch that he bore in his beak as a dove of peace. Contrary to recent fears, he told his interviewer, the likelihood of conflict in Europe was diminishing, not increasing. Any signs of strain in Anglo-German relations were subsiding 'owing largely to the wise and patient diplomacy of Sir Edward Grey' – an emollient reference to Lloyd George's cabinet colleague, the foreign secretary. Thanks to this new spirit of harmony, the chancellor continued, 'Sanity has been more or less restored on both sides of the North Sea.'

Indeed, the 'Welsh wizard' added, in a bullish swipe at another cabinet rival, the ever-belligerent young First Lord of the Admiralty, Winston Churchill, he was so confident that the year ahead would bring peace rather than war that he would stand fast against Churchill's demand for an increase in the year's naval estimates to keep Britain comfortably ahead in its naval race with Germany. The Kaiser's Germany, forecast the chancellor, was no longer interested in beating Britain at its own naval game, and would concentrate on building up its armies to defend itself against potentially hostile neighbours on its borders rather than on strengthening its High Seas Fleet. 'That is why I feel convinced that, even if Germany had any idea of challenging our supremacy at sea, the exigencies of the military situation must necessarily put it completely out of her head,' concluded the chancellor, complacently adding for good measure: 'Never has the sky been more perfectly blue.'

The peace message was born of wishful thinking (like all chancellors, Lloyd George liked to keep a firm grip on the government's purse strings and was against spending money unless it was absolutely necessary). Holding the lid down on naval expenditure suited his fiscal schemes, as well as dealing a satisfying snub to young Winston. The slightly smug confidence of this New Year interview was widely felt by many other Britons

LLOYD GEORGE AND CHURCHILL on Budget Day, 1910. Rivals and friends in the Liberal cabinet, the Welsh chancellor and his younger colleague would lead their country respectively in the two world wars.

WARLORD: Winston Churchill as First Lord of the Admiralty, 1914. When war came, he at least would be ready for it.

– particularly those who shared Lloyd George's radical views. The socialist journalist H. N. Brailsford, for example, confidently opined:

> In Europe the epoch of conquest is over, and save in the Balkans, and perhaps on the fringes of the Austrian and Russian Empires, it is as certain as anything in politics that the frontiers of our national states are finally drawn. My own belief is that there will be no more wars among the six Great powers.

This faith in peace was often curiously allied, among progressive thinkers, with a fervent admiration for Germany. Ignoring the evident militarist nature of the Wilhelmine empire, along with its obvious ambition to supersede Britain as Europe's premier power, many on the Left looked enviously at the advanced social welfare structures that the Iron Chancellor, Otto von Bismarck, had put in place to appease the growing power of his country's social democratic movement. The rudimentary skeleton of a welfare state – old-age pensions and health insurance – that Lloyd George introduced with his 1909 'People's Budget' had existed in Germany for several decades, and few wished to contemplate the awful possibility that the millions of socialist-minded workers whose toil and sweat had driven Germany to top place among Europe's industrial powers could, with a swift change of uniform, become a conquering horde trampling the continent under their jackboots. Another Liberal minister, the Lord President of the Council John Morley – the embodiment of Gladstonian rectitude – even called Germany the 'high-minded, benign and virile guardian of Europe's peace'.

THE PROPHECY OF POETS

If politicians were happy to bask in the warm glow of contentment generated by their own complacency, it was left to poets – those unacknowledged legislators of the world, as Shelley had called them – to pick up the more disturbing vibrations of the prevailing *Zeitgeist*. In Russia the great poet Aleksandr Blok told his readers prophetically, 'If you only knew the darkness that is to come', while in Germany the young Expressionist Georg Heym, who would fall through the ice of Berlin's Havel River to drown before his dark prophecies became grim reality, described a hallucinogenic vision in his poem 'The War':

> Tower-like he crushes the embers' dying gleams,
> And where day is fleeting fills with blood the streams,
> Countless the corpses swept into the reeds,
> Covered with white feathers, where the vulture feeds.

More pragmatically, another young poet, the handsome and well-connected Englishman Rupert Brooke, gave a newspaper interview, while on a world tour, that was considerably less optimistic than Lloyd George's fatuous Panglossian fluff. Under the headline 'General European War is Opinion of Political Writer from Great Britain', Canada's *Calgary News Telegram* reported that Brooke predicted the imminent outbreak of a global 'struggle in which practically every country will participate'; the paper then added that Britain needed to build more and still more of Brooke's friend Churchill's Dreadnought battleships to counter the German threat. Unlike the politicians, more sensitive souls were clearly tapping into waves from the future – waves as yet unseen but deeply felt nevertheless.

Back in London, a rather different sort of poet, Osbert Sitwell, an aesthetic young aristocrat, had recently joined the elite Grenadier Guards, stationed at the Tower of London. In his autobiography *Great Morning*, Sitwell recalled how his brother officers in 1914 – amidst their routine round of humdrum duties interspersed with pleasurable nights at the music halls and West End clubs – were wont to consult a palm-reader so fashionable that even Winston Churchill was reputed to use her services:

> My friends, of course, used to visit her in the hope of being told
> that their love affairs would prosper, when they would marry, or
> the directions in which their later careers would develop. In each
> instance, it appears, the cheiromant [palmist] had just begun to read
> their fortunes, when, in sudden bewilderment, she had thrown the
> outstretched hand from her, crying 'I don't understand it! It's the
> same thing again! After two or three months, the line of life stops
> short, and I can read nothing…' To each individual to whom it was
> said, this seemed merely an excuse she had improvised for her failure:
> but when I was told by four or five persons of the same experience, I
> wondered what it could portend…

'Beneath it all,' wrote a later poet, Philip Larkin, 'the desire for oblivion runs.' In 1916, under the influence of the war, the father of psychoanalysis Sigmund Freud would postulate the idea of the 'death instinct' – the notion that, parallel to our appetite for life, a darker stream shadows us always, tending towards our extinction. It seems clear that, beneath the evident bursting energy of the Edwardian world with its inventiveness, passion for new technology and forward-looking thought, other powerful forces were stirring in the subterranean collective unconscious – a force resembling a gigantic blind mole fumbling towards the surface, tunnelling its way beneath the smooth lawns of tranquillity.

The writer J. B. Priestley has described how he spent the first seven months of 1914 'running at a standstill' – on the surface engaged in a frenetic round of activity, yet accomplishing very little. It was as if he – and with him the whole nation – were waiting for something, anything, to happen. 'Historic rationality cannot reach it,' mused Priestley:

> We can of course point out – and it is wise to do so – that the very
> things that were supposed to preserve peace did in fact greatly help
> to end it. Thus the great powers… were prepared for war, whereas
> if they had all been unprepared for war there would not have been

one. Again, the very system of alliances, interlocking for better protection, pulled one country after another into war: the powers were like mountaineers roped together but with the rope itself nowhere securely fastened above or below them. Even so, and at the risk of offending every historian, I believe it is useless examining and brooding over every document, telegram, mobilisation order, putting the blame first on one foreign office, then on another. If the war had not arrived one way, it would have arrived some other way. What was certain was its arrival.

EUROPE TAKES SIDES

According to the popular image, the crisis touched off by the shots at Sarajevo that culminated in the Great War arrived out of Lloyd George's 'perfectly blue' sky, unexpectedly and savagely interrupting the sedate concert of European nations with the force of a cloudburst ruining a summer garden party. The image is false. It may not have been conscious of the fact, but Europe had been gearing up for war for more than a decade. In April 1914 Britain and France were celebrating ten years of the Entente Cordiale, the informal agreement that had ended almost a millennium of hostility and intermittent but fairly regular warfare between the two neighbours.

Officially merely a tidying-up of colonial rivalries and disputes between the British and French empires, in Egypt, Morocco and elsewhere in Africa, the Entente in fact marked the end of almost a century of 'splendid isolation' in which Britain had held herself loftily aloof from European affairs. Ever since finally trouncing Napoleon at Waterloo in 1815, Britain had steered clear of continental involvement. Mistress of the greatest empire the world had ever seen, ruling dominions covering a quarter of the globe's surface on which the sun never set, Britain smugly sat behind the steel castles of her navy – easily the strongest fleet in the world – and gazed down condescendingly upon the quarrels of 'lesser breeds without the Law', as the bard of empire, Rudyard Kipling, had called them.

Kipling, in fact, was far from the unthinking jingo imperialist he is often portrayed as being. In 'Recessional' (the poem in which he refers to the 'lesser breeds') he issued a stark warning against imperial hubris, cautioning that Britain's empire – for all her 'Dominion over palm and pine' – was doomed, like those of the ancient world, to crumble into dust. 'Recessional' was written in 1897, after Kipling had seen Queen Victoria's Diamond Jubilee review of the fleet at Spithead and watched with pride as no fewer than 195 grim, grey warships had steamed by. But, despite being hugely

THE FLEET LIT UP: Britain's sea power illuminated at George V's coronation review, June 1911. Two years later England expected another Trafalgar, but didn't get it.

impressed by this stupendous display of power, Kipling had foreseen the certainty of imperial overstretch and decline:

> Far-called, our Navies melt away;
> On dune and headland sinks the fire:
> Lo, all our pomp of yesterday
> Is one with Nineveh and Tyre!

As late as the 1860s, Britain's prime minister, Lord Palmerston, had still been building forts along her southern coastline to repel the threat of a

cross-Channel invasion by another Bonaparte emperor, Napoleon III. But in the early years of the new century – perhaps taking Kipling's warnings on board – Britain's post-Victorian rulers had initiated overtures to the old enemy, France. However, when the brash new kid on the European block, Bismarck's Germany, had contemptuously smashed France's armies in the 1870–1 Franco-Prussian War, proclaiming a new German empire in that holy of holies, the Palace of Versailles itself, the news came as a cold douche of realism for Britain: a wake-up call to look to her defences anew.

With the benign approval of Victoria's son Edward VII – a frequent visitor to belle époque Paris, with his own louche reasons for wanting good relations with France – diplomats cautiously extended the hand of amity across the Channel. The result was the eventual signing of the Entente, followed by a similar understanding with Germany's other principal potential enemy, Russia. Thus, by the end of the twentieth century's first decade, Europe was divided into two armed camps: the Triple Entente of France, Russia and Britain; and the Central Powers of Germany, Austria-Hungary and Italy (though when push came to shove, Italy would throw in her lot with the Entente, to be replaced as a German ally by Turkey).

The Entente, however, was still an informal and loose alliance. Britain continued to rely on its navy as its main weapon to maintain its global empire and protect it from invasion, while its small army acted as a gendarmerie policing the far-flung empire. Almost alone among European nations, Britain scorned to conscript its youth into the army. The same game spirit of amateurism which still dominated its cricket and football teams pervaded its military thinking too. But events in Europe were exercising a magnetic force, pulling Britain along in their wake. Just as far-sighted diplomats awoke to the German threat and made their dispositions with France accordingly, so too did two able and clear-thinking men: one a politician, the other a general.

Richard Burdon Haldane was a ponderous, portly Scottish lawyer whose agile brain belied his elephantine appearance. As secretary of state for war in the multi-talented cabinet of giants that was the 1906–14 Liberal government, Haldane pushed through a thorough-going reform of the army that gave Britain at least the nucleus of a modern, professional fighting force. In 1907–8 Haldane had created the Territorial Army out of the hodge-podge of militia, volunteer and yeomanry units that had formed the army's reserve since the Napoleonic Wars. The Territorials would learn the soldiering trade at weekend and summer camps.

Haldane, like so many progressives, was a passionate admirer of things Teutonic. (He translated the words of the gloomy German philosopher Schopenhauer, and even described a German philosophy seminar as 'My spiritual home'.)

But notwithstanding his open sympathies – which would cost him his cabinet job when a hysterical anti-German press campaign drove him from office after the war began – Haldane was a clear-eyed realist who knew that if war came, it would be with his beloved Germany. His Territorials were a first tentative step towards girding Britain for an all-encompassing industrial conflict like none she had seen before.

Despite his unsoldierly appearance and the military top brass's cheerful contempt for the 'Frocks', as they called frock-coated politicians, Haldane worked well with soldiers – especially with his fellow Scot, Douglas Haig, the future commander of the British Army in the war, and with the unlikely figure of Sir Henry Wilson, the gangling, arrogant Irish Unionist who was appointed Director of Military Operations at the War Office in 1910. Wilson's unprepossessing appearance – not helped by a facial scar that made him reputedly 'the ugliest man in the Army' – concealed a shrewd mind and unmatched skills as a backstairs intriguer. Informal 'conversations' between the British and French military high commands had been underway since December 1905, shortly after the Entente had come into force. A fervent Francophile, Wilson was determined to upgrade these casual chats into a proper, full-blown military co-operation.

Even more sure than Haldane that a war with Germany was inevitable, Wilson was equally certain where the coming conflict would be fought: on the rolling downs and among the slagheap-strewn coalfields of north-eastern France, and on the flat, featureless polders of Belgian Flanders. To spy out the lie of the land, the incongruous figure of the lanky, snaggle-toothed soldier could often be seen, in the years before 1914, laboriously pedalling a bicycle around the future battlefields. So sure was Wilson that war was coming that he devised a plan to move an army of four divisions, called the British Expeditionary Force (BEF), across the Channel in double-quick time as soon as war was declared, or even looked likely.

The French warmly welcomed the plan for the deployment of what they called 'L'Armée Wilson'. The French commander, General Joseph Joffre, laid his war plans for resisting a German invasion on the assumption that a strong British force would be deployed on his left wing, guarding the Channel ports. To quell French fears that the BEF would be far too weak to stand up to a German juggernaut numbering nearly a million, Wilson declared that the fighting quality of his troops, with their special skill at rapid musketry, would more than make up for their inferiority in numbers.

If the French were well aware of Wilson's plans to back them up to the hilt in the coming war, his political masters were not so well-informed. A convinced Conservative politically, Wilson despised the Liberal cabinet as 'dirty, ignorant curs', told them as little about his plans as he possibly could, and did what he could to obfuscate and conceal his real bellicose intentions. Only a semi-secret civil-military committee, the Committee of Imperial Defence (CID), containing a small core of select ministers, was vouchsafed a hint of the extent of the planned British deployment in France in the event of war. As a result, as the true scale of Britain's commitment to France became clear when the crisis broke in 1914, it came as a rude shock to the more pacifist or neutral-minded Liberals.

Britain's maritime dominance, unchallenged since Trafalgar a decade before Waterloo, was also threatened by a resurgent Germany. In 1907, the year that Haldane proposed his Territorial Army, at least partly in response to Germany's growing military might, Berlin's naval supremo, the fierce, fork-bearded Grand Admiral Alfred von Tirpitz, had created the High Seas Fleet, a modern force specifically designed to menace the Royal Navy in her own back waters: the North Sea.

Tirpitz was realistic enough to know that his fleet, however powerful, was unlikely to be able to inflict a decisive Trafalgar-style defeat on the all-powerful Royal Navy in its own home waters. However, the existence of the High Seas Fleet, his 'risk strategy' postulated, would compel Britain to keep the bulk of its navy on guard in the North Sea in case of a German sortie and would thus make it impossible to hold the sea lanes to the empire open and safe.

Britain, too, had its own belligerent Tirpitz in the fantastical figure of Admiral 'Jacky' Fisher, an ageing, contradictory naval supremo, still fizzing with energy and exuberant ideas and schemes as he entered his seventies, whose sardonic, impassively oriental features barely betrayed the throbbing dynamo within. It was Fisher who, as First Sea Lord, had junked as so much useless scrap many of the ships that had so awed Kipling at the 1897 Spithead review. Utterly unsentimental and as ruthless with ships as he was with men, Fisher had derided the ageing Victorian battle fleet as 'too weak to fight and too slow to run'. In their place he had introduced in 1906 the Dreadnought – a new class of battleship that packed a knockout punch with ten twelve-inch guns hurling their shells across eight miles of ocean, and which ran on oil rather than coal, unlike the warships of yesteryear. To back up his Dreadnoughts, Fisher introduced another new ship – the battle-cruiser, which gained in speed what it lost in defence. Its thin armour would prove an Achilles heel in the ultimate test of war at Jutland in 1916.

Fisher, like Lloyd George and his young political boss at the Admiralty, Churchill, was a human whirlwind who rightly described himself as 'ruthless, relentless and remorseless'. Not caring who he annoyed and alienated, he was an arch-modernizer who advocated inflicting a 'Copenhagen' on the High Seas Fleet: a pre-emptive knockout, in the manner of his hero Nelson, to blow the Germans out of the water without the formality of a declaration of war. Lacking the fourth 'R' in Fisher's lexicon – recklessness – the government preferred the more cautious, and more expensive, method of simply keeping ahead of the Germans in the great naval race. Pledged to maintain a superiority of at least two to one in warships, and supported by public opinion that was intensely patriotic and naval-minded,

MEN OF WAR: General Sir Henry Wilson (left) with French friends General Ferdinand Foch (centre) and Colonel Victor Huguet, the French military attaché in London, in 1914. Wilson did more than anyone to bring Britain into the war on France's side.

even the Liberals, with Lloyd George's increasingly expensive welfare bill to meet, kept comfortably but not ridiculously ahead in the race.

Nonetheless, suspicion of Germany and her future intentions remained intense, sometimes shading into outright paranoia. One manifestation of such fears was the genre of 'invasion literature' in popular print; another was the equally widespread terror of enemy espionage amounting to a veritable spy fever.

IMAGINED INVADERS AND ENEMIES WITHIN

Invasion literature had come into being as far back as 1871 with the publication of *The Battle of Dorking*, initially as a serial in the popular *Blackwood's Magazine* and subsequently as a novel. Strangely, the author was a serving soldier, Colonel (later Sir George) Chesney, who would end his days a general and Conservative MP for Oxford. Impressed, and not a little frightened, by the speed and overwhelming power of the German conquest of France in the recently concluded Franco-Prussian War (the conquest lasted a matter of weeks), in response Chesney had penned at lightning speed a futuristic fantasy in which he envisaged an enemy power – never named but quite clearly Germany – crushing Britain with the same cruel thoroughness.

In Chesney's tale, Britain is rendered defenceless by a mysterious, if convenient, wonder weapon which eliminates most of the Royal Navy at a stroke before an invading army from the region of the Netherlands lands on the Essex coast. The British Army, weakened by short-sighted government cuts and absent in India and Ireland, hastily cobbles together a defence with a mixed bag of enthusiastic but poorly trained amateur volunteers. This scratch force is cut to pieces by the invader in a great battle around Dorking in the Surrey hills, and a conquered England is turned into a vassal state of Prussia, and her empire dismembered.

Chesney was a gifted writer, and his story was given extra veracity by being told through the words of a veteran volunteer, looking sadly back on the years of great defeat that followed. The story struck a disturbing chord with the public, not only in Britain but across Europe, where *The Battle of Dorking* swiftly appeared in translations and inspired many imitative works – notably in France, where a thirst for '*revanche*' for the defeat of 1871 was a dominant theme. Even in Germany, Admiral Tirpitz used an alarmist nationalist novel *Wehrlos zur See* ('Defenceless at Sea', 1900) by a patriot called Gustav Erdmann, which warned of the dire consequences of naval defeat, as propaganda to boost his campaign to build the High Seas Fleet. In the three decades following *The Battle of Dorking*'s phenomenal

SEA LION: aggressive, opinionated and visionary, as First Sea Lord Admiral 'Jacky' Fisher modernized the Royal Navy with his Dreadnought battleships. But when war came he was past his peak and fell out with Churchill.

Castle of Steel: the original
HMS *Dreadnought* launched
in 1906. This class of fast, oil-
fired battleships began a new
naval era. But Germany was in
the race, too – and coming up
fast on the inside track.

publishing success, a whole genre of invasion literature sprang up across the continent – it is estimated that some 400 such titles appeared – proving that fears about future wars and invasions were by no means confined to Britain.

But it was in Britain that the far-seeing young novelist H. G. Wells, a writer who utilized the huge strides in science and technology of the late Victorian age to fuel his imaginative fiction, took the genre to an entirely new plane when he postulated an invasion, not by Germans or any other earthly enemies, but from outer space. In *The War of the Worlds* (1898) Wells describes an attack by Martians equipped with a fearsome array of hi-tech weaponry – including heat rays and chemical weapons – as yet undreamed-of by earthlings. Once again, as with *The Battle of Dorking*, much of the action takes place in Surrey, capital of the London commuter belt, and battles are fought around Woking, home of the novel's narrator. And again, as in the earlier story, the inter-terrestrial war ends with a complete victory of the invader and Martian rule over the earth.

More earth-bound than Wells, though his fantasies had a Walter Mittyish character, was the journalist and prolific popular novelist William Le Queux – he churned out more than 150 novels. Half-French himself, Le Queux perhaps had a particular animus against the Germans, but his first effort in the invasion literature genre, written when colonial tensions between Britain and France were high, foresaw a coming war with France. In *The Great War in England in 1897* (1894), Germany actually comes to Britain's rescue, joining her in a victorious alliance against Russia and France.

By 1906, with the Entente Cordiale firmly in place, the ever flexible Le Queux had changed his literary tune. In *The Invasion of 1910* Le Queux foretells a full-blown invasion of England by Germany across the North Sea. Written in co-operation with – indeed, under the instructions of – Lord Northcliffe, founder and owner of the *Daily Mail*, the best-selling popular newspaper that had revolutionized the reading habits of the country on its foundation in 1896, the path of Le Queux's invaders followed no known plan of military strategy, but was dictated by the needs of the

THE INVASION OF 1910.

WITH A FULL ACCOUNT OF THE SIEGE OF LONDON.

WHAT LORD ROBERTS SAYS TO YOU:

Speaking in the House of Lords on the 10th July, 1905, I said: "It is to the people of the country I appeal to take up the question of the Army in a sensible, practical manner. For the sake of all they hold dear, let them bring home to themselves what would be the condition of Great Britain if it were to lose its wealth, its power, its position."

The catastrophe that may happen if we still remain in our present state of unpreparedness is vividly and forcibly illustrated in Mr. Le Queux's new book, which I recommend to the perusal of everyone who has the welfare of the British Empire at heart.—ROBERTS, F.M.

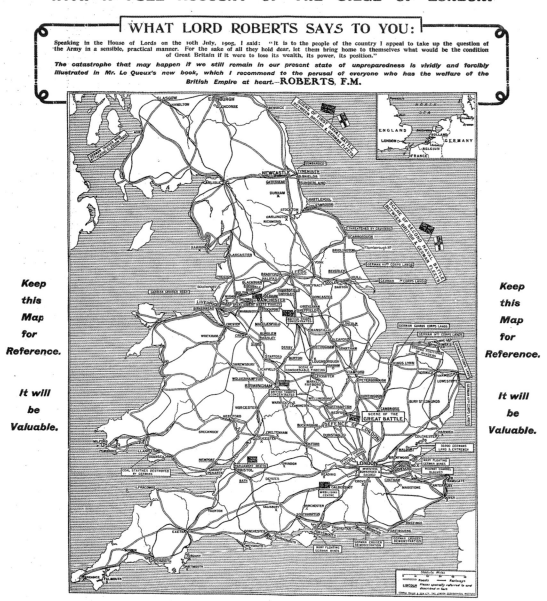

Keep this Map for Reference.

It will be Valuable.

Keep this Map for Reference.

It will be Valuable.

This Intensely Interesting Narrative by Mr. Wm. Le Queux begins in the

LONDON "DAILY MAIL" TO-MORROW.

ORDER THE "DAILY MAIL" TO-DAY.   ORDER THE "DAILY MAIL" TO-DAY.

Mail's circulation department, who made sure that large towns where the paper's circulation required a boost lay directly in the path of the meandering invaders: they travelled to London via destinations as far-flung as Chelmsford, Royston and Sheffield, before finally fetching up at the capital, where the book culminated in a horrific siege of London that recalled the real-life German investment of Paris in 1871.

Serialized in the *Mail* and backed by Britain's aged military hero Lord Roberts of Kandahar, as part of his National Service League's campaign for conscription, Le Queux's fantasy – which sold an extraordinary one million copies – served the triple purpose of increasing the *Mail's* already healthy circulation, deliciously terrifying its readers, and putting them in a lather about the presence of German spies in their midst. At the same time it exerted pressure on a reluctant new Liberal government to increase spending on the army – and especially on the navy.

Three years before Le Queux's *Invasion of 1910*, a work of infinitely superior literary merit – indeed, the only example of invasion literature that still finds readers today – appeared. *The Riddle of the Sands* (1903) by Erskine Childers was specifically aimed at arousing an apathetic public to what the author saw as the very real danger of a German seaborne invasion. An intense, tortured Anglo-Irishman, Childers – like his compatriot and contemporary Roger Casement – would eventually change from being an eager servant of the British empire to a bitter opponent of it in the cause of Irish republicanism. Also like Casement, Childers would be executed for his pains. However, in Childers's case, his executioners would not be England's hangman, but his fellow Irish republicans, who never fully trusted this once faithful servant of the empire.

Childers was a keen amateur yachtsman who spent all his spare time on leave from his job as a House of Commons clerk sailing not only in Britain's home waters but also around the treacherous, mist-shrouded islands and sandbanks off the north German coast where he set his enthralling yarn. The *Riddle* is often regarded as the first modern spy story, but it is also a hymn to the Edwardian Englishman's love of messing about in boats. In the book Carruthers, a stuffy Foreign Office box-wallah, and his rough-hewn yachtsman chum Davies stumble on and foil a dastardly German plan – aided and abetted by Dollmann, an English traitor – to transport an army across the sea to the Norfolk Wash.

In the years that followed, the drizzle of invasion books became a blizzard, with titles such as *When the Eagle Flies Seaward*, *The Death Trap* and *The Message* (all 1907). Allied to the same basic scenario – a German invasion and conquest of a complacent England – was the increasingly

CHRONICLE OF DEATHS FORETOLD: *The Times* promotes one of the many alarmist dystopian novels of the era foretelling war and a future invasion of an unprepared England. A self-fulfilling prophecy?

explicit message that such an invasion would be carried out, or at least aided and abetted, by a 'secret army' of Germans already resident in Britain. There were, in fact, plenty of Germans living in Britain, whose numbers fuelled the flames that were being eagerly fanned by the invasion literature. Although most of the panic surrounding 'alien' settlement in the nineteenth century had focused on Jewish immigrants from the Russian empire who had settled in large numbers in London's impoverished East End, a survey in 1911 revealed that there were more than 53,000 Germans living in Britain, mostly in the capital. (This was the year that Winston Churchill took personal charge of the Siege of Sidney Street, a shoot-out in the East End between the army and police and a cornered group of immigrant Russian anarchists.)

Like many migrants, their main motivation was economic – German waiters and barbers were particularly prominent – but there was among the genuine refugees a smattering of professional spies and secret agents: the paranoia stoked by the press and the invasion novels had a small kernel of truth. Gradually, as time went by, the invasion literature began to focus on the 'enemy within' who would betray Britain and lay the country open to the marauding invader. In Walter Wood's *The Enemy In Our Midst* (1906) a secret council of Germans meets in London to plot a takeover, while Captain H. Curties's *When England Slept* (1909) portrayed a hidden army of Germans fiendishly infiltrating England in disguise. The indefatigable Le Queux muscled in on the trend with *Spies of the Kaiser* (1909) in which he made his many readers' flesh creep with a vision of a nation honeycombed with German spies living incognito among their English neighbours.

In the same year, the peak of invasion literature, the invasion theme was adapted for the stage when Guy du Maurier's melodrama *An Englishman's Home* became a West End hit. Pseudonymously written by 'A Patriot', du Maurier's play depicted an 'ordinary Englishman' shooting dead a foreign – and clearly German – officer who had dared to violate his home and being executed by the occupiers as a result. Ironically, du Maurier, scion of a famous literary and theatrical family, would die in the Great War.

The same fate would befall another prophet of German invasion, H. H. Munro, who wrote under the pen name 'Saki'. This sardonic satirist of Edwardian manners and morals penned a bitter warning – *When William Came: A Story of London under the Hohenzollerns* – in 1913, when invasion literature had apparently passed its peak. The novel's hero, Murray Yeovil, like Saki himself, returns from the colonies to find a strangely changed England. Conquered by Wilhelm II's Germany, the country has been deserted by the British royal family and most of the ruling class, who have decamped to Delhi, leaving a new class of collaborators to rule as obedient slaves of the Germans. Continental cafés line Regentstrasse and a sort of soft power keeps an obedient populace quiescent under their new masters. In an eerie way, Saki's fiction foretells the reality of German occupation of France and French collaboration with the conquerors during the Second World War – a conflict he would not live to see. Saki famously died on the Somme in 1916, killed by a sniper after urgently hissing to a comrade – too late – 'Put that bloody cigarette out!'

Warnings about future wars were not entirely confined to the shock fiction and drama of invasion literature, however. One of the most influential books of the pre-war period was a tract for the times, *The Great Illusion,* written in 1909 by Norman Angell, a radical Liberal journalist (later, with the decline of Liberalism, Angell, like Haldane, would become a Labour supporter). Angell wrote at a rather more elevated intellectual level than his fellow Northcliffe scribe Le Queux (Angell edited the European edition of the *Daily Mail*). His book was superficially a rationalist, pacifist plea that in an increasingly interlocking world, war no longer made economic – or any other sort of – sense. It was, argued Angell, ruinously expensive, never paid for itself, and in the end was as bad for the interests of the 'victors' as it was for those of the vanquished.

Beneath the high-flown prose, Angell's book, as well as being a high-minded protest against Europe's gathering militarist clouds, was also a plaintive plea to the powers in Berlin from a British imperialist scared stiff by ever-increasing German economic clout and sabre-rattling. Influenced by the prevailing invasion literature and spy mania that he could read in his own newspaper, Angell was attempting to persuade Germany that, even if it succeeded, invasion and conquest of Britain would merely result in mass impoverishment and starvation, as would any attempt to dismember the British empire – which was a force for stability and prosperity in the world. Essentially, Angell's argument is a plea for the status quo, and an attempt to deflect Germany's *Griff nach der Weltmacht* ('grab for world power') by the force of sweet reason. Addressed from a power already in decline to one all too obviously on the rise, it was doomed to failure.

SPY FEVER: THE BIRTH OF THE SECRET SERVICE

By 1909, the year that Curties and Le Queux published their lurid espionage warnings, the government – admittedly sluggishly and with laughably few resources – stirred itself to respond to the danger their novels had highlighted. That year saw the birth of the modern British intelligence community. Britain had always had an informal secret service, which tended to wake from long periods of torpor at times of national emergency when the threat of invasion was high: under Elizabeth I's spymaster Francis Walsingham; under the spy chief of Cromwell's Commonwealth, John Thurloe; and during the Napoleonic Wars. But in the Victorian age, when Britain's naval supremacy and empire meant that it felt secure from foreign attack, intelligence efforts were concentrated on the ever-active eruptions of Irish nationalism, combating which was left largely to the Metropolitan Police and its Special Branch, founded in the 1880s. In the empire, military intelligence concentrated on playing what Kipling, in his novel *Kim*, called the 'Great Game' – a power play to frustrate imperial Russia's designs against India, the jewel in the British empire's crown.

In 1903, in the wake of the less than brilliant conduct of the Boer War in South Africa, a Royal Commission of Inquiry had concluded that military intelligence had been undermanned and underfunded. In response, the War Office had bestirred itself to set up two new departments: MO2, to look after foreign intelligence; and MO3, to keep an eye on domestic affairs – and specifically to counter foreign espionage. These two tiny outfits were the direct ancestors of today's secret intelligence and security services, MI6/SIS and MI5. A Special Branch detective, William Melville, who had proved very effective in countering Irish Fenian terrorists, was brought in to serve both departments – an indication of their tiny size.

Melville was the mainstay of the secret service until the formal foundation of MI5 and MI6 in 1909. At first he directed his energies at the menace posed by Russian revolutionaries living in London and even co-operated with his German opposite number – Gustav Steinhauer, the Kaiser's combined personal bodyguard and secret service chief – against the Russians. By 1909, however, Melville's active mind was chiefly focused on Germany, whither – espionage being a two-way street – he had despatched his deputy, Herbert Dale Long, on a spying mission as early as 1904.

There is no doubt that the craze for invasion literature, merging into a panic about German spies roaming every street and dockyard, was the chief spur behind the creation of a more professional intelligence apparatus than Melville could muster. It came about despite the fact that the invasion scare had been discounted in 1908 by a high-powered special subcommittee of the Committee for Imperial Defence set up to consider the alleged threat. The committee was chaired by the prime minister, Herbert Asquith, and attended by his top cabinet colleagues and the armed service chiefs. After no fewer than sixteen meetings spread over a year, the committee pronounced a surprise invasion an impossibility. But, despite their reassuring conclusion, public alarm refused to be assuaged.

PRESS LORD: the influential newspapers of Alfred Charles William Harmsworth, 1st Viscount Northcliffe, including the Establishment *Times* and the populist *Daily Mail*, shaped and articulated the hopes and fears of the elite and the masses alike.

With Northcliffe – who now owned that voice of the Establishment, *The Times*, as well as the *Daily Mail* – whipping it along, and vociferously backed by the Tory opposition, public opinion settled on a demand for the immediate building of eight new Dreadnought battleships – two more than the Admiralty itself were asking for. 'We want eight and we won't wait!' ran the slogan. Faced with such a patriotic campaign, the Liberal government, terrified of being accused of weakness, caved in and agreed to the construction of the ships.

Meanwhile, a new broom had taken over the direction of intelligence at the War Office. While Henry Wilson was reputedly the ugliest soldier in the British Army, Sir James Edmonds was allegedly the cleverest – a reputation secured by his passing out first in his year among the cadets of Sandhurst, Britain's leading military academy. Edmonds, who would one day write the official history of the Great War, had lived in France as a child, where he had witnessed the aftermath of the Franco-Prussian War. Like Colonel Chesney (see page 28), he had been much impressed by the efficiency of the German conquest and occupation, which he believed had been assisted by an unseen host of German spies.

Placed in charge of the War Office's intelligence department in 1909, Edmonds was almost immediately inundated by a stream of reports from concerned citizens, mainly members of the public who had read invasion literature and believed that they had identified German spies. Much of this spy fever was the work of the ubiquitous William Le Queux, who had just produced his new shocker, *Spies of the Kaiser*, which, though billed as fiction, was, the author claimed, based on his own private investigation into the existence of 'a vast army of German spies'. Le Queux passed on the letters and reports from his own vast army of readers to Edmonds, who took them all very seriously – sometimes sending his assistants scurrying down to dockyards such as Chatham and Portsmouth to investigate reports of foreigners and strangers acting suspiciously – and in turn passed them to his boss, war minister Haldane.

The newly popular Edwardian pastimes of cycling and photography aided the spy scare no end. Hitherto remote parts of the countryside were becoming used to the sight of young gentlemen in tweed caps and Norfolk jackets, swishing silently through their lanes on bicycles, often dismounting to photograph a particularly pleasing view. With a little imagination, such sights were swiftly translated into stories such as the one that appeared in the popular *Graphic* newspaper in 1908. This reported how a bike-borne trio of German spies had rented a house in rural Essex, from which they had allegedly sallied out to photograph a 'secret magazine' of munitions and even – presumably to allay local suspicion – organized musical evenings around the piano at Ye Old Thatched House Hotel in Epping.

The dizzy heights of absurdity reached by some of the espionage and invasion fever were not lost on writers with a more developed comic turn of mind than the unintentionally hilarious Le Queux. Invasion literature gave birth to a spoof sub-genre which mocked the wilder fantasies of its parent. In 1909, with scare stories at their height, A. A. Milne, creator of Winnie the Pooh, writing in *Punch* magazine, had the Kaiser himself alighting at Basingstoke station and asking for the restaurant. In the same year P. G. Wodehouse penned a whole novel, *The Swoop, or How Clarence Saved England: A Tale of the Great Invasion* – a conflation of all previous invasion stories in which the combined armies of Germany, Russia, China, Morocco and Turkey, accompanied by the Mad Mullah from Somaliland, and even pacific Switzerland and little Monaco overrun England, only to be foiled by the book's eponymous hero. Even Heath Robinson, one of the great cartoonists of the era, got in on the act the following year, publishing an illustrated series on the theme in *The Sketch* in 1910.

In spite of the mockery, one important person who did take the dire warnings of spying and subversion seriously was Haldane. Though initially sceptical that his dearly beloved Germany could be employing such underhand methods on a large scale, Haldane allowed himself to be persuaded by Edmonds that there was serious substance behind Le Queux's claims. Haldane's credulity was due at least in part to his admiration for the German qualities of thoroughness and meticulous military preparedness, which he had witnessed during a recent visit to Berlin – the so-called 'Haldane mission' – in an abortive effort to persuade the Germans to call off the arms race.

Haldane's response to Edmonds's alarm was to set up yet another cabinet sub-committee, chaired by himself, to inquire into the nature and extent of the espionage threat. Like Haldane, the subcommittee members were dubious at first, but allowed themselves to be persuaded by the stream of reports of foreigners behaving strangely supplied by Edmonds and Le Queux, many of them apparently emanating from the fevered brain of the novelist. Even the sober-minded foreign secretary, Sir Edward Grey, was infected by spy fever; he believed that a 'great number of German officers spend their holidays in this country… along the East and South coast… for no other reason except that of making strategical notes about our coast'.

Eventually, perhaps to justify their own existence, the subcommittee approved the setting-up of a new 'Secret Service Bureau', with a dual brief to monitor the activities of enemy agents at home and to control British spies abroad. In this haphazard and indeed absurd way, as a response to a newspaper scare campaign, the revered modern British secret services, which were to achieve spectacular spying successes over the next century and to survive equally extraordinary fiascos of treachery and betrayal, came into being.

From the start, the new service's activities were cloaked in the strictest secrecy. Indeed, the very existence of any British intelligence service was officially denied by the state until towards the end of the twentieth century. The blanket of secrecy was, however, torn asunder early in January 1910 by none other than the ever-busy William Le Queux, who wrote indignantly to the (then *Manchester*) *Guardian,* then as now the leading voice of Britain's Liberal Left, which had cast doubt on the extent of German espionage, claiming that it was a 'myth'. Cut to the quick, Le Queux openly revealed that a new spy service had been born when he boasted:

> The authorities in London must have been considerably amused by
> your assurances that German spies do not exist among us, for it may be
> news to you to know that so intolerable and marked has the presence
> of [these] gentry become that a special Government Department has
> recently been formed for the purpose of watching their movements.

Though strictly guarded, the vaunted secrecy of the new secret service was always open to penetration.

When founding the new bureau, Edmonds decided to convert the two existing War Office bureaux, MO2 and MO3 (the latter having been renumbered MO5), into two distinct departments with clearly divided responsibilities for foreign and domestic intelligence and counter-intelligence. The department which would become MI6, often called the 'Secret Intelligence Service' (SIS), would be responsible for running Britain's agents abroad. MI5, or the 'Security Service', would counter the threats of enemy espionage and subversion by home-grown traitors both in Britain and throughout the British empire. To head up – indeed, at first, so limited were the available resources, to provide the sole staff members for – the new apparatus, Edmonds chose two remarkable men: one military, Major Vernon Kell, to run MI5; and, after consulting with the Admiralty, the other naval, Captain Mansfield Smith-Cumming, as chief of MI6.

Both men had already been involved in intelligence work. Kell, who was half-Polish, was an intellectual – small, asthmatic and sporting pince-nez – who spoke half a dozen languages fluently. Cumming, in contrast – a bluff, broad, monocled figure, whose active naval career had been brought to an end, ironically, by his seasickness – had once journeyed through Germany in disguise, picking up intelligence titbits despite not speaking a word of German. These two contrasting characters were allotted an office to share at 64 Victoria Street, behind Buckingham Palace and close to where Edmonds's office was located.

SUPER SPOOK: Sir Vernon Kell, first head of MI5, ran Britain's internal secret service throughout the Great War, dismantling many German spy networks. He stayed in charge until sacked by Churchill in 1940.

They moved in in October 1909 and started work. There was no shortage of things for the odd couple to do. Despite the random nature of the often spurious spy stories and rumours that had brought their Secret Service Bureau into being, there certainly was at least one genuine German espionage network at work in Britain – though it was nothing like as widespread as popular opinion believed. Between August 1911 and the outbreak of war three years later, ten German spies were arrested, and six were jailed for espionage. Berlin's espionage effort was mainly directed at ferreting out Britain's naval secrets, and many of her spies were centred on naval bases such as Portsmouth, Plymouth, Chatham and Rosyth outside Edinburgh.

Gustav Steinhauer, the Kaiser's bodyguard, spymaster and master of disguise, had established his own spy ring largely by the bizarre and rather too blatant method of writing out of the blue from his HQ at Potsdam, outside Berlin, to Germans resident in Britain, asking them to spy for the Fatherland. Since one of Kell's earliest successes had been to establish an office within the Post Office to intercept suspicious letters to and from German citizens, MI5 soon got wind of the network and monitored it closely. Immediately on the outbreak of war in August 1914, thirty-one members were arrested in one fell swoop. Germany's intelligence-gathering within Britain was neutralized at a stroke.

THIRTY-NINE STEPS TO WAR

The supreme example of spy literature – a thriller which continues to fascinate today – was completed in the summer of 1914, when the events it dealt with were already moving towards the climax of a European, then a world, war. Its author, John Buchan, a Scottish polymath of titanic energy combining the roles of novelist, historian, biographer, statesman and – not least – intelligence officer, had long been worried about the threat from Germany.

In the summer of 1914, while convalescing from a duodenal ulcer brought on by worry and overwork, Buchan and his family took seaside lodgings in Broadstairs on the Kent coast – an area also favoured by Lord Northcliffe, another Germanophobe, who had taken his title from his home there. Buchan was accompanied by his wife Susan and their six-year-old daughter Alice, who had also been ill, having had a mastoid operation. Though Buchan spent much of the holiday in bed, Alice ventured out, descending a wooden staircase to a private beach on Broadstairs' North Foreland. She told her father that she had counted the steps and that there were thirty-nine of them. Somehow, the figure stuck in the writer's head.

Buchan began writing a 'shocker' which became perhaps the most famous spy thriller in history. Repeatedly filmed and staged, *The Thirty-*

Nine Steps owes its enduring popularity to its theme of a single man on the run from two enemies – the British police who believe he is a murderer, and a gang of German spies who know he is the key to undoing their nefarious schemes to plunge the world into war. Many cuts above Le Queux, and more exciting than its only peer in the genre, Childers's *The Riddle of the Sands*, Buchan's fiction – the first of several books featuring the same hero, Richard Hannay – reflects the febrile atmosphere of a world plunging into the abyss.

That abyss yawned wide when the Serb nationalist Gavrilo Princip fired his shots in Sarajevo on 28 June of that fateful year, 1914. Although much of the press, the public and even the more sober minds in Britain's government were concerned to the point of obsession with what they perceived as the growing threat from Germany, there were signs in plenty that not all was well within England either.

Beneath the placid surface of Edwardian England, seething currents were stirring. The historian George Dangerfield famously alluded to the eddying of these undercurrents in the title of his 1935 book *The Strange Death of Liberal England*. In this he identified the murderers of that idyll, like the many suspects on board Agatha Christie's Orient Express, variously as the suffragettes, Green and Orange Irishmen, foreign terrorists, trade unionists, socialists, and the great constitutional clash between Peers and Commons, Liberals and Tories, compromising 'Hedgers' and die-hard 'Ditchers'. In the summer of 1914, all these long-bubbling cauldrons of discontent seemed to come to the boil together.

Civil war was widely expected to break out in Northern Ireland. It was here with, in the inimitable words of Winston Churchill, the British Cabinet gloomily considering the limited options open to them, caught as they were between the rock of intransigent Ulster Protestantism and the hard place of rising Catholic nationalism, the quiet voice of Sir Edward Grey began reading aloud a document just bought him from the Foreign Office. Churchill recalled:

> It contained the terms of Austria's fatal note to Serbia. He had been reading or speaking for several minutes before I could separate my mind from the tedious and bewildering debate which had just closed… but gradually, as the sentences followed one another, impressions of a wholly different character began to form in my mind… The parishes of Tyrone and Fermanagh faded back into the mists and squalls of Ireland, and a strange light began immediately, but by perceptible gradations, to fall and grow upon the map of Europe.

2. ULSTER WILL FIGHT

NO SURRENDER: Sir Edward Carson inspects armed members of the Ulster Volunteer Force (UVF), 1914. A brilliant Dublin barrister and orator, Carson would go far to defend Ulster's Protestants. But the hard men behind him would go further.

2. Ulster Will Fight

Rumours of wars in Europe were not the only crisis facing the Asquith government as 1914 opened. No sooner was the clash between Lloyd George's Treasury and Churchill over the Admiralty's demand for more money resolved by a compromise in the Admiralty's favour than the spectre of Ireland loomed again over the cabinet's counsels. The battle over the naval estimates had been smoothed over by the emollient prime minister, as Churchill conceded, praising Asquith's 'unswerving patience'. The lawyerly Asquith's greatest political gift was indeed that of a suavely efficient chairman, holding together his brilliant cabinet – especially its two most extrovert stars – like a skilful coachman driving a fractious team of wild horses. But it would take more than the prime minister's buttery tact – as smooth as his flabby features – and patience to bring peace to rocky, knotty Ireland.

Pacifying Ireland had proved beyond the skills of even William Ewart Gladstone, the greatest figure in Liberal party history, during his stints as prime minister in the late nineteenth century. Asquith, who had cut his teeth in the Grand Old Man's cabinet, proved no more successful than his mentor in sorting out the Irish imbroglio. His temperament – ponderous, magisterial, patient – was the exact opposite of the Celtic stereotype, as his decades-long duel with the mercurial Welsh wizard Lloyd George would prove. Asquith never understood Ireland, or its infuriatingly warring tribes, and his failure to do so is one of the more explicable aspects of the Strange Death of Liberal England.

With the support of the moderately nationalist Irish Parliamentary Party, and at the cost of splitting his own party when a group of radical imperialists led by Joseph Chamberlain broke away to join the Tories as Liberal Unionists in 1886, Gladstone pushed through the House of Commons two Home Rule Bills (1886 and 1893) that gave Ireland devolved government within Britain. But both were squashed before becoming law by the Tory-dominated House of Lords. The scandalous divorce case that ended the career of Charles Stewart Parnell, the charismatic Irish parliamentary nationalist leader, in 1890–1 split Gladstone's own party in its turn – and, as it turned out, fatally wounded the cause of parliamentary Irish nationalism at Westminster.

IRISH PARLIAMENTARY nationalist leader John Redmond speaks in 1912. In an age of extremes, his voice of moderation was muffled, and Redmond's cause of peaceful Home Rule was to be drowned in blood.

When the Liberals returned to power in London in 1906, the Irish Parliamentary Party had reunited under the impeccably reasoned leadership of John Redmond, one of Parnell's loyal lieutenants and a member of an old Catholic gentry family. The nationalist movement was stirring again in Ireland, with a cultural revival manifested in a passion for Gaelic sports and a serious attempt to save the Irish language, which had been in steady retreat for centuries. The prospect of striking third time lucky with a new Home Rule bill, again introduced by the Liberals, was intoxicating to the Irish, especially after the Liberals had curbed the powers of the Lords to destroy legislation in the constitutional crisis touched off by Lloyd George's People's Budget of 1909.

The tantalizing chance of Home Rule became a certainty after the two general elections caused by the Lords crisis in January and December 1910. Both whittled down the Liberal majority to a dead heat, and the year 1911 opened with the Tories and Liberals level-pegging with 272 Westminster seats each. Redmond's nationalists held eighty-four seats, so once more, as in Parnell's time, a Liberal government depended on Irish votes, and the price for that Irish support, also as in Parnell's time, was Home Rule.

HOME RULE, ROME RULE

Inevitably, the hopes raised in the nationalist hearts of Ireland's Catholic majority found an answering echo in the fears of Ireland's substantial Protestant minority. The Protestants were themselves divided between the small, Anglican, mainly middle- and upper-class elite in and around Dublin, who formed the Anglo-Irish Ascendancy and from whom many of Ireland's leaders – her lawyers, soldiers and politicians (including Parnell) – had traditionally been drawn.

Most of the island's Protestants, however, were concentrated in Ulster in the north-east, the only one of Ireland's four provinces where they formed a narrow numerical majority. Of Scottish working-class origin, imported to 'plant' the province in the seventeenth century, and Presbyterian rather than Anglican in religion, Ulster men and women were dour, determined folk, motivated by a fierce pride in their harsh heritage and an almost obsessive terror that 'Home rule means Rome rule'. Treasuring their links with Britain and her empire rather than resenting and rejecting them as many of their Catholic neighbours in the south did, Ulster's Protestants formed a natural alliance with the Tories on the British mainland as they prepared to do battle against the Home Rule Bill.

The Tories had adopted the title Conservative and Unionist Party after Joe Chamberlain's anti-Home Rule followers had joined them in 1912. Now their commitment to the Unionist cause would carry them up to and over the brink of constitutional politics and onto the rocky shores of support for armed sedition. The two men mainly responsible for this new hard line were the new Tory leader Andrew Bonar Law, the Canadian-born but Scots-descended son of a Presbyterian preacher, and the equally bleak and austere figure of Edward Carson, the brilliant but destructive leader of the Ulster Unionists and their resistance to Home Rule.

Bonar Law, a tough, unflinchingly honest, wealthy Glasgow business-man, opened the door to a bracing cold wind in Tory politics when he was unexpectedly elected party leader as a compromise candidate after the resignation of the laid-back and ineffectual Arthur Balfour in November 1911. The Tories – hungry for office and what they regarded as their natu-ral birthright in government, and increasingly resentful of the Liberal-led erosion of wealth and privilege – had finally despaired of Balfour's languid leadership after his failure to stop the swingeing taxes on the aristocracy and the emasculation of the House of Lords touched off by the People's Budget. His equally hesitant reluctance to take sides in the great debate between Tory free traders and the imperial protectionist tariff reformers championed by Joe Chamberlain finally sealed his fate. After a spirited 'Balfour Must Go' campaign led by the high Tory journalist Leo Maxse's *National Review*, the aristocratic Scot duly went – though he was to remain an influential and feline presence in politics for years to come.

Given Bonar Law's austere Presbyterian background, Home Rule, and Ulster's violent objection to it, was the one issue that he really cared about – and he was prepared to use the harshest language and go to the very brink of propriety to pursue his chosen cause. Bonar Law was certainly not the kind of aristocratic gentleman that the Tories were used to electing as leader, and his elevation to the role was the sort of startling innovation that the party would have the imagination – or desperation – to contemplate only in moments of crisis (other instances are the Jewish-descended Disraeli's elec-tion in the 1860s and Margaret Thatcher's emergence in the 1970s).

Now the rough, tough, taciturn Canadian Scot was the Tory man of the hour. 'I shall have to show myself very vicious, Mr Asquith, this session,' Bonar Law told the prime minister as they walked side by side to the open-ing of the new parliament in February 1912; 'I hope you will understand.' Mild-mannered, reasonable Mr Asquith never did fully understand the raw passions and principles that Bonar Law embodied, but the gritty, accusa-tory 'new style' that the Tory leader brought to their Commons exchanges proved to be a permanent feature of parliamentary life. Bonar Law meant what he said, and he meant business.

So too, in spades, did Sir Edward Carson, whose sunken cheeks, leathery features, mournful hound-dog eyes, and lips betraying a sneer of cold command advertised his chilly, contradictory character all too well. Strangely for the man whose outsize Stormont statue still symbolizes the inflexible steely will of what was the Protestant province, Carson was not an Ulsterman but a Dubliner – albeit a member of the city's Protestant Ascendancy class. A contemporary of Oscar Wilde at Trinity College, the Ascendancy's alma mater, Carson became a formidably brilliant barrister whose brutal forensic courtroom destruction of his old friend during Wilde's fateful libel action against the Marquess of Queensberry in 1895 has passed into legal legend.

Carson became a Dublin MP for his old college, and his appearance – this time on the side of the angels – as advocate in the 1908–11 Archer-Shee case, another courtroom *cause célèbre* in which he successfully defended a naval cadet falsely accused of theft and fraud (dramatized by Terence Rattigan in his hit 1946 play *The Winslow Boy*), cemented his reputation and his fame. Invited in 1910 by the less oratorically gifted and sharp-brained but equally determined chief of the Ulster Unionist Council, Sir James Craig, to become Ulster's political leader, Carson hurled himself into the fray with fanatical zeal. Craig was his deputy, the administrative grafter behind Carson's menacing rhetoric. Craig was a slab-faced, hard-nosed Ulsterman with a rock-like attachment to the austere and narrow values of his people. And it was Craig, not Carson, who began to organize Ulster's male population for what looked very much like civil war.

On 23 September 1911 Craig called the first of the monster rallies that would become a recurrent feature of the Ulster crisis in the grounds of his estate, Craigavon, overlooking Belfast Lough. Carson told the massed ranks of grim-faced Ulster folk that the government's plan to introduce Home Rule was 'the most nefarious conspiracy ever hatched against a free people' and warned that Ulster would set up its own provisional government if Home Rule ever came to pass. In February 1912, Winston Churchill – whose own father, Randolph, a radical Tory, had supported Ulster's resistance to earlier Home Rule plans in the 1880s by famously declaring 'Ulster will fight – and Ulster will be right' – was chased out of Belfast's Ulster Hall by hostile Protestants and forced to deliver his Home Rule message to a largely Catholic audience in Celtic Park, a Gaelic football ground in the heart of the city's Catholic area.

On 11 April 1912, blandly ignoring such pre-shocks of the earthquake to come, Asquith introduced a third Home Rule Bill in the House of Commons, proposing to give all Ireland – including Ulster – devolved

SIR EDWARD CARSON: legal nemesis of the playwright Oscar Wilde; implacable opponent of Irish Home Rule and – for generations of Ulster loyalists – the creator of a Northern Ireland free of 'Rome rule'.

government as a self-ruling dominion of the British empire. Two days previously, in an ominous precursor of things to come, Carson and Bonar Law had reviewed 100,000 Ulstermen, marching in military-style columns, all pledged to resist Home Rule to the death. Carson heartened his followers when he told them – in a prophecy that would prove accurate when put to the test in 1914 – that the British Army would never agree to coerce their own Ulster 'kith and kin'.

There followed a long, hot summer of rising discontent and increasingly angry words. In June, Bonar Law, using language not heard in Britain from a political leader for centuries, issued a veiled warning of civil unrest. There were things, he told a rally darkly, more important than mere parliamentary majorities. He added that there was more chance of a London mob lynching Liberals in London than there was of Ulster Loyalists being shot by British troops in Belfast.

On 29 July at another monster rally held at Blenheim Palace in Oxfordshire – ironically Churchill's family estate and birthplace – Bonar Law lashed the Liberal government as 'a revolutionary committee which has seized by fraud upon despotic power'. He pledged the support of the Conservative and Unionist party for Ulster, concluding that he 'could imagine no lengths of resistance that Ulster would go to in which they would not be supported by the Unionist party, [and] the overwhelming majority of the British people'.

A COVENANT IN BLOOD

More mass meetings and rallies in Ulster and on the mainland culminated, on 'Ulster Day', 28 September 1912, with the signing of the Ulster Covenant. This document, displayed on a Union Flag-draped table in Belfast City Hall, pledged its signatories to 'use all means which may be found necessary to defeat the present conspiracy' to impose Home Rule. Carson and Craig signed first, followed by an impressive roll of 471,414 Ulster men and women – some signing in their own blood. Nor were signatures confined to Ulster. The Covenant was signed in mainland British cities too, especially those with significant Protestant populations such as Glasgow, Edinburgh, Manchester and Liverpool.

Support for the Ulster cause spread like wildfire in Unionist circles. Rudyard Kipling pledged £30,000 to the Ulster Fighting Fund, and a British League to support Ulster received the endorsement of 100 peers and 120 MPs. In another innovatory move, which was then unprecedented in British politics but has since become commonplace, Bonar Law demanded a referendum of the whole nation on the Home Rule issue on

WRITTEN IN BLOOD: half a million Ulster Protestants signed the Solemn League and Covenant – some in their own blood – pledging resistance to Home Rule in 1912. By 1914 civil war threatened all Ireland.

the grounds that the Liberals had not signalled their intention of granting Home Rule in their December 1910 general election manifesto.

The agitation whipped up over the Ulster issue dismayed the government and even alarmed the phlegmatic Asquith. But, foreseeing some resistance to their bill, they had already secretly prepared fall-back lines of defence. Asquith had agreed that if significant public resistance was encountered beyond the normal opposition in Parliament, then 'special treatment' should be granted to Ulster. In effect, this meant that *in extremis*

Ulster's Solemn League and Covenant.

Being convinced in our consciences that Home Rule would be disastrous to the material well-being of Ulster as well as of the whole of Ireland. subversive of our civil and religious freedom. destructive of our citizenship and perilous to the unity of the Empire. we. whose names are underwritten, men of Ulster. loyal subjects of His Gracious Majesty King George V.. humbly relying on the God whom our fathers in days of stress and trial confidently trusted. do hereby pledge ourselves in solemn Covenant throughout this our time of threatened calamity to stand by one another in defending for ourselves and our children our cherished position of equal citizenship in the United Kingdom and in using all means which may be found necessary to defeat the present conspiracy to set up a Home Rule Parliament in Ireland. ¶ And in the event of such a Parliament being forced upon us we further solemnly and mutually pledge ourselves to refuse to recognise its authority. ¶ In sure confidence that God will defend the right we hereto subscribe our names. ¶ And further. we individually declare that we have not already signed this Covenant.

The above was signed by me at_____
"Ulster Day." Saturday. 28th September. 1912.

———— God Save the King. ————

the government would be prepared to exclude Ulster – or some counties of the province – from the Home Rule Bill's provisions if the Protestants kicked up enough fuss about it.

But Asquith was in no hurry. True to his maxim 'Wait and see', he preferred to sit and watch, apparently doing nothing at all, while patiently anticipating a moment when he could intervene most effectively. Meanwhile the Home Rule Bill was making its laborious way through Parliament. In January 1913, having been passed by the Commons with the aid of Redmond's votes, the bill was decisively rejected by the Lords by 326 votes to 69. So it was reintroduced into the Commons, and the whole grinding parliamentary process began again.

In the same month, the Ulster Unionists decisively upped the ante. For more than a year Ulstermen had been parading and drilling, marching and rallying unofficially, and they were getting restless. It was time, the leadership of the Ulster Unionist Council decided, to organize and discipline them, both in the interests of good order and also to wield a more effective weapon against Home Rule. The result was the foundation of the Ulster Volunteer Force (UVF) – a province-wide paramilitary organization, largely based on the Protestant Orange Order and Ulster's rifle clubs.

The Ulstermen set about their work with grim determination. To procure arms and ammunition for the new movement, they appointed Major Frederick Crawford, a member of the Council with a military background (he had fought in the Boer War) and fearlessly militant views (he was one of those who had signed the Covenant in his own blood). Crawford contacted arms manufacturers in Germany and Austria and began negotiations to buy weapons in industrial quantities.

TO DO OR DIE FOR IRELAND

Irishmen in the south had been observing the activities of the Ulstermen and the Unionists with increasing anxiety. Redmond knew that his best policy was to keep quiet and not offer needless provocation to his thoroughly aroused Unionist fellow countrymen. There were, however, Irishmen more militant than he who were not only determined to face down the Ulster Unionists, but were hostile to Redmond's milk-and-water brand of constitu-

tional nationalism on the grounds that it did not go nearly far or fast enough.

The most ardently nationalist strand in Irish politics was the physical-force republicans, loosely known as the Fenians, who – aided and funded by the large Irish emigrant diaspora in the United States and across the empire, and embittered by memories of the Great Famine of the 1840s – had kept up an intermittent campaign of terrorism both in Ireland itself and in Britain from the 1860s to the 1880s. The chief Fenian grouping in Ireland was the secret society called the Irish Republican Brotherhood (IRB). Its members were admitted by invitation and sworn in by oath. The IRB was organized in a cell structure designed to obstruct the traditional British police penetration of similar nationalist societies, and its members were dedicated to achieving an Irish republic by violent means.

By the 1900s, its terrorist strategy having failed to end British rule, the IRB was quiescent. Then a new generation was sworn in and enthused by the example of Tom Clarke, a Dublin tobacco shop owner who had spent fifteen years in a British jail and whose militancy burned as bright as ever. Men such as Sean McDermott, Sean McBride and Padraig Pearse – the latter a half-English lawyer who had founded a school, St Enda's, to inculcate the Gaelic tongue and Irish culture into its children – eagerly joined the IRB. Personally gentle, Pearse was nonetheless infused with a mystical adoration of blood and violence, writing longingly on the outbreak of war in 1914 that 'the earth's old heart needed to be warmed by the red wine of the battlefields'.

Also wholly prepared to do or die for Ireland were the socialist revolutionaries of the Irish Citizen Army. This small militia was born of the great Dublin strike and lockout which had paralysed the city for months in 1913 and into 1914. The inspiration for both the strike and the Citizen Army was James 'Big Jim' Larkin, a bellow-lunged socialist organizer who built up Ireland's first mass trade union, the Transport and General Workers, founded the Irish Labour party, and succeeded in calling out most of the city's workforce in a strike which brought about bloody battles between strikers and police.

The Citizen Army was originally a bunch of heavies armed with hurling sticks formed to protect strikers and teach the police, in Larkin's words, some 'manners'. When the strike wave collapsed, a disillusioned Larkin departed for the US, but the Citizen Army survived under the command of Larkin's deputy, a ball-headed, heavily moustachioed Scots-born socialist named James Connolly. Drilling under the direction of a renegade British army officer named Major Jack White, the Citizen Army soon grew into an enthusiastic, if tiny, force of disciplined worker-soldiers distinguished from their Fenian rivals of the IRB by their belief in the imminent arrival of international socialism.

The third element of Irish nationalism outside the ranks of Redmond's Parliamentary Party was a small grouping calling itself Sinn Féin ('We Ourselves'). Sinn Féin was founded in 1905 by a Dublin journalist named Arthur Griffith, who took his inspiration and his model for a future Ireland from Hungary's achievement of dual statehood alongside Austria: his ambition was for Ireland to emulate Hungary and achieve parity with Britain as an equal dominion or republic. He differed from the IRB in rejecting violence and organizing and campaigning openly rather than covertly, and from the Parliamentary Party in refusing to take seats at Westminster and advocating the establishment of Ireland's own Dáil – a parliament in Dublin. Griffith's 'middle way' and his esoteric foreign inspiration had little appeal for those who believed in the romantic ideal of a republic established by force of arms, and by 1914 his movement was treading water and struggling to survive.

As part of their preparations for armed revolt, the IRB had built a drill hall off Parnell Square in central Dublin, where they gave military training to members of the youth movement Fianna Éireann and Gaelic sporting associations. Aware that they were being closely observed by the vigilant Dublin police and wishing to draw other nationalist groups under their umbrella, IRB journalist The O'Rahilly persuaded an eminently respectable Trinity College academic, Eoin MacNeill, a nationalist professor of medieval history of impeccably moderate views, to write an article advocating the formation of a national volunteer force in response to the foundation of the UVF in Ulster.

MacNeill's article 'The North Began' triggered exactly the favourable reaction that O'Rahilly had anticipated. In November 1913, amidst scenes of great enthusiasm, 7,000 people attended an overflowing meeting in Dublin to inaugurate the new volunteer force. Secret IRB members were prominent on its council, which was headed by MacNeill, but so were Sinn Féin and the Parliamentary Party. Though intensely suspicious of any form of violent militarism, John Redmond saw the Irish Volunteers as a useful counter to the UVF, and anyway he knew that his party had to join the new body if he was to have any hope of restraining those nationalists who favoured violence.

The year 1914 opened with the whole of Ireland poised on a cliff edge. The rival Ulster and Irish Volunteers were drilling and parading with every appearance of earnestness – albeit as yet without lethal weapons. The two tribes seemed deadly serious in their intentions and civil war was looking more than an ominous possibility.

A SIX-YEAR STAY OF EXECUTION

At Westminster, where the House of Lords had rejected the Home Rule Bill
for a second time, Asquith decided to invoke the plan to exclude Ulster – or
some of its counties – from Home Rule's provisions. Prompted by the new
king, George V, a former naval officer of high Tory views and a stickler for
constitutional propriety who was terrified of the monarchy being drawn into
a new civil war, the prime minister had been holding secret talks with Bonar
Law at Cherkley Court, the Surrey country home of Bonar Law's friend and
Canadian compatriot, the press magnate Max Aitken, owner of the *Daily
Express*. When these proved inconclusive, Asquith turned to Carson, who,
as a fellow member of the bar, he knew better, but drew a blank there too.

Continuing pressure from the king, who correctly predicted that many
army officers would refuse to enforce Home Rule against a reluctant Ulster,
persuaded Asquith to make concessions. He moved from offering Ulster
the right to veto any Act passed by a Dublin parliament that it found
objectionable to agreeing to exclude the majority Protestant counties of
the province from the Act altogether for three years, a period subsequently
extended to six years.

A reluctant Redmond was prevailed upon to agree to the concessions,
but Carson would not be so accommodating. When Asquith rose in the
Commons to move the third reading of the Home Rule Bill on 9 March
1914, the Ulster Unionist leader scornfully rejected the six-year exclusion
as a 'sentence of death with a stay of execution for six years'. Days later,
in a fine theatrical scene, he declared 'my place is with my people' – and
stormed out of the chamber to take the boat train for Belfast, cheered
on his way by the Tories. The government was left in some doubt as to
whether he intended to proclaim the threatened provisional government
of Ulster when he got there.

Unnerved, the government began precautionary moves to use the army
in the event of a breakdown of law and order in Ulster. They planned to
occupy key buildings in Ulster's capital Belfast and elsewhere and to defend
armouries in the province against any attack from the UVF. But when
these plans were outlined to military chiefs, the government faced the first
stirrings of open disobedience from the officer corps. The secretary of state
for war, Jack Seely – a bluff, hook-nosed, horse-riding soldier-politician (he
had been decorated during the Boer War) and friend of Winston Churchill
since their Harrow schooldays (he had joined his friend in defecting from
the Tories to the Liberals over the free trade issue in 1904) – quietly gave
permission for officers stationed in Ireland who had close family connec-
tions with Ulster to go on leave or otherwise 'disappear' if ordered north to

put down any disturbances. However, any other officer who refused orders for 'conscientious' reasons, warned Seely sternly, would be dismissed.

The army commander in Ireland, General Sir Arthur Paget, a soldier who had even less political nous than Seely and who only knew that he detested what he called 'those swines of politicians', interpreted the war secretary's nod and a wink rather loosely, and upon landing in Dublin told his seven most senior subordinates that any officer who felt disinclined to deploy in Ulster would be excused that distasteful duty. He talked wildly of Ulster being 'ablaze', giving the distinct impression that the army would be expected to engage the UVF in armed combat, rather than merely securing buildings from possible attack.

THE CURRAGH MUTINY

One of Paget's seven subordinates was Brigadier-General Hubert de la Poer Gough, commander of the 3rd Cavalry Brigade based at the Curragh Camp outside Dublin. Gough was himself, like so many of his brother officers, an Anglo-Irishman and an ardent sympathizer with the Ulster cause. He had a reputation as an impetuous 'thruster', which his rash, ill-prepared assaults in the Great War, when he commanded a whole army, would prove only too tragically justified. Having heard Paget out, Gough hurried off to consult his own officers, returning with the news that all sixty officers in his unit would prefer to accept dismissal rather than go north to 'coerce' Ulster. Similar answers came from the officers of two lancer regiments.

On 20 March Paget sent a panicky telegram to London reporting what soon became known as the 'Curragh Mutiny': 'REGRET TO REPORT BRIGADIER AND 57 OFFICERS 3RD CAVALRY BRIGADE PREFER TO ACCEPT DISMISSAL IF ORDERED NORTH'. Faced with this collective and unanimous disobedience, the government itself panicked – and beat a hasty retreat. Asquith swiftly ascribed the 'mutiny' to a 'misunderstanding' and soon found a scapegoat for the crisis in the not terribly bright Jack Seely.

The mutinous Gough, accompanied by a couple of his colonels, had arrived at the War Office and insolently demanded an assurance that the army would never again be used to 'coerce Ulster'. In response, Asquith issued a typically vague piece of fluff, which Seely, on his own initiative, 'sexed up' with a pair of closing paragraphs, assuring Gough and any other concerned officers that, while the government reserved the right to use the army as it saw fit, it had no intention of ordering troops to crush the 'political opposition to Home Rule'.

Even this was not enough to satisfy Gough. But at the War Office he was among friends: the Chief of the Imperial General Staff, Sir John French,

and the WO's chief military advisor, that inveterate intriguer Sir Henry Wilson, were both Anglo-Irishmen and hot partisans of the Unionist cause. They too, like Bonar Law and Carson, were determined to defeat Home Rule. French added his endorsement to Seely's unauthorized sentiments, and with a piece of paper in his pocket signed by the secretary of state for war and Britain's chief soldier, pledging that troops would never be used to intimidate Ulster, Gough, satisfied at last, boarded the boat train back to Dublin. The Curragh Mutiny was over.

Its political fallout, however, was not. We have a fascinating inside view of the crisis from the Olympian viewpoint of the prime minister himself. Early in 1912 Asquith had, in a fit of folly at the age of sixty, fallen in love with a young woman some forty years younger than himself. Venetia Stanley, a friend and contemporary of Asquith's devoted daughter Violet, was a daughter of Lord Stanley, later Lord Sheffield, an aristocratic Liberal peer and landed magnate who often entertained the Asquiths at one or

MUTINEERS: the men might march – but where were the officers? British troops of the Duke of Cornwall's Light Infantry parade at Ireland's Curragh camp in March 1914. Most of their officers refused orders to deploy against the UVF in Ulster.

other of his two palatial country houses, Alderley Park in Cheshire or Penrhos on Anglesey. Asquith's mounting obsession with Venetia grew steadily, and she soon became first among equals in the group of half-a-dozen women – known to his tolerant family as 'the harem' – with whom he maintained flirtatious pen friendships.

It was long thought that the ageing Asquith's romantic infatuation with Venetia was, however absurd and 'inappropriate' for the married statesman, an innocent and non-sexual affair that went no further than 'spooning' and groping on sofas and in the back of chauffeured limousines. But recently it has been plausibly claimed that the relationship was far more intense than previously thought, and in fact resulted in the birth of an illegitimate child, Louis Stanley, whose photographs do indeed show a remarkable resemblance to the last prime minister of a Liberal government.

Whatever the truth of that, Asquith's surviving letters to Venetia, beginning in 1912 and lasting until 1915, when she threw him over in favour of marriage to one of Asquith's own ministers, Edwin Montagu, offer an unparalleled inside view of British high and low politics in the run-up to and early days of the war. Asquith wrote to his mistress on an almost daily basis – sometimes even more often – scribbling the impassioned *billets doux* in the midst of cabinet meetings, when his colleagues were doubtless flattered to believe that he was making furious notes on their contributions to the discussion. Just as a modern minister might text or tweet, so Asquith would fire off his gossipy, indiscreet screeds to his lady love, who became his confidante and the repository of state secrets, as well, probably, as his lover.

The Curragh Mutiny was just one of the recurrent crises of Asquith's premiership to which Venetia was given a ringside ticket, courtesy of the prime minister, and it is from his letters to her – hot, urgent and unbuttoned – that we get the real story behind his Olympian, smooth and unflappable public façade. On first learning of the mutiny, Asquith, typically, was taken by surprise by the gravity of the crisis, which, he told Venetia, should have been 'cleared up in a few hours'.

By the next day, 22 March, he had awoken to the uncomfortable fact that 'about half the officers in the Army would strike' if ordered to coerce Ulster, and on learning that the army's rank and file were of the same pro-Protestant opinion as their officers, he started to beat a cautious retreat. Asquith's normal tactics when confronted by a crisis seemingly in need of an urgent resolution was to stall and obfuscate until tempers cooled and attention wandered to another topic. He was a past master at these can-kicking games, and once again on this occasion they did not fail him. After days of procrastination he accepted the resignations of Seely and the army's commander, General Sir John French, and proposed what he called the 'bombshell' idea that he himself should assume control of the War Office alongside the premiership. Although the Conservatives catcalled 'Cromwell!' when he announced the plan in the Commons, the idea that the urbane and avuncular Asquith was a new military dictator in the making was evidently absurd, and the crisis, as he had anticipated, blew over.

But the legacy of the Curragh Mutiny was more serious than Asquith, with his lazy optimistic ebullience and his assumption that sweet reason would always prevail, would allow. The crisis had demonstrated that, when push came to violent shove, the government would buckle under pressure and surrender. Although Churchill, with characteristically bellicose impetuosity, had ordered the navy to take up stations in the Irish Sea, where their shells, he threatened, could 'reduce Belfast to ruins', and was all for dissolving the existing mutinous army and creating a new one from scratch,

Asquith rightly saw that this was, as he told Venetia, 'nonsense'. Instead of Belfast, it was his policy of granting Home Rule to the whole of Ireland that had been blown away. Bereft, he pottered along the uncertain route of allowing Ulster to be excluded from Home Rule for a vaguely indefinite period. In meetings with Tory leaders and in messages to the king, Asquith indicated that a compromise along these lines, effectively agreeing to the partition of Ireland, was now his policy. The southern Irish themselves, in the words of historian Robert Kee, 'were being squeezed out'. Asquith was hoping, as usual, for the best, and meanwhile waiting and seeing.

To put extra pressure on the still imperturbable premier and to demonstrate that Ulster was a popular issue for the great patriotic majority of the population, the Tories staged a monster 'Ulster rally' in London's Hyde Park on 4 April 1914. Under a sea of Union and St George's flags, columns representing different sections of society – the City, lady imperialists and last but not least the working class – converged on fourteen platforms arranged in a giant circle to sing patriotic hymns and listen to speeches denouncing Asquith and Churchill (who was called 'a Lilliput Napoleon') and to demand that Ulster's future be put to a popular referendum.

THE RACE FOR ARMS

In the meantime, the Ulstermen themselves had not been idle and were looking to their own defences with characteristic pugnacity. Crawford's attempts to buy arms and so give the Ulster Volunteer Force some serious military muscle had continued throughout 1913, approved by Carson and Craig, and financed by Ulster businessmen and industrialists and by wealthy Tories, including Lord Milner, in England. (Hitherto the UVF had been drilling, comically, with wooden rifles and had sported shotguns.) At first Crawford had sought to buy weapons in Britain, but after his efforts had been frustrated by vigilant customs officers who had spotted his purchases in transit, he turned to continental Europe.

Though ostensibly the most patriotic of Britons, the Ulstermen had no qualms about seeking their weapons from the countries – Austria and Germany – which, within a few months, would be at war with the country to which they swore such undying loyalty. After months of secret negotiations Crawford clinched a deal with the international arms dealer Benny Spiro to purchase, for some £45,000, 10,000 brand new Mannlicher rifles, each with a bayonet, and 12,000 Mauser 88 rifles, also with bayonets, together with three million rounds of ammunition to fit both weapons. In addition to these modern rifles, Spiro threw in several thousand aged Vetterli rifles and another million rounds.

To carry this lethal cargo across to Ulster, Crawford spent a further £5,000 to buy a steamer, the *Clyde Valley*. The landing of the arms at the ports of Larne, Bangor and Donaghee on the night of 24 April, just a month after the Curragh Mutiny, was carried out with faultless military precision. Convoys of cars and lorries converged on the ports under cover of darkness – the first time in history that motor vehicles had been used en masse for military purposes – and the arms and ammunition were unloaded and distributed with brisk efficiency to UVF units throughout the province. Any police officers who showed signs of taking an interest in this illegal operation were discouraged with varying degrees of gentleness, and by morning some 40,000 guns, together with weapons already in the province, were in the hands of a paramilitary force sworn to resist the lawful government.

Appalled at this open flouting of the law by their mortal enemies, the Irish Volunteers resolved to follow Ulster's route into illegal arms acquisition – albeit on a far smaller scale. The southern gun-running was masterminded by two renegade and repentant former Anglo-Irish imperialists – men destined to die violently as a direct result of their espousing Irish republicanism midway through their apparently blameless and conventional careers in the service of the empire they would reject so forcefully: Erskine Childers and Sir Roger Casement.

Childers – author, as we have seen, of that superior example of the invasion literature genre, *The Riddle of the Sands* – though half-English and English-born, had come under the influence of his American wife Molly and become a fierce critic of the British empire generally and of British policy towards Ireland in particular. His companion in the arms-running venture, Sir Roger Casement, from an Ulster Protestant background, had become disillusioned with European colonialism during his work as a consular diplomat in Africa and Latin America, when he had attracted worldwide fame for his courageous exposure of the evils of King Leopold's slave empire in the Belgian Congo, and later for his similar reports on the cruelties of the commercial rubber trade in the Putomayo region on the Peruvian–Brazilian border. Taking early retirement after accepting a knighthood for his humanitarian efforts, Casement had plunged ever more deeply into Irish nationalism.

He and Childers co-operated with Molly Childers and Casement's friend Alice Stopford Green in a committee to raise funds to buy arms for the Irish Volunteers. Spurred into action by the Curragh Mutiny and the Larne arms landing in Ulster, by May 1914 the committee had raised sufficient funds to buy a small quantity of arms through the same German

RIDDLE OF THE SANDS: patriotic spy writer-turned-Irish republican Erskine Childers – seen here on his yacht *Asgard* with his American wife Molly – used the boat to run rifles to the Irish Volunteers in 1914.

city of Hamburg where the Ulster arms deal had been clinched. However, the funds available – some £2,000 – were only sufficient to purchase a tiny quantity of arms, compared to the mass of rifles imported into Ulster, and the rifles themselves – a mere 1,500 – were antiquated Mausers, which, together with a small quantity of equally ancient black-power cartridges, dated from the 1870–1 Franco-Prussian War. Childers offered his private yacht, the *Asgard*, to bring in the cargo, which was finally ready to be shipped in late July – just when the eyes of the rest of the world were on the fast-approaching war.

The small amount of arms to be landed, together with the fact that the landing, on 26 July, was made in broad daylight and that 1,000 Irish Volunteers and the Fianna, the youth section of the Citizen Army, were mobilized to receive the weapons on the quayside at Howth harbour outside Dublin, suggests that the arms running was very amateurish compared to the slick professionalism of the UVF. There is, however, an alternative explanation: that the whole operation was a propaganda stunt designed primarily for popular consumption, rather than a real threat to the government. The amateurishness is underlined by the fact that the Volunteers moved the rifles from the harbour in carts and wheelbarrows, slowing down the operation and alerting the authorities, who had, anyway, been kept abreast of the whole operation by at least one spy in the Volunteers' ranks.

A company of the King's Own Scottish Borderers regiment at Kilmainham Barracks was mobilized to hamper or prevent the landing, but failed to seize more than a handful of the arms, most of which were spirited away by the Volunteers or hidden on the premises of the ultra-Catholic Christian Brothers Order. As the Borderers disconsolately returned to their barracks, they were jeered and taunted by the Dublin crowds, and at a quay on the Liffey called Bachelors Walk, the soldiers turned and fired at their tormentors, killing three people and injuring thirty-eight.

The shooting at Bachelors Walk enraged Irish nationalists, who pointed out the gross discrepancy between the harsh way that they had been treated and the apparent kid-glove attitude the authorities had adopted towards the UVF. Grimly, both sides drew the same conclusion: the only language the government would understand was violence, or the threat of it. Ulster's embattled Protestant population had won an impressive victory over the democratically elected government of Great Britain: they had faced it down and thwarted a central plank of its programme by means of a militant campaign in which they had enlisted the official opposition party, much of England's ruling caste and its army. Militant Irish republicans redoubled their efforts to follow Ulster's suit.

BARRED: a soldier of the Scottish Borderers closes his barrack gates after his unit shot civilians in Dublin's Bachelors Walk during the smuggling of arms to the Irish Volunteers at Howth, 1914.

ENGLAND'S DIFFICULTY, IRELAND'S OPPORTUNITY

In victory, the Ulstermen could afford to be magnanimous. As ever more menacing war clouds darkened the skies over Europe in the high summer of 1914, Bonar Law, Carson and Craig made what to them was a statesmanlike concession: they would allow the Home Rule Bill to become law without further ado, with the important proviso that Ulster would be excluded from it for at least twelve months – or for the duration of the war, in the unlikely event that the conflict lasted longer. At a moment when even pessimists conceded that the fighting would probably be done

Formed to match the UVF, the Irish Volunteers – seen here on a Dublin rooftop – were less well armed than their Ulster rivals, but their spirit was just as strong.

by Christmas, a year's grace seemed like an eternity. And during that year, the Ulster Volunteers would prove their burning patriotism on the field of battle by enlisting en masse in the British army bound for France.

For their part, the overwhelming majority of Irish Volunteers felt the same. Ostensibly, Britain had entered the war on behalf of 'gallant little Belgium', a small nation which, just like Ireland, had been violated by an alien invader. The leader of the Irish Parliamentary Party, John Redmond, who had fought so hard and so patiently to get Home Rule on the Westminster statute book, saw whole-hearted Irish participation in the war as the surest means of holding the government to their promise to implement Home Rule in full when the war was won. His brother, Willie Redmond, was one of the first to enlist. Of approximately 200,000 Volunteers in the summer of 1914, 180,000 heeded Redmond's call and joined the British Army to fight.

One of them was Tom Kettle, a brilliant young poet, barrister and nationalist MP. As a war correspondent in Belgium for the Liberal *Daily News* in the opening weeks of the war, he witnessed with incredulous horror the massacres of Belgian civilians and other atrocities committed by the German army and pronounced the conflict a war of 'Civilisation against barbarians'. He too joined the colours and, like Willie Redmond, was destined to die fighting, as he saw it, for Ireland.

Other Irishmen saw things differently. A hard core of the Volunteers, encompassing most of the movement's leaders, who had founded the organization as 'cover' for their secret republican agenda, refused to join Redmond and declared their intention of continuing to work for an Irish republic, war or no war. True to their Fenian traditions, they saw England's difficulty as Ireland's opportunity. The dispute divided the Volunteers. The Redmondite majority called themselves the National Volunteers, while the republican minority kept the name Irish Volunteers. And while the Redmondites marched off to join Europe's war, the republicans began to organize for a war of their own. England had put Ireland on the back burner for the war's duration, but it was burning still and would soon boil over.

FREE AT LAST: suffragette leader Emmeline Pankhurst (fourth from left) with daughter Christabel (smiling, in black) celebrate their release from one of many prison terms. But by 1914 both they and their campaign were exhausted.

3. Votes for Women

SHORTLY BEFORE ELEVEN O'CLOCK on 10 March 1914, a small woman, dressed smartly but inconspicuously in a grey coat with large buttons and matching skirt, entered the National Gallery in London's Trafalgar Square. Mingling unnoticed with the crowds of art lovers, she made for Diego Velázquez's seventeenth-century masterpiece, the *Rokeby Venus*, and stood for a few moments contemplating the picture.

The painting, which – uniquely in the Spanish master's œuvre – depicts a female nude, shows a rear view of the goddess of love reclining on a draped couch, considering her own reflection in a mirror held by her son Cupid. Brought from Spain in 1806 by the Duke of Wellington during the Peninsular War, the picture had been acquired by the National Gallery a century later, and was one of its major glories.

Suddenly, the whispered calm of the gallery was shattered by the sound of breaking glass. The woman had drawn a foot-long butcher's chopper from beneath her coat, broken the plate glass protecting the painting, and was furiously hacking at the canvas. An attendant and a police constable darted forward and grabbed her arm, but not before she had inflicted half-a-dozen vicious downward slashes to the picture, leaving it hanging in tatters.

As she was escorted away, the woman, speaking in a transatlantic accent, called out: 'Yes, I am a Suffragette. You can get another picture, but you cannot get another life and they are killing Mrs Pankhurst.' The assailant was swiftly identified as a well-known militant in the cause of female suffrage, a thirty-one-year-old Canadian-born journalist named Mary Richardson. Appearing before Bow Street magistrates the following day, she was sentenced to six months' imprisonment for vandalizing the picture.

A press statement was issued by sympathizers on Richardson's behalf explaining her action:

I have tried to destroy the picture of the most beautiful woman in mythological history as a protest against the Government for destroying Mrs Pankhurst, who is the most beautiful character in modern history. Justice is an element of beauty as much as colour and outline on canvas. Mrs Pankhurst seeks to procure justice for womanhood, and for this she is being slowly murdered by a Government of Iscariot politicians.

The hushed, reverent tone and the biblical reference are no accident, for to her followers Mrs Emmeline Pankhurst, founder of the Women's Social and Political Union (WSPU) – in whose name Mary Richardson claimed to be acting – was no less a goddess than the woman whose image had been so grievously defaced.

Mary Richardson was a veteran suffragette activist, belonging to the movement's most militant wing. She had appeared before the courts on no fewer than nine previous occasions for her violent acts on behalf of the suffrage cause, including arson. Richardson had been released from jail as recently as October under the notorious 'Cat and Mouse' Act, under which suffragettes who had been on hunger strike were freed to fatten themselves up sufficiently to be re-arrested and re-incarcerated.

The previous June, Richardson had had been with Emily Wilding Davison on Derby Day at Epsom when she became the only suffragette to have martyred herself in the cause. Davison had flung herself into the path of the galloping horses and had been struck by Anmer, a colt owned by King George V, bringing down the horse and its jockey. Davison herself succumbed to her multiple injuries. Richardson was chased by the incensed crowd of race-goers to the nearby Epsom Downs station, where she was saved from the mob's fury by the (male) stationmaster.

GENTLEWOMEN GENTLE NO LONGER

So how had it come to this? That respectable gentlewomen should be driven to the extremes of committing serious crimes – acts, in twenty-first-century terms, of political terror – against Britain's seemingly stable body politic? The Edwardian suffragette movement traced its roots through the English radical tradition spawned in the Civil War era, and even as far back as the 1381 Peasants' Revolt. The feminist movement received its Urtext in 1792 with the publication of Mary Wollstonecraft's *A Vindication of the Rights of Woman*, written in a blaze of anger by its brilliant author as a distillation of her thirty years' experience of male oppression.

In the century between Wollstonecraft's work and Mrs Pankhurst's foundation of the WSPU in 1903, women had made huge strides in the social and professional spheres. Writers such as Jane Austen, George Eliot, Elizabeth Gaskell and the Brontë sisters were at the forefront of the nineteenth-century flowering of the English novel. Social reformers such as

DIRECT ACTION:
suffragette Mary
Richardson arrested after
slashing Velázquez's *Rokeby
Venus* at London's National
Gallery in March 1914.
Between the wars she
became a keen fascist.

Elizabeth Blackwell and Elizabeth Garrett Anderson – Britain's first female doctors – and Emily Davies, founder of Cambridge's Girton College, had shattered the barriers to female advancement in medicine and education. Josephine Butler, meanwhile, had linked the inequality of the sexes to the exploitation of women epitomized by the epidemic of Victorian prostitution and venereal disease. Politically, however, women had failed to make comparable headway, and although Catholics, Dissenters, Jews, even unpropertied members of the working class had all gradually been granted the vote, women had not.

Efforts to extend the franchise to women were spearheaded by radicals and socialists of the late nineteenth century such as John Stuart Mill, George Bernard Shaw and Henry and Millicent Fawcett. The Fawcetts were strict constitutionalists, and until Emmeline Pankhurst arrived on the scene, the campaign for the female franchise, if still confined to the radical political fringe, remained eminently respectable, consisting largely of pamphlets, polite petitions and discreet pressure applied to sympathetic MPs.

Emmeline Pankhurst, widow of Dr Richard Pankhurst, a Manchester physician, and mother of five children, drank in feminism at her progressive parents' knee. A pillar of radical causes as well as the establishment in provincial society, she was a magistrate, a school governor and a Poor Law governor, which made her aware of the conditions of abject poverty in which so many women lived. Passing rapidly through her husband's liberalism and the infant Labour party of James Keir Hardie, she arrived at the conclusion that women must rely on their own strength to gain the vote. Increasingly, she came to see the enemy not as the government of the day – whether Liberal or Tory – but as the male political Establishment of whatever colour. In 1903 she founded the WSPU, dedicated to fighting for the vote and increasingly inclined over time to a militancy that was rare in British politics and utterly unheard of among women.

At first Mrs Pankhurst, supported by her daughters Christabel, Sylvia and Adela, relied on the tried and trusted (albeit failed) methods of constitutional feminism. They lobbied and petitioned Parliament, they pressured sympathetic MPs to introduce bills for women's suffrage, they wrote newspaper articles, and they demonstrated. Under the Tory administrations of Lord Salisbury and his nephew Arthur Balfour, there was little chance of change, but with the landslide Liberal victory of 1906, suffragette hopes were high. The party contained many members who were sympathetic to the cause and the Pankhursts confidently expected that votes for women would be one of the major reforms that the new government would introduce: they were destined to be deeply disappointed.

SINGING FROM THE SAME SONGSHEET: suffragette composer Ethel Smyth composed music for the coronation of George V in 1911. But when the Establishment refused to listen, a different song was sung.

Not only were several leading Liberals – above all Asquith, who succeeded to the premiership in 1908 – opposed to female suffrage on principle; there was a wider feeling in the party that women were by nature more conservative than men and that granting them the franchise would ensure permanent Tory government. There was, therefore, no serious attempt during the early years of the Liberal government to introduce the measure.

Despairing of male support, in 1907 Emmeline and Christabel resigned their membership of the Independent Labour Party and began a new policy of harassing Liberal leaders, singling out Asquith, Lloyd George and Churchill in particular. They and their closest supporters heckled their targets at public meetings, and even badgered them in private when they were relaxing on the golf course. Increasingly authoritarian, Emmeline Pankhurst carried out the first of several purges of the WSPU the same year, when she expelled leading members who questioned the lack of democracy within the organization.

The years 1908 and 1909 saw Emmeline serving the first of her many spells in prison for inciting riots. The first overt violence from the WSPU came when its members stoned the windows of 10 Downing Street soon after Asquith had assumed the office of prime minister. In 1910, after the Liberals had won a general election, Mrs Pankhurst proclaimed a 'truce', hoping against hope that a cessation of violence would encourage the re-elected government to give women the vote. Once again, she was to be disappointed.

THE PANKHURSTS DECLARE WAR

Although in 1911 Asquith announced a Manhood Suffrage Bill extending the franchise to hitherto disenfranchised working men, women of whatever social station were conspicuous by their absence from the measure. Asquith, it seemed, despite his fondness for them in his personal sphere, was setting his flabby face like flint against votes for women. The government's intransigence infuriated the suffragettes, and Mrs Pankhurst, egged on by her even more extreme elder daughter Christabel, declared war on the Liberals in general, and on Asquith in particular. She personally led militant women on another stone-throwing expedition to Downing Street, shattering the panes of the prime minister's home.

The government responded to the violence by mass arrests of more than 200 suffragettes. Mrs Pankhurst and Christabel were repeatedly arrested and released when they refused food under the 'Cat and Mouse' Act. Suffragette tactics grew ever more violent: the windows of exclusive department stores like Swan & Edgar were smashed in Oxford and Regent

THE MOUSE THAT ROARED: a 1914 poster protests against the Prisoners (Temporary Discharge for Ill-Health) Act, otherwise known as the 'Cat and Mouse' Act, which temporarily freed hunger-striking suffragettes from jail only to re-arrest them when they had regained their strength.

Streets; postboxes were set alight; churches and historic houses were damaged; golf courses were vandalized. Female members of the aristocracy like Lady Constance Lytton joined the campaign, much to the bemused outrage of their families.

The astonishment and anger of most of Britain's male population at the 'unladylike' behaviour of the militant suffragettes are slightly surprising – not to say hypocritical – in the context of increasing political violence across the globe. In the last years of the nineteenth century and the early years of the twentieth, a worldwide wave of anarchist assassinations and bombings had taken the lives of US president McKinley, President Carnot of France, Empress Elisabeth of Austria-Hungary, Umberto I of Italy, two Spanish prime ministers, and numerous assorted victims of less exalted status. Closer to home, such incidents as the Siege of Sidney Street and the mobilization of the Ulster and Irish Volunteers had provided yet more evidence of the efficacy of violence or the threat of violence in changing the political weather. Beneath the deceptively tranquil surface of Edwardian England, disturbing currents were stirring.

Mrs Pankhurst and Christabel took note and upped the ante accordingly, calling for 'civil war' and increased attacks on what Emmeline called the 'sacred idol of property'. Other, less fanatical members of the WSPU took fright. In 1912 Emmeline and Frederick Pethick-Lawrence, a wealthy couple whose deep pockets had helped fund the organization, met Christabel Pankhurst in Paris, whither she had fled to direct operations from the safety of exile while her mother was in prison. The Pethick-Lawrences voiced their worries about the violent strategy of the Pankhursts – and were promptly expelled from the WSPU for their pains. It is worth noting that, although the WSPU hogged the headlines with their violent acts, they were never more than a minority within the women's movement, with a membership of 2,000 compared to the 50,000 who belonged to the less militant Women's Freedom League.

Having purged the Pethick-Lawrences, Mrs Pankhurst and Christabel felt free to pursue their increasingly militant campaign unimpeded by caution. In 1913 they ascended the twin peaks of their campaign, when four rooms of Chancellor Lloyd George's country house in Surrey were fire-bombed in February, and Emily Davison made her suicidal Derby Day protest in June. These acts were carried out against a fiery background of arson attacks throughout the country, while Mrs Pankhurst spent the year in and out of prison. Within the prison walls hunger and thirst strikes by jailed suffragettes were answered by the authorities with forced feeding. Though no one had the nerve to attempt to force-feed Mrs Pankhurst herself, the idea of rubber tubes being shoved up the delicate nostrils and into the stomachs of respectable ladies while they were held down by brutish warders gave an invaluable new propaganda weapon to the suffragettes' formidable armoury.

The potent image of male prison doctors force-feeding helpless, pinioned women only reinforced the elder Pankhursts' insistence on the moral purity and superiority of women, and by extension the vile immorality of all – or almost all – men. Emmeline Pankhurst proclaimed the battle of the sexes a 'Holy war', while Christabel became increasingly obsessed with the twin evils of 'white slavery' and venereal disease. When the former moral panic – the idea that white women were being kidnapped en masse off Britain's streets and sold into slavery in the menacing Orient – was shown to be a fantasy, Christabel turned to the 'Great Scourge' of the pox, claiming that up to 80 per cent of married women were infected with VD by their husbands and advocating chastity as the only safe course for women.

A FAMILY DIVIDED

The year 1914 opened with the splits and schisms inside the WSPU reaching the very heart of the Pankhurst family itself. Mrs Pankhurst's second daughter, Sylvia, was an independent spirit with a mind and will of her own. Believing that feminism and socialism were two aspects of the same transforming force, she had maintained close contacts with the Labour party while her mother and elder sister had become bitterly anti-Labour, blaming it for propping up the detested Liberal government in Parliament.

An element of snobbishness was also a factor in the elder Pankhursts' disdain for Labour. Forgetting her own husband's role as a physician to the Mancunian poor, Mrs Pankhurst became, paradoxically, ever more inclined to mix with and favour the upper stratum of society, the more she assailed it.

Sylvia's closeness to Labour's leaders extended to her becoming the lover of the party's grizzled Scots founder, Keir Hardie – a relationship deeply disapproved of by her mother. Though nominally still in the WSPU, with her mother frequently in jail or touring America lecturing and her sister in Parisian exile, Sylvia had turned the movement's East End branch into her personal fiefdom, acting almost autonomously in relation to the rest of the WSPU and pursuing socialist projects in tandem with feminist ones.

In the autumn of 1913, Sylvia committed the ultimate sin of appearing at a rally in the Albert Hall alongside not only the Labour leader George Lansbury and James Connolly of the Irish Citizen Army, but also Frederick

Pethick-Lawrence, so recently excommunicated from the WSPU. In vain did Sylvia protest that with 10,000 people hearing her, this was one of the few ways left to the beleaguered and increasingly marginalized WSPU to reach a mass audience: she had finally stepped beyond the Pankhurst pale.

In January 1914 Sylvia was summoned, like an errant schoolgirl, to meet her mother and big sister in Paris. Christabel read her the riot act, concluding by denouncing the democratic structure of Sylvia's East London Federation. The elder Pankhurst daughter claimed that this meant that working-class – and therefore less educated – women were being promoted by Sylvia to the forefront of the movement. 'We want picked women, the very strongest and the most intelligent,' Christabel declared. The meeting concluded with Sylvia and her federation being expelled from the WSPU and cast into outer darkness.

Christabel's open declaration of elitism foreshadows the later political development of her mother and herself, and also of other leading WSPU members, three of whom, including the *Rokeby Venus* attacker Mary Richardson, became impassioned supporters, between the wars, of Sir Oswald Mosley, the incarnation of British fascism. Uncomfortably for admirers of the elder Pankhursts and the WSPU, it must be admitted that their sexual politics – authoritarian, elitist, anti-democratic – came very close to fascism.

Sylvia was not the only member of the family to feel the wrath of Emmeline and Christabel. The youngest Pankhurst daughter, Adela, a passionate and accomplished public speaker, had also blotted her copybook by striking an independent line and attempting to make a life of her own. She too was summoned to Paris and – literally – given her marching orders. In her case these consisted of a one-way ticket on an emigrant boat bound for Australia, together with a £20 parting gift from her imperious mother, who would never see her again.

TAKING THE STRUGGLE TO THE GATES OF THE PALACE

In the early months of 1914 Mrs Pankhurst was living the underground life of the hunted guerrilla leader she had become. To avoid the constant round of arrests and releases, she went to ground, staying in a succession of safe houses lent by wealthy friends and supporters. Only a select few – not even including her self-styled 'bodyguard' of strapping, physically robust suffragettes armed with rubber clubs – knew her whereabouts, and that favoured few were not telling.

In the first week of March 1914, Mrs Pankhurst emerged from her hiding place to address a packed meeting in Glasgow. With the WSPU's

ROCKING THE NATION: Christabel Pankhurst directed the militant suffragette campaign from exile in Paris. But when war came she and her mother Emmeline threw their patriotic support behind Britain's cause.

habitual military efficiency, members of the bodyguard had been secretly summoned the day before, travelling from London on the night train disguised as a theatrical troupe and using their rubber clubs as pillows. On arrival at the city's St Andrew's Hall, an hour before the meeting was due to begin, the bodyguard was distributed around the platform, which was further protected by a barbed-wire barricade, thinly hidden by bunting and bouquets. The besieged suffragettes were surrounded by a cordon of police keeping a sharp lookout for the most wanted woman in Britain, while eagle-eyed detectives on the doors checked the credentials of members of the public as they arrived.

One frail and elderly white-haired lady failed to attract more than a cursory glance as she tottered in. But on being admitted, Mrs Pankhurst – for it was she – shed her elderly persona and made her way down the aisle towards the platform in triumph. Raucous cheers greeted her as she was recognized, and she immediately launched into her scheduled speech, during which she made a direct link between 'the militancy in Ulster and the militancy of women'.

Angered at being fooled so easily, the police rushed the platform as the bodyguard rallied to defend its leader. Mrs Pankhurst's slight figure disappeared under a sea of flailing truncheons and rubber clubs as the two sexes joined battle. When she was finally apprehended, the suffragette leader was roughly handled by a Glasgow constabulary more used to throwing pub drunks onto Sauchiehall Street at closing time than to handling an upper-middle-class English gentlewoman with kid gloves. Her dress was ripped, her handbag stolen, and her necklace torn from her throat as she was unceremoniously dragged from the hall, her legs kicked and pummelled the while. She was thrown bodily into a black maria, insulted, and made to lie on the floor as she was taken to a police station.

Although she was released after five days' incarceration because of her customary hunger strike, it was this rough treatment of her beloved leader that so incensed Mary Richardson and caused her, the following day, to attack the *Rokeby Venus* in protest at what she called the 'slow murder' of Mrs Pankhurst.

The WSPU leader, undaunted by her Glasgow experience, was busy planning her next piece of street theatre. To demonstrate her contempt for the parliament that was refusing the vote, she declared that she would by-pass the Lords and Commons and take the women's case to the third pillar of constitutional authority in the kingdom: the king himself. After demanding an audience with the monarch (which was predictably refused), the WSPU, with its usual organizational care, put into place plans to 'rush the Palace' – on the same lines as it had 'rushed Parliament' in the past – hoping to overwhelm the guards by sheer weight of numbers.

The attempt to breach the defences of Buckingham Palace was made on 21 May 1914 – a sunny spring day. For three days preceding the demonstration, suffragettes – eventually including Emmeline Pankhurst herself – had secretly infiltrated and occupied the house of a sympathizer in Grosvenor Place, close to the palace. By the day of the demonstration there were 200 women in the house, and at a pre-arranged signal they issued forth, with a phalanx from the bodyguard leading the way, marching ten abreast to clear a path for Mrs Pankhurst. The formidable spearhead of the bodyguard managed to penetrate the police cordon around the palace, but a fierce battle erupted in which police on foot and mounted used their batons freely to beat women to the ground. The suffragettes retaliated by throwing marbles under the hooves of the horses and cut their reins – even in one case neatly severing the braces of a policeman, causing him to lose both his trousers and his dignity.

In the midst of the mêlée Mrs Pankhurst was arrested by an enormous police officer who swept her up bodily in his arms and carried her off, her trim ankles a full foot off the ground. An iconic photograph was taken of the scene as the WSPU leader, with a touching faith in her sovereign and his sympathy for her cause, called out 'Arrested at the palace gates – tell the King!' She was released a week later in the course of her eighth – and penultimate – hunger strike.

COMPROMISE IN THE SHADOW OF WAR

The rushing of Buckingham Palace proved to be the last hurrah of the militant suffragettes. Ironically, a Pankhurst would secure a partial promise from the hated politicians that the franchise would be extended to (at least some) women: but, certainly in the eyes of the WSPU leader, it was the wrong Pankhurst. Sylvia Pankhurst declared that she would carry out her next hunger strike in public – at the entrance to the House of Commons to shame its members. When she executed her threat by being carried on a stretcher to the entrance to the Strangers' Gallery, she won private meetings with the government's two leading lights: Asquith and Lloyd George.

Despite – or perhaps because of – the bombing of his house, Lloyd George had always believed in giving women the vote, and even Asquith now overcame his disdain for the suffragettes by making Sylvia a Delphic and ambiguous pronouncement: 'If the change has to come we must do it boldly and on a democratic basis.' Both men privately pledged that the next Liberal government would – at long last – give votes to women.

PATRIARCHY: suffragette leader Emmeline Pankhurst cries in protest as she is arrested during a demonstration outside Buckingham Palace, May 1914.

In fact, the Liberal leadership, rather than making a magnanimous gesture, was responding to irresistible political pressure from both Left and Right. The rising Labour party, on which the Liberals depended for getting progressive legislation on the statute book, had firmly allied itself with the constitutional wing of the women's movement, thus vindicating the view of moderate 'suffragists' that quiet pressure rather than noisy and violent protest was the most effective means of securing the female franchise. Meanwhile, on the Right, the Conservatives were planning to steal a march on the Liberals by promising to grant the vote to women – at least women with property – in their next election manifesto.

Caught in this cleft stick, the Liberals had little option but to give way. But it was important – particularly to Asquith, smarting from years of taunts, abuse and even physical attacks from Mrs Pankhurst's army – that he should not be seen to be surrendering to intimidation or violence. Hence his receiving, together with a delegation of women from her East London Federation, the Pankhurst daughter who had been anathematized by her mother.

Too late, Mrs Pankhurst attempted to follow Sylvia's example. Typically, she made her move in a letter to the Establishment's favourite newspaper, *The Times*. She announced that she intended to appear in public, get herself arrested with the 'usual accompaniment of brutality and insult', and, once inside prison walls, resume her hunger strike, challenging the authorities to do their worst and force-feed her 'as they had her friends'.

Anticipating the move which she had so publicly announced, the authorities tried a different tack. Mrs Pankhurst may have steeled herself against the prospect of being force-fed, but she had not expected the utter indignity of a strip search. Overcome by the physical force of the Holloway wardresses, she then refused to dress and lay naked on the floor of her cell. She also resumed her hunger strike as promised, but instead of force-feeding her, the authorities played the usual game of releasing her after a week's confinement – during which she lost a stone in weight.

It was, however, to be her final prison experience. For the suffragettes, as for so many in the final season of peace and the old world, the summer of 1914 changed everything. On 4 August, Britain declared war on Germany. Recuperating from her jail ordeal in the French port of Saint-Malo, Emmeline Pankhurst was for once caught off guard. However, she soon recovered her customary poise, perceiving that the war offered a way out of the impasse of fruitless violence and pointless protest into which she had driven her movement.

She offered a truce to the government which had persecuted her for the duration of the conflict, and the home secretary, Reginald McKenna, responded by ordering the release from jail of all detained suffragettes on 10 August. Mrs Pankhurst explained her new policy at a public meeting. Men, she now conceded, were not all sex-crazed beasts bent only on brutalizing women. 'The war has made me feel how much there is of nobility in man, in addition to the other thing which we all deplore.'

Christabel returned from her two-and-a-half years of exile in France, and mother and daughter put their shoulders to the patriotic wheel, bringing their formidable organizational skills to their new tasks with as much energy and dedication as they had previously given to the WSPU. Mrs Pankhurst became one of Lord Kitchener's most effective recruiting sergeants, storming halls up and down the land just as she had done for the past decade, but now urging men to go and fight and women to encourage them to do so and to take their place in factories and offices. Christabel for her part transformed the WSPU newspaper, *The Suffragette*, into a patriotic paper, which was renamed *Britannia* and offered editorial comment harping on the need for war to 'purify the race'.

The war also made final the breach in the Pankhurst family ranks. Just as the conflict shifted the stream of Emmeline and Christabel's molten energy from feminism to patriotism, so it changed Sylvia from a feminist socialist to a feminist communist. She changed the name of her East End wing of suffragism from the Women's Suffrage Federation to the Worker's Socialist Federation, supported international peace conferences in a bid to halt the war, and even helped hide men fleeing the draft – all at a time when her mother and sister were campaigning for compulsory conscription. Sylvia deplored her mother and sister's flag-wagging, while Emmeline and Christabel were appalled and 'ashamed' by her left-wing pacifism.

Historians of the women's movement still argue about the effectiveness or otherwise of the suffragette campaign. Images of their struggle are now an inseparable part of our picture of the Edwardian era and the run-up to war: the women marching with their green and purple trimmed banners; the noisy demonstrations; the violent arrests; the oratory from public platforms which defied Dr Johnson's misogynist dictum that to see a woman preaching was like watching a dog walking on its hind legs – 'It is not done well; but you are surprised to find it done at all.' The Pankhursts may, as their more moderate opponents alleged, have been authoritarian, undemocratic, shrill and fanatical man-haters whose violence set back rather than advanced their ostensible objective. But none can deny that, in the eyes of posterity, it was the suffragettes who made the sultry social and political weather – even if it was the war that finally changed the law.

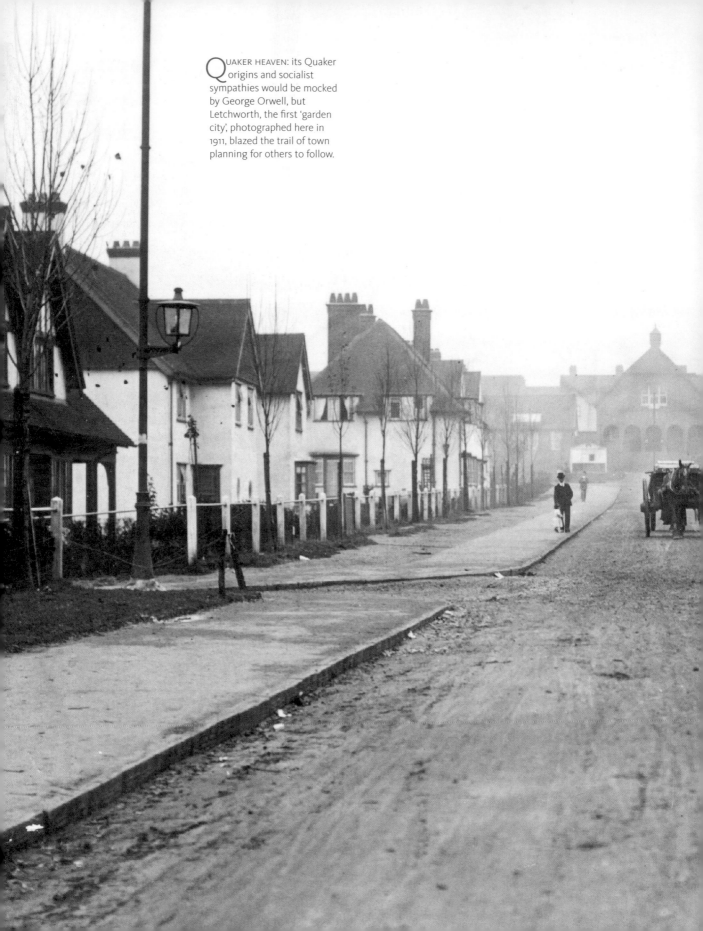

QUAKER HEAVEN: its Quaker origins and socialist sympathies would be mocked by George Orwell, but Letchworth, the first 'garden city', photographed here in 1911, blazed the trail of town planning for others to follow.

4. Home Fires

Britain in 1914 was a land of extreme inequalities in income and wealth distribution. Just under half of the national income went to some five million of the working population, while another fifteen million industrial and agricultural workers earned less than £160 a year – below the threshold for income tax. Almost one third of the working population was classed as living below the poverty line. Low wages failed to keep pace with a constantly rising cost of living, and – despite the minimal protection offered by the then chancellor of the exchequer David Lloyd George's 'People's Budget' of 1909 – the threat of unemployment was a constant fear, and the cramped, cold and ill-lit tenements, terraces and tumbledown cottages in which most people lived bred diseases such as tuberculosis, diphtheria and scarlet fever which carried off many years before their time.

Recruiting for the army at the time of the Second Boer War (1899–1902) had revealed a stunted generation. The typical working-class recruit was concave-chested and pigeon-toed, with limbs bent by rickets caused by dietary deficiencies (they lived largely on bread, dripping and tea). They wheezed and were smaller, thinner, had fewer teeth and lived shorter lives than their European counterparts.

AN AGE OF POVERTY

For the great mass of the population – perhaps 90 per cent of those living in cities – life remained a grinding struggle in which poverty, overcrowding, sickness, premature death, and poor housing, health and hygiene were an everyday reality. The workhouse for the truly indigent – and weekly visits to the pawnshop, as well as the pub – broke families as often as the frequent visitations of the grim reaper. The agricultural slump at the turn of the century had driven many of the rural poor into the overcrowded cities, where there was little space to house them. In 1914 just under 10 per cent of the population were living more than two to a room, and in London the figure was almost double that at 17 per cent. In the East End's poorest boroughs, such as Shoreditch, more than 36 per cent lived in such squalor, and the figures were much the same for the poorest northern cities such as Newcastle and Sunderland.

WORKING-CLASS HEROES? Machinists pose for the camera in a Burnley factory, c. 1905: the rise of organised labour was a threat to Tories and Liberals alike.

Even in prosperous, progressive Birmingham, fiefdom of the Liberal-turned-Unionist Joseph Chamberlain and his programme of 'municipal socialism', where the pre-war population had swollen to 530,000, 10 per cent were still living more than two to a room in 1914, and 40,000 were still dependent on a single tap serving at least thirty people. Such overcrowded and insanitary conditions bred and spread disease. In 1911 there were 5,000 new cases of tuberculosis reported in the city, which was served by just 300 acres of green parks. Eddie Marsh, Churchill's private secretary, records a visit with his boss to a working-class area of Manchester, where Churchill had a parliamentary seat from 1906 until 1908. 'Fancy living in one of these streets,' Churchill mused to Marsh. 'Never seeing anything beautiful, never eating anything savoury, never saying anything clever.' Yet such was the lot of the vast majority of Churchill's constituents.

The situation was no better for the rural poor. In February 1914, Lloyd George – himself hailing from a rural Welsh background – acted on the recommendations of the Rowntree Committee, which had found that 60 per cent of agricultural workers were even worse off than their urban brethren, earning less than eighteen shillings (ninety pence) a week. Lloyd

George had begun a campaign to alleviate such poverty – he was working on proposals for doing so in his next budget while fighting the general election, expected in 1915 but never held – when he was overtaken by the war. Like so much else, ending rural poverty was put on hold for the duration.

Given the plight of both industrial and agricultural workers, it is scarcely surprising that one of the major developments of the Edwardian age was the rise of the Labour party, dedicated to bettering the conditions of the poor. And it is little surprise that, partly as a response to this threat on their Left, the governing Liberals – who in the nineteenth century had been the apostles of unfettered free trade, capitalism and the liberty of the individual – should have moved towards collectivism and the state amelioration of poverty.

AN AGE OF REFORM

The result was a raft of sweeping social reforms. These included the provision of school meals; the abolition of solitary confinement in jails; the introduction of Borstal reformatories for young offenders; health insurance, which by 1914 was providing a minimum safety net for thirteen million people against illness and infirmity; old-age pensions (970,000 elderly people applied for their new pensions in 1914 at a cost of £8 million); and a shake-up of the ancient Poor Laws, dating back to Elizabethan times, which spelled the end of the notorious Dickensian workhouses.

In 1914 an Act was passed by Parliament which extended the school meals scheme by compelling local education authorities to provide meals at the central exchequer's expense. By then, the school meals service was providing fourteen million free lunches a year to some 158,000 needy children. Startlingly for those who know him as the fiercely imperialist Tory of his later years, among the most radical of the Liberal reformers was Winston Churchill, who introduced labour exchanges as job-finding agencies for the unemployed. By 1914 there were 430 of them dotted across the land.

Most members of the middle classes, having only recently escaped from the underclass themselves, preferred to turn a blind eye to the sad state of their fellow Britons and hastened to move to the leafy suburbs spreading out from the cities. Some, however – notably the socially progressive Quakers and the Fabian Society with its own socialist agenda – resolved to do what they could to ameliorate the conditions in which the majority languished. Company towns like Port Sunlight, built by the soap manufacturer Lever Brothers, and the Quaker Cadbury company's Bournville near Birmingham established the principle of spaced-out housing in green fields, far from the smoke and smog of city factories. By 1914 the first

URBS IN HORTO: a railway poster extolling the joys of urban life in rural Essex. Harlow, later a New Town, was one of several planned attempts to escape the clutter and squalor of Victorian slums.

garden city – at Letchworth in Hertfordshire, founded by another Quaker, Ebenezer Howard – was already a decade old. Such experiments in planned living seemed to point the way to a healthier, happier future for working folk – until the shots at Sarajevo in June.

But it was an ill wind that blew no one any good. The war would give a shot in the arm to the ailing parts of industrial Britain. Leicester, for instance, the traditional home of the boot and shoe industry, not only raised service battalions of volunteers to enrol in Kitchener's New Armies, but benefited from government contracts to make the boots in which they would march. By the end of 1914 the Leicester Boot and Shoe Operatives Union noted with some satisfaction that for the first time ever not a single one of its members was drawing on the union's own unemployment fund. The rag trade in woollens and cottons in such cities as Leeds also benefited from government contracts to make uniforms.

As the front lines in France and Flanders stabilized and then solidified into trenches and dugouts, miners found their tunnelling skills much in demand. A skilled underground worker – known in the army as a 'clay kicker' – could be on five or six shillings a day 'danger money', earning as much as five times what his surface counterpart, the ordinary Tommy, made from putting his life on the line. Despite the desperately dangerous and hellishly unpleasant conditions beneath the trenches, there was no shortage of volunteers for this perilous duty, where death from collapsing tunnels or counter-mines laid by the enemy was a daily occurrence. Nonetheless, by December 1914 14 per cent of all miners had joined the colours, and there was a shortage of skilled pitmen to dig the coal at home. As a result some schools had to close their doors that winter, and by the beginning of 1915 the price of coal had rocketed by 20 per cent.

THE WORKERS UNITED...

In stark contrast to its rival Germany, Britain's industrial infrastructure had remained mired in the ways of the nineteenth century – modes and methods appropriate to the first country to have experienced the Industrial Revolution, but not to the new century that had now begun. The advent of the reforming Liberal government in 1906 had coincided with a cyclical economic slump, creating a perfect storm in which the growing expectations of the working class for a radical improvement in their conditions met a rise in the cost of living, a slowdown in growth, shrinking exports and rising unemployment.

The result was a series of devastating strikes which – beneath the superficially tranquil surface of Edwardian social stability – shook the country to its very core. In 1908 alone more days were lost to stoppages than in the previous decade. In the north-east, where shipbuilding in the Tyneside yards was peculiarly vulnerable to cycles of boom and bust, empty order books led to wage cuts. This in turn led to a prolonged four-month strike, followed by an employers' lock-out. In the same region, engineering workers staged a seven-month wildcat strike against wage cuts.

In 1909 industrial unrest moved underground. Strikes spread like brushfires through the coalfields of Yorkshire, Northumberland and Durham. Nowhere was miners' militancy more bitter than in South Wales, where, in 1910, miners in the village of Tonypandy refused to accept lower wage rates offered for working a new seam and were locked out. Five other pits went on strike in solidarity, bringing 30,000 pitmen out, and – notoriously – the then home secretary, Winston Churchill, ordered troops into the area to restore order after riots threatened to get out of hand. This became an urban legend within the Labour movement, caricaturing Churchill as a monster who sent soldiers to shoot down starving miners and their families, and the strike left a lasting legacy of bitterness that poisoned industrial relations in mining for decades.

In 1911 it was the turn of seamen, dockers and transport workers in the ports to come out in protest at their working conditions and low pay. Spurred on by the oratory of the London dockers' leader, Ben Tillett, they demanded eightpence an hour for a ten-hour shift. The unrest, enflamed by the heat of a long, hot summer, spread from Southampton to Hull, and this time there was real blood on the streets and genuine fatalities as troops fired on rioters in Liverpool and Wales. Printers who produced a pamphlet entitled *Don't Shoot*, urging soldiers not to fire on their fellow workers, were jailed, though its author, the revolutionary socialist Tom Mann, was spared as he was thought to be too popular to prosecute. The situation was exacerbated by 'blackleg' non-union labour being brought in, protected by police and soldiers, to break the strikes, and by dark threats from Prime Minister Asquith that he would use all the resources at the state's disposal to enforce order. A suggestion that the new Territorial Force of part-time soldiers should be brought in to repress the strikes was vetoed for fear that the untested army reservists would side with the strikers.

As in many trade disputes of the era it was Lloyd George who finally defused the situation. The Welsh wizard poured his voluble Celtic emollience on these troubled waters. Calling both sides – employers and strikers – in for conciliation talks, the silver-tongued chancellor found a peace formula and persuaded the suspicious strikers to end their action and return to work. Lloyd George, with his own humble Welsh

background, sympathized with the strikers, telling his hard-line Liberal colleague Churchill in 1910: 'Listen. There were 600 men turned off by the Great Western Railway Works last week. There is not a man in those Works who does not live in terror of the day when his turn will come to go. Well, I am against a social order that admits that kind of thing.'

The state had become queasily aware of the less than perfect condition of the poor in England as a result of the wave of industrial unrest that had spread through the land between 1910 and 1912. In this time the numbers involved in industrial disputes doubled from half a million to a million, while the number of disputes rocketed from 521 to 872. Trouble peaked in 1912 when a million and a half workers went on strike and the number of days lost to industrial action grew to forty million – ten times that of any previous year. Once again the miners – as so often in the vanguard of industrial militancy – spearheaded the stoppages with a demand for 'five and two': a minimum wage of five shillings per shift for men at the coalface, and a two shilling minimum for teenage boys who worked down the pits with them. For the first time, sporadic local strikes became an organized national walk-out in February when the Miners' Federation

WAISTCOAT REVOLUTIONARY: a nattily dressed Ben Tillett, leader of the crippling dock strikes of 1911–12, addresses a London strike rally. But when war came in 1914 Tillett's backing proved his patriotism to be stronger than his socialism.

called their members out. Two million men went on strike, pits lay idle, and in the midst of winter coal stocks dwindled.

The government was panicked into rushing a Minimum Wages Bill into law, which granted the strikers' demand for a national minimum wage – although they did not receive the 'five and two' they had been demanding. No sooner was the strike settled, however, than another national dispute broke out: this time paralysing London's dockland, where workers struck in a failed protest against non-union labour.

LABOUR ON THE RISE

The prolonged wave of stoppages was driven by a labour market in which real wages were falling and by an ever present and growing terror of joblessness – despite Lloyd George's tentative introduction of a skeleton welfare state. The industrial unrest was also indicative of a newly confident Labour and trade union movement. Many Liberals were sympathetic to the aims of the Labour party, which had seen thirty MPs elected in the Liberal landslide election victory of 1906; what they did not see is that the newcomer to the radical wing of British politics would one day replace them. One of the Liberal government's first initiatives, therefore, had been the 1906 Trades Disputes Act, which for the first time legalized such novelties as picketing, sympathetic strikes and secondary boycotts; it also gave the unions a degree of protection against claims for compensation and damages.

Along with Labour's growing political influence, trade union membership was also increasing, especially among unskilled trades, rising by more than 60 per cent in the four years from 1910 to 1914. The clout and bargaining power of the unions was also enhanced by the merger and amalgamation of small unions into powerful national bodies, such as the National Transport Workers' Federation in 1910 and the National Union of Railwaymen in 1913. In 1914 the three largest unions, representing miners, transport workers and railwaymen, formed the 'Triple Alliance', agreeing to co-ordinate contracts and co-operate in future industrial action.

Even as strikes engulfed the country, most trade union leaders remained impeccably moderate. There were running disputes within the unions between a leadership wedded to improving pay and conditions, preferably by peaceful bargaining, and more militant rank-and-file local leaders in the workplace, such as Tom Mann, who were prepared to reach for the strike weapon more readily and were often inspired by revolutionary social goals. At least since the Chartist movement of the 1840s, and 1848, the year of European revolutions, Britain – and London in particular – had provided a welcome environment for foreign revolutionaries, including such figures as

Marx, Engels and Kropotkin. In the mid-1900s the Russian revolutionaries Lenin, Trotsky and Stalin had all visited London and held their party congresses in the city.

The syndicalist movement, which saw the revolutionary strike as the best weapon in the struggle for socialism, gained little traction in Britain, despite the frequent presence of so many foreign revolutionaries. The leaders of the Labour party, then as now, saw their militant rhetoric fade away the older they grew and the closer they got to real power. This moderation, in which the influence of the Nonconformist churches proved stronger than that of the various Marxist political sects, was maintained despite horrifying social inequality. Of a population of just over 46 million in 1914, under half a million earned more than £500 a year. Only those earning more than £160 paid income tax, and there were less than a million people liable to do so.

FABIANS AND SOCIALISTS

The wretched condition of the British working classes was also brought home by the reports of social reformers such as the Quaker Seebohm Rowntree and by the activities of groups such as the Fabian Society, which boasted the talents of such socialist luminaries as Sidney and Beatrice Webb and the writers George Bernard Shaw and H. G. Wells. Wells himself was a typically unhealthy product of late Victorian and early Edwardian working-class life, being the son of a professional cricketer and a domestic servant and lacking a lung. He was both a champion of the class from which he came and an atypical representative of it, having bettered his condition by his own brilliantly original talents. An idiosyncratic socialist, his brand of the doctrine was authoritarian and even presaged fascism with its call for the breeding of Nietzschean supermen and the weeding-out of the unfit and the inferior in the name of the fashionable doctrine of eugenics.

But for all their nominal adherence to international socialism, the Fabians – as Lenin acutely perceived – were ultimately insular Little Englanders, concerned with domestic detail and pettifogging parochialism rather than the wider picture. An analysis of the contents of the weekly *New Statesman* of July 1914 – then, as now, the house journal of what passes for England's radical Left intelligentsia – reveals that as the rest of Europe spun towards war, the magazine's writers were concerned with such subjects as stage censorship (Ibsen's *Ghosts*, which deals with vene-real disease, had just been licensed for a private London performance); Diaghilev's modish Russian ballet; a review of a book on eugenics; and Mrs Webb's thoughts on 'Personal Rights and the Women's Movement'.

PLAYING THE GAME:
a football team from
Malmesbury, Wiltshire,
during the 1913/14 season.
Sport provided a diversion
from humdrum lives for
players and spectators alike.

Letters to the editor did not mention the coming war, but waxed lyrical on a woman's right to motherhood, the crime of poverty and the rising cost of divorce.

The *New Statesman* issue of 18 July carried an advertisement for the Fabians' summer school, while the following week – as final ultimatums were issued, ambassadors packed their bags and armies mobilized across the continent – the editorial gave the quietly smug reassurance that 'Germany is entirely opposed to a military upheaval in Europe just now'. A week later, the continent was at war.

'PLAY UP! PLAY UP! AND PLAY THE GAME!'

While the eggheads of the *New Statesman* were engaged in their earnest debates, members of H. G. Wells's class, in their millions, were improving – or amusing – themselves by participating in or watching competitive sport.

Sport had come into its own as a mass leisure activity during the late Victorian and Edwardian period. The middle classes embraced cricket, tennis and golf; while the workers followed the great football clubs born in the last decades of the nineteenth century. The Football League had been founded in 1888, its twelve member clubs – Accrington, Aston Villa, Blackburn Rovers, Bolton Wanderers, Burnley, Derby County, Everton, Notts County, Preston North End, Stoke F.C., West Bromwich Albion and Wolverhampton Wanderers – drawn from the industrial Midlands and North of England rather than the 'soft south'. In 1914, for the first time, football received a royal seal of approval when, on 25 April, George V became the first reigning monarch to attend an FA Cup final, then always played at Crystal Palace's south London ground. The sovereign saw Burnley defeat Liverpool 1–0 with a goal scored in the fifty-seventh minute by the prolific centre-forward Bert Freeman.

In cricket, the era from 1890 to 1914 has come to be seen as a 'golden age'. Cricketers like the dazzling Surrey opening batsman J. B. ('Jack') Hobbs and Yorkshire's all-rounder Wilfred Rhodes became national heroes. Between 1895 and the early 1900s India's prince of cricketers, K(umar) S(hri) Ranjitsinhji, formed a well-nigh invincible partnership for Sussex with the great C. B. Fry. Ranjitsinhji, who in 1907 became the Maharaja Jam Sahib of the Indian state of Nawanagar, was so magical a batsman that the cricket writer Neville Cardus would describe him as 'the Midsummer Night's dream of cricket' (and 'Ranji' even earned a playful reference in James Joyce's novel *Finnegans Wake*). Fry was an Edwardian Renaissance man and an athlete of such stature and renown that he was as much in demand on the football field as on the cricket pitch: he was Kipling's 'flannelled fool at the wicket and muddied oaf at the goal' made into glorious flesh. The 'ultimate all-rounder', as his epitaph would describe him, he played for his country in both games and represented Southampton FC in a cup final in 1902.

The venerable bearded figure of Dr William Gilbert Grace – known variously as 'The Doctor', 'The Old Man' or just plain 'W. G.' – played first-class cricket for an extraordinary forty-four seasons, from 1865 until 1908, continuing to notch up first-class centuries when he was well into middle age. He played his last innings in a competitive game as late as 25 July 1914, a week after his sixty-sixth birthday, when he scored 69 not out for Eltham cricket club in a match played in the nascent south-east London suburb of Grove Park.

On 26 August 1914, after hearing news of the casualty figures at the Battle of Mons (see page 235), Grace wrote a letter to *The Sportsman* newspaper calling for the cessation of the county cricket season and for county cricketers to set an example by enlisting in the forces forthwith. In the event, one further round of matches was played in the County Championship before the season was brought to a premature end on 2 September. The man who topped that truncated season's bowling averages, Kent's epileptic, violin-playing left-arm spinner Colin Blythe, joined the King's Own Light Infantry on the outbreak of war and was killed near Passchendaele on 8 November 1917, a victim of random shell-fire. He was one of some 210 first-class cricketers who joined the armed forces, of whom thirty-four would perish before the county championship resumed in May 1919. Hobbs and Rhodes survived the war to recommence their cricketing careers: the Surrey man eventually scoring a record 197 first-class hundreds; the Yorkshireman appearing in more first-class matches than any man before or since.

And as for 'W.G.', the indomitable leviathan of cricket's golden age still had the energy to shout and shake his fist at German Zeppelins as they drifted over his south London home in 1915, the year of his death from a cerebral haemorrhage.

A BATSMAN AND A GENTLEMAN: Charles Burgess Fry was the ultimate Edwardian all-rounder, playing in an FA Cup final, breaking the world long-jump record – and even turning down an offer of the throne of Albania.

FINAL FAREWELL: the *Titanic* leaves Ireland on her fatal maiden voyage, April 1912. Her loss failed to halt the fashion for transatlantic travel by luxury liners.

5. Liners

THE TWENTY-SIXTH OF FEBRUARY 1914 dawned dank, grey and cold in Belfast – a typical cheerless Ulster winter day. A raw wind whipped the Irish Sea and the chilly waters of Lough Neagh into white horses, yet the squat terraces surrounding the giant Harland and Wolff shipbuilding yard challenged the dismal day with a brave display of red, white and blue bunting. It was not, however, the gathering campaign against Irish Home Rule that had set the hearts of the stolidly Protestant shipyard workers and their families a-flutter on this particular morning, but the event that was taking place that day: the launch of the yard's latest pride and joy, the third and last of the White Star shipping line's giant Olympic-class transatlantic liners, HMHS *Britannic*.

As those on board the still-incomplete ship cheered and fluttered white handkerchiefs from decks and portholes for the benefit of the newsreel cameras and the crowds watching on shore, the huge ship slid smoothly down the slipway and into the waiting waters of Lough Neagh. This was indeed a moment of triumph to savour for the workers who had built the ship, the 860 members of her crew, and the directors of the ill-starred White Star line who had commissioned her. Weighing 48,158 tons, displacing 53,200 tons and 882 feet 9 inches long from stem to stern, the *Britannic* – with her nine decks and twenty-nine coal-fired engines, whose 50,000 horsepower could push her through the waves at a maximum speed of twenty-three knots – was indeed a marvel of modern maritime design and engineering. But it was more than her technical superlatives that the crowds witnessing her launch that chilly February day were celebrating.

The *Britannic*, marvellous as she was, was no ordinary new ocean-going liner. Her birth, for the thousands watching, signified the arrival of a new live child following the death of a much loved elder sibling. In a symbolic sense, she was the assertion of new life over a tragic death. For the sibling which had gone before was none other than *Britannic*'s sister ship, the *Titanic*.

ABOARD THE FLOATING PALACES

Transatlantic travel in the first decade of the twentieth century had become more than the grim necessity it had been for the millions of storm-tossed, near-penniless migrants who had made the crossing to the New World in

DOOMED: the *Titanic*'s White Star line sister ship *Britannic* is launched in Belfast in February 1914. She would sink in the Aegean Sea in November 1916 while being used as a wartime hospital ship.

the nineteenth century. Sea voyages, for those who could afford them, had become both a luxury and a pleasure: a change brought about by increasing prosperity and higher expectations, coupled with the advances in marine design made by Brunel and his successors, such as the turbine-propulsion engine, which from 1903 allowed crossings from Liverpool and Southampton to New York to be made in unheard-of and record-breaking times.

As a result, the rigid class stratification of Victorian and Edwardian England had been transposed to the ships that crossed the Atlantic, with palatial luxury on the upper-class decks descending progressively down to the sweat-box, chicken-coop-like cabins endured by those travelling 'steerage' deep in the bowels of the same ships. Out of the welter of shipping lines competing to transport passengers across the Atlantic, by the dawn of the new century two major leaders had emerged, Cunard and White Star.

Cunard had originated in the 1870s from a steamship packet company founded in 1839 by a Canadian, Samuel Cunard. In 1902, nettled by the

fact that the German liners *Deutschland* and *Kronprinz Wilhelm* were regularly winning – and keeping – the coveted Blue Riband awarded for the speediest westbound Atlantic crossings, the British government decided to support Cunard's bid to win back the title. This backing took the substantial form of a massive £2.26 million subsidy loan to Cunard at a low 2.75 per cent interest rate, together with an annual top-up of £150,000. The loan was made on the understanding that the line would use the cash to build two turbine-driven liners, each capable of travelling at twenty-five knots – more than the top speeds with which their German rivals had snatched the Blue Riband.

There was a secret clause in the lending agreement between the government and Cunard, to the effect that the new liners, to be named the *Lusitania* and the *Mauretania*, would be designed so that they could easily and quickly be converted into warships in the event of war. The Anglo-German naval race which saw the two powers striving to outdo each other in building fleets of warships had now spilled over into the civil sphere.

There was competition, too, within Cunard itself between the two new liners, which were built at rival Scottish and English shipyards: the *Lusitania* at John Brown's on the Clyde, and the *Mauretania* at Swan Hunter on the Tyne. So massive was the *Lusitania* – fitted with four huge bronze propellers and weighing in at an unprecedented 44,000 tons, making it the biggest ship afloat – that the River Clyde itself had to be dredged deeper and wider in order to accommodate her.

It was, however, the *Mauretania* that won the race to be launched first, in September 1906. The *Lusitania* snatched the Blue Riband back from the Germans in October 1907, but her sister ship would pluck the accolade from her in September 1909, and would thereafter hold the Blue Riband until 1929. Though built for speed, the *Mauretania's* interior designers did not stint on luxury inside the great ship. Her main staircase was modelled on a fifteenth-century Italian palazzo, her woodwork was made from stained French walnut, and the first-class lounge and music room echoed a French salon of the eighteenth century. Not for nothing did brochures advertising the liner's delights describe her as a 'floating palace'.

Faced with the twin threat presented by her deadly rival's new ships, the White Star Line rose to the challenge. Since 1899, when he had inherited the line from his father, Thomas Ismay, the man in charge of the White Star's destiny was its chairman J. Bruce Ismay. An astute and ruthless businessman, Ismay decided that, if he could not compete with Cunard's speed, he would outdo them in luxury. He commissioned Harland and Wolff to build two new super-liners simultaneously at their Belfast yard.

GOLDEN AGE: a poster of the White Star Line's luckier rival Cunard promotes their luxury liner fleet as the last word in sophisticated, comfortable transatlantic travel.

The new vessels would be the last word in size and magnificence, catering for their passengers' every creature comfort. They were to be called the *Olympic* and the *Titanic*.

THE UNSINKABLE GIANTS

The Belfast yard had never been faced with building ships of such monstrous size before, and Sir William Arrol, architect of Scotland's famous Forth Rail Bridge, was called in to make a gantry of sufficient size and strength to accommodate the sister ships as they were put together alongside one another. The man in charge of the project was Harland and Wolff's managing director and chief designer Thomas Andrews. Though he was said to know everything there was to know about ships and the sea, the scale of the task was beyond even Andrews's experience. Nevertheless, undaunted, he set about it with all the confidence and enthusiasm he could muster.

A White Star promotional brochure produced in 1910 for the *Titanic* and *Olympic* stated that 'these two wonderful vessels are designed to be unsinkable'. Andrews designed a double-bottomed hull which he hoped would be proof against all but the sharpest rock; and to make assurance doubly sure, both ships were divided into sixteen watertight compartments so that if one were pierced, the others would stay dry. He did not reckon with a deadly tear ripping through more than one compartment like a tin-opener.

White Star's chairman Ismay, eager to accomodate as many luxurious features as possible, sacrificed safety for the comfort of his passengers and the convenience of the crew. Not wishing to clutter up the decks with lifeboats, he provided only enough to accommodate about one third of those on board. He certainly did not stint on the liners' internal fittings and furniture. There were lounges, libraries, a swimming-pool, gymnasium and Turkish bath – though the best of the facilities were reserved for first-class passengers only.

The first liner down the launch slipway was the *Olympic*, which made her maiden voyage in June 1911 – ten months before the infamous and ill-fated uncompleted Atlantic crossing made by her bigger and slightly younger sister, the *Titanic*. In her first year, before the *Titanic* briefly took the prize, the *Olympic* was the largest ship afloat, and she escaped the notoriety of both the *Titanic* and the *Britannic* because, unlike them, her career did not end in shipwreck and tragedy. After a blameless and humdrum quarter-century of service, *Olympic* was laid up and scrapped in 1935. Neither of her sister ships would be so lucky.

After the *Titanic* came so spectacularly to grief when she collided with an iceberg on her maiden voyage to New York in April 1912, there were calls to scrap the whole concept of super-liners. Ismay, widely castigated for cowardice after he left the sinking ship, resigned in disgrace to live out his days in shameful humiliation, but the directors who took over the White Star Line were determined that not even a disaster as spectacular as the *Titanic*'s sinking should be allowed to stand in the way of luxury sea travel.

Reasoning that attack was the best form of defence, they gave orders for the construction of *Britannic*, the third ship in the Olympic class of liners, to go ahead as planned in the same shipyard where *Titanic* had been built. There were rumours that the new liner was to have been called *Gigantic*, but in the wake of the *Titanic*'s fate this was thought to be too hubristic and the name *Britannic* was substituted. As concessions to an outraged and alarmed public opinion, however, White Star authorized major modifications to both the *Olympic* and the *Britannic* as a direct result of the *Titanic* tragedy, to make sure that the disaster which had cost more than 1,500 lives would never be repeated. Above all, these improvements included the provision of enough lifeboats to hold everyone on board.

FEEDING THE WORM OF DOUBT

The loss of the *Titanic*, terrible as it was, did not seem to many observers to be entirely a bolt from the blue. It was one of several such reminders of the fragility of human existence, which the enormous pomp and overweening confidence of Edwardian England could not completely conceal. Barely a month before the great liner upended and slid beneath the icy sea, a man who, in direct contrast to the cowardly Ismay, was represented as the quintessential British hero, the Polar explorer Robert Falcon Scott, had also perished in unforgiving ice, as he struggled back from the South Pole, a goal to which he had been beaten by the less gentlemanly, but more realistic Norwegian Roald Amundsen.

If the soaring super-liners, with their rows of gleaming portholes illuminated by electricity and their mighty engines pounding through the seas, were the ultimate symbol of Edwardian society's triumph over nature, it was very clear that nature had nasty ways of hitting back. Another symptom of the unease worming its way beneath the seemingly solid foundations of a secure society was the vogue for the supernatural, which particularly manifested itself around the time of the *Titanic*'s catastrophic end. Some passengers were said to have dreamed of the disaster in advance – including one of its more famous victims, the campaigning journalist W. T. Stead, editor of the *Pall Mall Gazette*, whose sensationalist exposures of London vice and paedophilia had both titillated and shocked a prurient public – and earned Stead a jail sentence. Later in life Stead had become a spiritualist and was said to have fatalistically awaited his end on the liner and his transition to another world without attempting to escape his destiny.

Like the vogue for invasion literature, a number of books and stories appeared prior to the *Titanic*'s final voyage which appeared eerily to predict her fate. Most strangely prophetic among these was the 1898 story *Futility* by Morgan Robertson, an American author of seafaring tales whose novel featured an enormous Atlantic liner called the *Titan*, carrying a cargo of rich and complacent characters, which had come to grief and foundered after striking an iceberg on a cold April night.

There were other striking similarities between Robertson's fiction and the awesome facts of the *Titanic*. The real *Titanic* displaced 52,310 tons, while Robertson's *Titan* was only slightly larger at 70,000. The *Titanic* was 882.5 feet long, and Robertson's imagined leviathan 800 feet. Both vessels had three propellers which powered them along at twenty-five knots; both could carry 3,000 passengers, but only had lifeboat space for a fraction of those aboard; and it was boasted that both were unsinkable.

The loss of the *Titanic* shattered the myth that Edwardian technology had tamed nature red in tooth and claw. Even one of the new wonders of the decade – the vaunted radio communications developed by Guglielmo Marconi – had failed to summon other vessels in the vicinity of the stricken ship in time to save more of her passengers. Indeed, the continuing vulnerability of large ships at sea was underlined only three months after the launch of the *Britannic*, in May 1914, when yet another transatlantic liner, the *Empress of Ireland*, sank in the St Lawrence Seaway, drowning no fewer than 1,012 people.

The sinking of the *Empress* has been almost completely overshadowed by the foundering of the larger *Titanic* just two years before, even though the loss of life was almost as great (1,514 died on the *Titanic*) and the circumstances just as dramatic.

The *Empress of Ireland* was operated by another of the large lines, the Canadian Pacific. Built at Govan shipyard on the Clyde and launched in 1906, the *Empress* was not as large as her White Star and Cunard competitors, being 570 feet long and only half as heavy. She had just embarked on her ninety-sixth Atlantic crossing on the Quebec–Liverpool route when disaster struck.

At around 2 a.m. on the morning of 29 May, the *Empress*, which had left Quebec soon after 4 p.m. the previous day, was nosing cautiously along the wide St Lawrence River, guided by the green, yellow and red river traffic

FORGOTTEN *TITANIC*: the *Empress of Ireland*, the liner that came to grief in Canada's St Lawrence Seaway in May 1914: more than 1,000 died.

lights. Her master, Captain Henry Kendall, was used to the route. A skilled sailor who had first gone to sea on sailing boats at the tender age of fourteen, Kendall had been given his first command in 1900 – the same year in which he survived his first shipwreck, in a ship ominously named the *Lusitania*, off Newfoundland. In 1908 he had worked with Marconi at the ship end of the Italian inventor's revolutionary ship-to-shore radio, and two years later Kendall achieved fame when he became instrumental in the arrest of the Edwardian era's most notorious murderer, Dr Hawley Harvey Crippen.

'O CAPTAIN! MY CAPTAIN! our fearful trip is done': Captain Henry Kendall walks with a passenger on the deck of his ship the *Empress of Ireland* off Quebec on 28 May 1914, the day before the disaster.

CRIPPEN AND THE BODY IN THE CELLAR

In 1910, Crippen, a tiny, mild-mannered, bespectacled American physician with a fondness for homeopathic remedies, either accidentally or deliberately administered a fatal dose of the drug hyoscine hydrobromide to his demanding and disaffected wife, a music-hall singer whose stage name was Belle Elmore. Crippen dismembered the body and hid most of it in the cellar of his house in Hilldrop Crescent, Holloway, north London. He then disappeared, accompanied by his surgery secretary and young lover, Ethel Le Neve.

Alerted by concerned friends of Belle and unconvinced by Crippen's story that she had deserted him, gone to America and died there, the police, led by Chief Inspector Walter Dew, searched the offending cellar and found parcels of Belle's flesh. (Crippen had burned her bones.) The doctor and Ethel, the latter unconvincingly disguised as a boy and posing as Crippen's son, had fled to the Flemish port of Antwerp and booked a passage to Quebec in the names of Mr and Master Robinson on board the Canadian Pacific liner SS *Montrose*, whose master was none other than Henry Kendall.

Reading of the hue and cry raised in London for the missing couple in the *Daily Mail*, Kendall viewed his strange passenger and his 'son' with a suspicious eye. Deciding to play the detective himself, he secretly searched their cabin for clues and began to stalk and even photograph them. Seeing the father and son kissing and canoodling when they thought they were unobserved, Kendall put two and two together and concluded that his passengers were the wanted pair. Using Marconi's wonderful ship-to-shore radio, he contacted Scotland Yard with the message:

HAVE STRONG SUSPICIONS THAT CRIPPEN LONDON CELLAR MURDERER AND ACCOMPLICE ARE AMONG SALOON PASSENGERS. MOUSTACHE TAKEN OFF GROWING BEARD. ACCOMPLICE DRESSED AS BOY; VOICE MANNER AND BUILD UNDOUBTEDLY A GIRL.

The Yard sent Inspector Dew in hot pursuit of his quarry aboard the White Star liner SS *Laurentic*, which had a faster turn of speed than the lumbering *Montrose*. Meanwhile, on the *Montrose*, Crippen and Kendall had struck up a friendly relationship. Once, little knowing that he was observing the instrument of his own doom, Crippen looked up at the *Montrose*'s radio mast and remarked: 'It's a wonderful invention.'

When they reached the St Lawrence Seaway, a heavy fog was blanketing the river – just as it would, fatally, when the *Empress of Ireland* foundered. As the *Montrose*'s foghorn sounded mournfully through the mist at regular intervals, a small cutter made its way towards the liner. Kendall explained to Crippen that the boat bore the pilots who would guide the ship into port. In fact it contained Inspector Dew, himself disguised in a pilot's uniform. The two disguised imposters, the policeman/pilot and Crippen/Robinson, met in Kendall's cabin, with the captain watching proceedings with a precautionary revolver stowed in his pocket.

As Crippen put out his hand in greeting, Dew whipped off his pilot's cap and announced he was arresting the doctor for the murder of his wife. It was Kendall's finest hour, and Marconi's 'wonderful invention' had proved its worth. But little did the captain know, as he watched the diminutive doctor, clad in an Ulster coat with his face muffled by a scarf, led down the *Montrose*'s gangplank by a grim and extravagantly moustachioed Dew to his eventual appointment with a Pentonville jail hangman, that his eagle-eyed triumph would be tragically trumped in the same fog-shrouded waters by a human catastrophe far dwarfing the death and dismemberment of Belle Elmore.

THE SINKING OF THE *EMPRESS*

Only promoted to command the *Empress* less than a month before, Kendall, despite knowing the St Lawrence so well, was cautious as he strained his eyes through the dark. He cursed softly as the first tell-tale threads of fog curled around the bridge. Soon visibility was down to nothing, and he was uneasily aware that his ship was not alone. He had seen a squat and ugly collier, the *Storstad* by name, which, though Norwegian, had been made in a British shipyard, nosing through the same waters with her sharp ice-breaking prow questing ahead like some bird of prey's beak. Kendall's alert seaman's eyes had taken this in, but he was confident that the old tub was safely on his port side.

Suddenly, with a tearing, terrifying crash, his confidence and his peace of mind were shattered as the *Storstad*'s sharp prow ploughed into the *Empress*'s starboard side, gouging an enormous hole in the liner through which the St Lawrence gushed. As the great ship listed, more water poured

VICTIMS: pages from the *Graphic* magazine, showing some of those who died in the sinking of the *Empress of Ireland*. Among the 1,012 victims of the disaster were the actor Laurence Irving (son of the great Victorian actor-manager Henry Irving) and his wife Mabel (centre).

THE PERSONNEL OF THE GREAT DISASTER
THE QUICK AND THE DEAD OF THE EMPRESS OF IRELAND'S COMPANY

SAVED—CAPT. KENDALL
Commander of the lost liner.

DROWNED—COMMISSIONER REES AND HIS WIFE
In charge of the Salvationists' deputation on board.

SIR H. SETON-KARR
The well-known big-game hunter.

MR. LEONARD PALMER
Of the "Financial News."

MR. J. W. FURNESS
The leading violinist on board.

SAVED—ROWALD FERGUSON
Senior wireless operator.

DROWNED—MRS. R. SPOONER, SEN.

SAVED—MR. J. FERGUS DUNCAN
After being nearly an hour in the water.

"TYPHOON." THE PLAY IN WHICH LAURENCE IRVING AND HIS WIFE MADE THEIR LAST APPEARANCE

SAVED—EDWARD BAMFORD
Junior wireless operator.

DROWNED—MRS. R. SPOONER, JUN.

DROWNED—COL. MAIDMENT
Of the Salvation Army.

THE OFFICERS OF THE EMPRESS OF IRELAND

STAFF BAND OF THE SALVATION ARMY, WHO WERE ON BOARD

in through the portholes in the lower decks, which, against all safety rules, were often open to let some warm spring air into the stifling cabins.

Kendall had barely time – less than a quarter of an hour – to order lifeboats to be filled and launched. The ship was listing further and further, and although there were heart-rending cries of panic as the freezing torrents of water gushed through cabins and corridors, many people had drowned in their beds before they had time to scream. Then the ship gave an almighty lurch, which propelled Kendall bodily clear of the bridge and straight into the icy waters of the river.

Helpless, he found himself being pulled under as the *Empress* – his ship – sank beneath the waves. Then – he never knew how – he rose to the surface and saw heads bobbing like discarded corks and heard the screams of drowning people. He kicked out and swam towards the dark shape of a lifeboat. Helping hands hauled him aboard, and, his natural authority asserting itself, he took charge of rescue operations, commanding the lifeboat to land survivors on board the nearest ship, which, ironically enough, was the *Storstad*, the cause of the catastrophe.

Of the 1,012 people – 840 passengers and 172 crew – who died on that terrible night, a disproportionate number were women and children, who had drowned in their cabin cots without even realizing they were in danger. Of 138 minors on board, just four survived. The last of them, the daughter of a Salvation Army musician on the way with his band to play a series of concerts in Britain, died as recently as 1988, aged eighty-nine.

At the inquiry into the disaster, the skippers of each ship tried to blame one another. The Norwegians claimed that Kendall had not stuck to his allotted course on the port side of the river, while Kendall charged that the *Storstad* had switched position from his port side to starboard in the fog without notifying him. Kendall was exonerated from all blame and resumed his career with Canadian Pacific.

When war came within weeks of the disaster, Kendall found himself reunited with his old ship, the *Montrose* – on which he had trapped Crippen – and in the same port, Antwerp, from which he and the disguised doctor had sailed on that occasion. This time he used the ship for purposes that were indisputably humanitarian – to rescue 600 Belgian refugees who were besieging the British consulate in the city, desperate to escape the advancing Germans. Later in the war, Kendall survived yet another shipwreck – the third of his seafaring career – when his HMS *Calgarian* (like the *Lusitania*) was torpedoed by a German U-boat off the Irish coast. He ended his long career with Canadian Pacific as the line's marine harbourmaster in Southampton and died aged ninety-one in 1965.

THE HANDSOMEST YOUNG MAN IN ENGLAND

A very different Englishman, who had also been in Antwerp at the time Kendall was performing his rescue of the refugees, was the handsome and charismatic young poet Rupert Brooke. In contrast to Kendall's mercy mission, Brooke was in Flanders bent on killing. He had enlisted as an officer in his friend Winston Churchill's newly formed 'private army', the Royal Naval Division (RND), telling friends that he believed that God wanted him only to 'get good at killing Germans'.

By strange chance, Brooke had also been crossing the Atlantic in another liner, the SS *Philadelphia*, in the very same week in May when the *Empress of Ireland* had come to grief, only learning of the disaster when he made landfall in Devon. The poet was returning from a globe-trotting tour which had seen him wow literary America; view the explosively expanding cities springing up in the Canadian wilderness; prophesy the coming war in newspaper interviews; explore the South Seas and fall for its charming, artless, uninhibited inhabitants; and – for the first time in his tortured sexual life – engage in unproblematic, sensual physical love-making with a beautiful courtesan of the islands named Taatamata, with whom he enjoyed a Gauguinesque interlude.

Most bizarrely of all, a letter from Taatamata to Brooke informing him, in broken pidgin English ('I get fat all time Sweetheart'), that she was very probably pregnant by him, was being carried in the hold of the *Empress*, went down with the ship, but was miraculously recovered by divers weeks after the wreck and posted on to Brooke. By then he had already enlisted in the RND and was training for war at Blandford in Dorset.

In the last weeks of peace, as the high summer of 1914 ripened and Taatamata's momentous letter still lay on the watery St Lawrence seabed, Brooke had retreated to the depths of rural England among the fruit orchards of Gloucestershire. Here, in a nest of singing birds, he had settled with a group of fellow poets in a desperate bid to shut out the looming roar of war with the sound of birdsong, haymaking and their own laughing voices.

'Bloomsbuggers': Lytton Strachey, Bloomsbury's high priest, surrounded by acolytes at Garsington Manor, near Oxford. (left to right) Lady Ottoline Morrell, Garsington's châtelaine; Mrs Aldous Huxley; Strachey; his lover Duncan Grant and Grant's lover Vanessa Bell.

6. Poets

Rupert Brooke knew that he had arrived home in England on 5 June 1914 before the *Philadelphia* actually made landfall at Plymouth, from the delicious smell of freshly mown Devonshire hay that wafted across the harbour and pricked his nostrils with nostalgia and his eyes with tears. The scent was a reminder that his homeland – or at least the England that he and his friends celebrated in their verses – remained a rural nation: a country where harvest home was still part of the seasonal round, where villages were not just quaint dormitories for city folk to spend weekends in, and where landless labourers tied to cottages they did not own remained bound in feudal bondage to an aristocracy that – despite the depredations of Lloyd George and his People's Budget – still held the reins of political and social power.

THE BRIGHTEST YOUNG THING

Brooke was gushingly but probably accurately described by W. B. Yeats as the 'handsomest young man in England' and, less flatteringly pinned down by his friend Frances Cornford: 'A Young Apollo, golden haired,/ Stands dreaming on the edge of strife,/ Magnificently unprepared/ For the long littleness of life.' Brooke was the object of doting admiration by an extraordinarily large gallery of the great and the good in Edwardian England. A list of his friends and acquaintances reads like a *Who's Who* of the era's political, social and literary elite: Henry James, H. G. Wells, H. H. Asquith, Winston Churchill, D. H. Lawrence, A. E. Housman, Ezra Pound, Yeats, the Keynes and Strachey brothers, Virginia Woolf, Lady Ottoline Morrell. All, at one moment or another, were dazzled by and/or attracted to the young poet.

Brooke was the shining star of several interlocking social circles: in Cambridge, where he was the love object of a secret academic society, the precious intellectual elite called 'the Apostles', clustered around the economist John Maynard Keynes and the caustic critic Lytton Strachey; in London where, through his wealthy patron Eddie Marsh, he knew Marsh's boss Winston Churchill and the Asquiths. And, most recently, in deepest pastoral England, after spectacularly falling out with the members of the Bloomsbury Set and violently rejecting their free-thinking, liberal-left, cynical mindset, he had taken up with a new group who epitomized the

'Young Apollo': poet Rupert Brooke, the golden boy of his generation (but with feet of clay), in a study by US photographer Sherrill Schell. In other snaps in the same series Brooke posed half-naked.

traditional rural values he loved – values that were about to be swept away, yet remained potent in their powerfully nostalgic appeal.

THE NEW GEORGIAN AGE

The Georgians, as the group of poets called themselves – after King George V, whose reign had begun in 1910 – did not see themselves as backward-looking ruralists but as a fresh wind blowing away the musty and artificial cobwebs of English poetry left hanging over from the Victorian age. The idea for an anthology celebrating, in the opening words of Marsh's preface, the fact that 'English poetry is now once again putting on a new strength and beauty' had come from a late-night conversation between Brooke and Marsh after the effete civil servant had returned from putting in a hard day's work grafting for his master, Churchill, as the First Lord's private secretary at the Admiralty. A great-grandson of Spencer Perceval, the only British prime minister to have been assassinated, Marsh was a beneficiary of a substantial inheritance voted by Parliament to support Perceval's descendants in the first shock after the assassination.

Marsh used this 'murder money', as he called it, to support a range of writers and artists – particularly poets and painters – who caught his fancy, enthusiastically buying and promoting their work. Besides Brooke, his protégés included the impoverished and individualistic artists Stanley Spencer, David Bomberg and Mark Gertler, D. H. Lawrence, and the future war poets Siegfried Sassoon and Isaac Rosenberg. Though conservative in his tastes, Marsh was also tolerant, and the large number of Jews among his protégés proves that he was free from the widely prevalent anti-Semitism then characteristic of his upper-crust caste. A career civil servant, Marsh was nonetheless given considerable leeway by his bosses to pursue his extracurricular cultural interests. Discreetly homosexual, and sterile since a childhood bout of mumps, Marsh had a bachelor pad in Raymond Buildings, Gray's Inn, which was a meeting place where figures such as the one-legged tramp poet W. H. Davies might be found around the breakfast table, along with Brooke – who often spent the night there – or Marsh's chief Churchill himself.

Marsh had hitched his star to Churchill's fiery comet as his private secretary when the young firebrand got his first ministerial post as a Tory at the Board of Trade in 1903. Thereafter, flouting all civil service rules, he contrived to stick by him with the tenacity of a limpet, as Churchill switched parties and jobs with bewildering rapidity. In early newsreel footage of the January 1911 Siege of Sidney Street, when a gang of Latvian-Jewish gunmen in the East End exchanged shots with police and Royal

Scots Guards called out by Churchill as home secretary, Marsh, elegantly clad in a silk hat, can be seen at his chief's shoulder, cautiously observing events. On another occasion at the Home Office, the two men responded to complaints about the severity of judicial birching in prisons by caning each other in their office. They concluded that the punishment was no worse than the beatings they had endured at their public schools.

They made an odd couple – the aggressive, thrusting young politician and the effete gay aesthete – but Marsh stayed close to Churchill throughout his early political career, remaining in post as private secretary up to Churchill's less-than-glorious stint as chancellor of the exchequer in 1924. Even after Marsh retired with a knighthood at the end of the 1930s, Churchill remained in close touch, sending his old secretary his own prolific literary productions for comments and corrections from Marsh's editorial pen.

It was this influential but largely unsung literary and artistic promoter who became the godfather of the Georgians, once the idea of a new poetic grouping had occurred to his and Brooke's fertile minds. It seems odd, with Ezra Pound, T. S. Eliot and James Joyce waiting in the wings, that the Georgians should have seen themselves as daringly modern, but the reading public were evidently ready for something fresh and new.

On publication day in December 1912, *Georgian Poetry* – published by Harold Monro, who would open his Poetry Bookshop in London's Devonshire Street in January 1913 – was a sell-out. The anthology, the first of five similar collections, would eventually shift some 15,000 copies – an astonishing figure for a book of verse by largely unknown poets. As a publicity puff, Marsh and Brooke had arranged for Prime Minister Asquith's chauffeur to be waiting in a limousine outside Bumpus, the Oxford Street bookshop, ready to rush a newly printed copy to Downing Street for the premier's perusal.

The contents of the book itself, after Marsh's grandiloquent introduction – 'The Georgian period may take rank in due time with… great poetic periods in the past' – were a bit of a let-down. Though several of the names – Brooke himself, W. H. Davies, John Masefield, G. K. Chesterton, Walter de la Mare, D. H. Lawrence – are still remembered today, some (Ronald Ross, Edmund Beale Sargant, R. C. Trevelyan) have fallen into well-deserved obscurity, while others (Lascelles Abercrombie, W. W. Gibson, John Drinkwater) are only recalled, if at all, because they were friends and heirs of Brooke. The poetry, like the poets, is so diverse in quality and subject matter as to be unclassifiable as the product of a single group or movement: Brooke, the occasionally cynical sentimentalist; de la Mare, the

mystical romantic; Davies, the cracker-barrel sage; Lawrence, the quirky free-versifier; Chesterton, the comic satirist. Such men were 'Georgian' only in the sense that they happened to be writing in the same epoch and – apart from Lawrence – using traditional verse forms.

In the light of the war and the birth of modernism, the Georgians would quickly come to be scorned as backward-looking, reactionary sentimentalists, projecting an image of cheese and cider, of apple-cheeked maidens and hearty, healthy youths totally at odds with modern, mechanized urban life. But looked at in the context of 1914, before the coming of war, their efforts do not seem so futile. Poetry before the Georgians was hidebound and heavy with Victorian pieties and the artifice of symbolism. If not a brick thrown through the glass of this hot-house, Georgian poetry was at least an open door letting in a breath of fresh air. The Georgians succeeded in their aim of writing directly about everyday, concrete things, in plain language unadorned by artificial flourishes. And it must be borne in mind that the poets made famous by the war – Wilfred Owen, Robert Graves,

ON SAFARI: Eddie Marsh, patron extraordinaire of poets and painters (second from left, back row), standing behind his unlikely boss Winston Churchill during a visit to Africa, 1907

Siegfried Sassoon, Edward Thomas, Charles Sorley, Edmund Blunden, Ivor Gurney – would also appear in the later Georgian anthologies. In its later incarnation, in fact, Georgian poetry was the iconic poetry of the Great War.

It was the war that brought the popular perception of the Georgians as fusty celebrants of a vanished England, rather than the fresh, modern voices that they aimed to be. As the critic John Wain put it: 'If the First World War had not happened, the new idiom in English poetry would have been a development of Georgianism… the seeds were there: the honesty, the dislike of cant, the "selection from the real language of men"; the dissatisfaction with the narrow tradition of poetry laid down by the literary establishment.' Wain cites two poets, Edward Thomas and Wilfred Owen, both victims of the Great War, as neo-Georgian voices muffled by the brute fact of their deaths:

> If their flight had been longer, there would have been no need for a modern poetic idiom imported from France via America… Owen and Thomas, abetted by the excellent poets who survived the war, by Graves, by Blunden, by the older poets like [Ralph] Hodgson and De la Mare [all Georgians], would have made a living tradition out of English materials arising naturally from English life.

THE SONGBIRDS OF DYMOCK

In June 1914, soon after his return from his global trotting, another poet who would not survive the war, Rupert Brooke, went to join his new-found friends in their rural idyll. The first singing bird to found the nest of poets clustered around the village of Dymock on the border between the pastoral western counties of Herefordshire and Gloucestershire had been Lascelles Abercrombie, who in 1912, with his wife Catherine and two sons, took a house bearing the macabre name of The Gallows, at Ryton, on a hill south-east of Dymock. Here he was visited in 1913 by Eddie Marsh, whose description in a letter to Brooke gives some idea of the primitive conditions endured by the poets in their pursuit of pastoral inspiration:

> It's the most delicious little house, black and white, with a stone courtyard, and crimson ramblers, and low-beamed ceilings. The bathroom is a shed out of doors, with a curtain instead of a door, a saucer bath which you fill by means of an invention of Lascelles': a long tube of red india rubber, with a funnel at the end, which you hang on a pump on the other side of the path – cold water, alas!

In 1913 Abercrombie was followed to the area by his friend and fellow northerner Wilfrid Gibson (known to Brooke as 'Wibson'), who, accompanied by his wife Geraldine, took another cottage, between Dymock and the Herefordshire town of Ledbury, called the Old Nailshop. Clothed in the same local vernacular architecture of red brick and black-and-white timber, the Old Nailshop was also visited by Marsh, who had been the angel of mercy supporting Gibson in London by paying him an anonymous pound a week to edit *Rhythm*, the arts magazine founded by Katherine Mansfield and John Middleton Murry, two more literary protégés of the ubiquitous Eddie. In their new lush surroundings the two poets wrote their highly romantic verse and planned to start their own literary magazine, *New Numbers*.

When they were not writing or editing, the two friends explored the local countryside, a pretty landscape of small well-watered and wooded fields and orchards bearing apples and the soft fruits for which Herefordshire was famous. In springtime the meadows were carpeted by a Wordsworthian sea of golden daffodils – a legacy of an earlier dyeing industry in the area. Abercrombie and Gibson walked where they willed only with the express permission of their landlord, William Lygon, 7th Earl Beauchamp (later the inspiration for Lord Marchmain in Evelyn Waugh's masterpiece *Brideshead Revisited*), who owned more than a thousand acres in the locality and the cottages that stood on his land. Although he was Lord President of the Council in Asquith's Liberal cabinet and had a reputation for 'progressive' opinions, Beauchamp maintained to the full the feudal rights inherited from his ancestors. And although he may have looked fondly and with a liberal eye on these strange, bespectacled poets who had chosen to nest on his land, Beauchamp's minions and gamekeepers took a far less kindly view of the intruders.

Until the war sharpened such suspicions into actual hostility, the bucolic idyll continued. The poets busied themselves with issuing their magazine *New Numbers*. They had somehow managed to sign up 500 subscribers, and after Gibson made himself ill by licking the backs of so many envelopes, Catherine Abercrombie and Geraldine Gibson parcelled up the magazine and sent it off from Ryton village post office to the four corners of the world.

A LITERARY MIGRATION

Through Marsh and their other metropolitan contacts, word soon spread of the doings of the 'Dymock poets', and before long other literary gents – and one literary lady – were heading towards Herefordshire to join them. The first to arrive, in March 1914, was the American poet Robert Frost. Although best known for his poems celebrating rural New England, Frost had failed as a farmer in the United States before bringing his wife and children to old England in 1912, in a bid to achieve his real ambition: to succeed as a poet. With scant actual literary production to support his aims, Frost nonetheless had firm – indeed, dogmatic – ideas of what poetry should be, emphasizing the importance of 'cadence' and the close relationship of verse to the spoken word. His strong character influenced his friend Edward Thomas and was decisive in turning this literary hack and prose writer into the major poet he became in the last years of his life.

Frost had been living in a cramped cottage at Beaconsfield as he tried to break into London literary life, and the offer to migrate to Dymock as the spring of 1914 arrived was an attractive one. He told an American correspondent:

> I have no friend here like Wilfrid Gibson whom I am going to join in Gloucestershire next week. We bid a long farewell to London to be near to him and Lascelles Abercrombie. The cottage is already found for us. Iddens it is called – in Ledington, Ledbury… I don't know but I suppose we shall sleep under thatch. Those other poets do.

Frost's cottage, Little Iddens, was a tiny tumbledown black-and-white timber-framed dwelling in the hamlet of Ledington.

As soon he and his family arrived, the American lost no time in hymning the joys of the place to others:

> We are far from any town. We are on a lane where no automobiles come. We can go almost anywhere we wish on wavering footpaths through the fields. The fields are so small and the trees so numerous along the hedges that, as my friend [Edward] Thomas says in the loveliest book on Spring in England [*In Pursuit of Spring*], you may think from a little distance that the country was solid woods.

Thomas himself lost no time in visiting his friend in his new surroundings. For years, since coming down from Oxford and a shotgun marriage to his pregnant childhood sweetheart, Helen, Thomas had lived the life of an impecunious hack, churning out a stream of books and reviews to support his growing family. They moved from one country cottage to another until they settled in the Hampshire village of Steep, where Helen got a job in Bedales, one of the progressive boarding schools founded in the era – all vegetarianism, mixed nude bathing and the healthy outdoor life.

Melancholy by nature and increasingly subject to black depressions, Thomas found solace in long solitary walks across the countryside. A prose writer rather than a poet, he had nevertheless established himself as one of the country's leading critics of verse, and one of the foundations of his friendship with Frost was the latter's hunger for recognition. Meanwhile, the American pressed Thomas to turn the more poetic passages of his prose into real poetry.

At the end of April 1914, accompanied by his two older children, Merfyn and Bronwen, Thomas rented rooms at Oldfields, a farm two fields away from Frost. Abandoning their families, the two men spent their days walking and talking, occasionally stopping at a style, but mostly loping across the fields and through the woods – 'tiring the sun down', as Frost would put it, 'with talking and walking the footpaths and stiles of Ledington and Ryton'.

A LAND FROZEN IN TIME

That country, the valley of the little River Leadon, which gave its name to Ledbury and Ledington, bounded to the north by the Malvern Hills and further away by the 'blue remembered hills' of Housman's *A Shropshire Lad*, now became, for the spring and summer months of 1914, an enchanted valley that seemed to encompass an England teetering on the brink of dissolution. The people who populated the valley's villages and hamlets – celebrated in the poetry of local Ledbury lad John Masefield – still lived much as their ancestors had for centuries: pressing the soft local fruits to make cider or perry, cutting and threshing the corn at harvest time. Though mechanization was beginning to creep into agriculture, with horse-drawn harvesters chopping down the corn, it was still hard, back-breaking work; a round of unrelenting labour from sun-up to sun-down.

The poets who walked the fields where the workers sweated and laboured around them certainly romanticized those they lived among, but they were poor too, and their reasons for coming to the country were economic as much as artistic. Country cottages could be rented for a few shillings a week – and remote Herefordshire was cheaper than the Home Counties around London. Lighting was provided by oil lamps rather than gas or electricity; running water and flushing toilets were unknown; and central heating was yet to be invented. But for these poets, the simple life under the sun and stars, and a diet of cheese, cider, home-cured bacon and home-grown fruit and vegetables, and the occasional chicken, were compensation enough.

Robert Frost, once he had settled in, saw the plight of the agricultural labourers around him with the more realistic eyes of a farmer, his view

'I HAVE COME TO THE BORDERS OF SLEEP': the poet Edward Thomas photographed in 1905. His decision to enlist, like that of Brooke, solved some of his problems but would lead to his death.

tempered by the egalitarian sensibility of the American outsider that he was. In a later letter he would write with barely suppressed indignation about the iniquities of the English class system and the condition of the rural poor:

> Those English in the hamlets and open country, the genuinely submerged classes, can give you some pointers on destitution, depression and dejection that are age-lasting. They are used to living on black bread and rancid cheese, mitey cheese. Now and then we would run into one of them in the fields poaching for a hare. We would see the gamekeeper following after, waiting for a chance to nab the poacher and hustle him off to prison. We found that like as not the gamekeeper had his eye on us, squinting out from under his cap. One had to show birth certificate to prove he wasn't a poacher and avoid arrest… Those poor devils in the country go around with snares to catch rabbits to get one little taste of meat for their families to take away the infernal smell of rancid cheese or worse out of their nostrils. The authorities were forever invoking the laws of William Rufus and the New Forest – laws that made it safer, as Emerson says, to kill a man than to kill a hare.

From The Gallows, where he was staying with the Abercrombies in late June, Brooke, blind to such grim realities, wrote gushingly of the cottage: 'The most beautiful you can imagine; black-beamed and rose-covered. And a porch where one drinks great mugs of cider and looks at fields of poppies in the corn. A life that makes London a very foolish affair.' But despite this eulogy to the joys of country life, Brooke could not keep himself away from the metropolis, where he was the centre of so much attention and adoration. By 26 June he was back in the capital for a reunion of the Apostles – including Strachey and Keynes – with whose pacifist opinions he would soon be in violent disagreement, as the sword of war divided opinion and severed old friendships.

MOMENTOUS MEETINGS

The following day, 27 June, the indefatigable networker Eddie Marsh brought Brooke together with an *enfant* even more *terrible* of English literature, D. H. Lawrence, when they lunched at London's Moulin d'Or restaurant and afterwards went on to an art exhibition. Brooke and Lawrence were as different as men and writers as it is possible for two human beings to be. Brooke, for all his apparent anguish at the role that

ROBERT FROST in a 1913 studio portrait. Frost's English sojourn (1912–15), was a creatively profitable one for the American poet: he published his first collection, *A Boy's Will*, in 1913 and moved in artistic circles that included Edward Thomas, the other 'Dymock poets' and Ezra Pound.

had been thrust upon him, was a pampered creature of the Establishment whose looks and charm were a passport into the highest circles of the land. Lawrence took an angry pleasure at flouting the same Establishment's rules and seemed to be fighting a one-man war against it – a war that the coming conflict would make all too real.

Meeting Brooke, Lawrence was accompanied by Frieda von Richthofen, the German-born aristocrat and married woman whose elopement with the Nottinghamshire miner's son had caused a scandal. In July Lawrence would marry Frieda, almost as an act of defiance in the teeth of the fact that their respective nations were plunging towards war. Despite their obvious differences, the two Midlands men hit it off and were observed in intense conversation, punctuated by roars of laughter.

On the day after Brooke met Lawrence, 28 June, Archduke Franz Ferdinand of Austria-Hungary was assassinated with his wife while on a visit to Sarajevo, the capital of the province of Bosnia, and the slow fuse that would explode in a month's time began to splutter. In Britain, the echoes of a shooting on a far frontier in the always troublesome Balkans passed more or less unnoticed, except among the diplomats whose job it was to keep an eye on the doings of distant foreigners. Certainly the poets and painters remained untroubled by the event that would shatter and overturn their – and so many other – lives.

July, the month of high summer that would see the end of the old world, dawned bright and clear. The same summer sunshine persisted throughout the whole month as Europe spun ever more rapidly into the vortex of war. At first, summer rituals – cricket fixtures, sailing races and rowing regattas – continued as if nothing were amiss.

Eager as always to bring his favoured protégés together, Eddie Marsh invited Siegfried Sassoon to breakfast on 9 July to meet Rupert Brooke. Sassoon, scion of a wealthy Anglo-Jewish dynasty, had been brought up in the Kentish countryside, devoting his youth to cricket, riding to hounds and poetry. Shy and diffident – except on the sporting field or galloping over hedges, when he displayed the wild courage that would serve him so well in war – Sassoon had been a contemporary of Brooke at Cambridge, but a retiring failure in academic terms. He had never met the shining star before.

They met over bacon and kidneys at Raymond Buildings (Sassoon was living elsewhere in the same block in the hope that Marsh might boost his literary career), but the two future war poets did not hit it off. Sassoon, secretly homosexual, could not help being dazzled by Brooke's blue shirt, bluer eyes and bare feet, and his hair worn, as Sassoon prissily noted, 'a shade longer than it needed to be', but he found his fellow poet both brash and offhand: 'I was unprepared to find him more than moderately likeable. Eddie's adoring enthusiasm had put me somehow on the defensive.' Ignoring their fellow guests – the garrulous Welsh poet W. H. Davies and the taciturn painter Paul Nash, later to make his own unforgettable visual record of the same war that Sassoon would set down in words – the two poets made literary chit-chat in an atmosphere of stilted strain, occasionally broken by Eddie's excited squeaks. After half-an-hour of this torment, Sassoon made his excuses and left – leaving Brooke, as he imagined, happy to enjoy 'his own unimpeded self'.

As the vortex that ended in war spun ever more furiously, a few nights later Brooke dined and enjoyed a musical evening with the Asquiths in Downing Street, still hoping against hope that war could be avoided. Then he squeezed in a visit to his soulmates at Dymock, staying with the Gibsons at the Old Nailshop, where he discussed his own contributions to *New Numbers*. It was to prove a final valediction, nostalgically recalled by Gibson in his poem 'The Golden Room':

Do you remember that still summer evening
When, in the cosy cream-washed living-room
Of the Old Nailshop, we all talked and laughed –
Our neighbours from The Gallows, Catherine
And Lascelles Abercrombie; Rupert Brooke;
Elinor and Robert Frost, living awhile
At Little Iddens, who'd brought over with them
Helen and Edward Thomas…

In August, as the war began, the poets acquired an honorary female addition when Eleanor Farjeon, a plain, bespectacled literary lady, who would later write the words of the Christian hymn 'Morning Has Broken' and whose love for Edward Thomas expressed itself in dumb adoration, came to stay at a farmhouse called Glyn Iddens, close to the Frosts at Little Iddens and to Oldfields, where the Thomas family was housed. Eleanor's hosts, an old country family called the Farmers, extended an invitation to all the poets for a 'last supper' of pie, ripe cheese and cider, after the imbibing of which they were all so drunk that they could only rise from the table with each other's support. It was a suitably festive way to end an agonizingly brief idyll.

THINK ONLY THIS OF ME...
The two Dymock poets who were to die in the war, Brooke and Thomas, were both unsure of what their role would be when the storm finally broke

like a summer cloud-burst. Torn between his evident love of life and a darker impulse that sometimes seems like a desire to dance with death, Brooke toyed with the idea of becoming a war correspondent and seeking a commission as an officer. Eventually, as so often, a reluctant Eddie proved the fairy godmother who magicked up the desired commission for Brooke in the Royal Naval Division – a marine corps dreamed up by Marsh's chief Churchill, First Lord of the Admiralty, designed to be carried on naval ships but to fight on land.

Thomas, for his part, at last found literary fulfilment in following Frost's suggestion that he should try his hand as a poet. In the final three years of his life he produced the major poems – lyrical, moving and yet ultimately mysterious – on which his ever-growing reputation now rests. Even after he had resolved his own dilemmas about what to do in the war – his hack writer's income having dried up for the duration – by enlisting in the artillery as a gunner (though he was already pushing forty), the poems continued to pour out: 'Adlestrop', recalling a railway trip to Dymock on the eve of war, 'Old Man', 'Rain' and 'Lights Out' among them.

Brooke was the first to die. After briefly witnessing the brutal facts of war when his unit marched to the Flemish port of Antwerp, only to see it pounded into surrender by the guns of Krupp, he returned to write a passionately patriotic clutch of five sonnets that sold in spades and caught the fervently sacrificial mood of the hour. 'Now God be thanked who has matched us with his hour/ And caught our youth, and wakened us from sleeping…' began one entitled 'Peace', advancing the dubious theory that a century of peace had produced a corrupt society that could only be purified by the cleansing sword of war.

The most famous – or notorious – sonnet in the sequence, 'The Soldier' ('If I should die, think only this of me:/ That there's some corner of a foreign field/ That is forever England…'), was quoted in St Paul's Cathedral in a sermon by Dean Inge. And after Brooke's unheroic death from septicaemia in April 1915, brought on by an insect bite en route to the bloodbath of Gallipoli, it was used as a poster poem to recruit England's youth to arms, not least by Winston Churchill, who hymned Brooke in *The Times*:

Joyous, fearless, versatile, deeply instructed, with classic symmetry of body and mind. He was all that one would wish England's noblest sons to be in days when no sacrifice but the most precious is acceptable, and the most precious is that which is most freely proffered.

The rolling Churchillian phrases, however sincerely felt, did not do justice to Brooke's complex and divided nature, which – as his many friends privately acknowledged – was very far from the shining, laughing simplicity presented by his smiling exterior. The deeper, darker Brooke – misogynist, for all his womanizing; duplicitous, scornful, deceptive and secretive – is a far less sympathetic, but much more interesting figure than the cardboard cut-out saint presented by his dewy-eyed admirers.

Thomas, too, has emerged, thanks to recent research, as a man with more than his share of contemporary complexes, contradictions and sheer nastiness – again, far from the almost ethereal husband and father presented in the adoring autobiographies of his grieving widow, Helen, and his over-admiring female friend Eleanor Farjeon. Far from merely melancholy, Thomas was clinically depressed, a man who took out his savage moods on his wife and children, emotionally blackmailing them with threats of suicide and escaping the stifling constrictions of his own home with the solitary tramps through the countryside where he found his only solace.

Both Brooke and Thomas briefly surfaced from the swirling dark currents of their neuroses and pessimism to find healing in the woods and paths around Dymock. 'I shall never forget this – never', Brooke told Catherine Abercrombie after staring fixedly on the poppy-flecked fields around The Gallows on his last visit to the area. Thomas also found his ultimate purpose at Dymock, where Frost's eloquent persuasions nudged him from prose to the poetry that made his name.

More sombrely, the two men experienced an encounter on one of their walks, when Thomas – more conscious of England's class divisions than his egalitarian American friend – fled from the threatened violence of Lord Beauchamp's over-officious gamekeeper, while Frost gamely stood his ground. It is this episode that may have pushed the new-found poet into taking his fatal decision to enlist rather than accept Frost's invitation to emigrate to America – if only to prove his manliness to his rugged farmer friend.

In the end, it was Frost who fled to a still-neutral America while Thomas faced the German guns. 'Two roads divided in a wood,' Frost wrote, recalling their walks and talks. 'And I took the one less travelled. And that has made all the difference.' Asked what he was fighting for when he announced his decision to join up, Thomas stooped and picked up a pinch of English soil at his feet. 'Literally for this,' he said. At Easter 1917, as the bombardment heralding the British offensive around Arras opened, a shell passed close to Thomas at his observation post near a gun battery. It left his body unmarked – but stopped his watch, and his heart.

'A CRISIS OF BRILLIANCE': the pre-war generation of artists at the Slade School picnic, 1912. The group includes Mark Gertler, Stanley Spencer, Isaac Rosenberg, David Bomberg, Richard Nevinson and Dora Carrington.

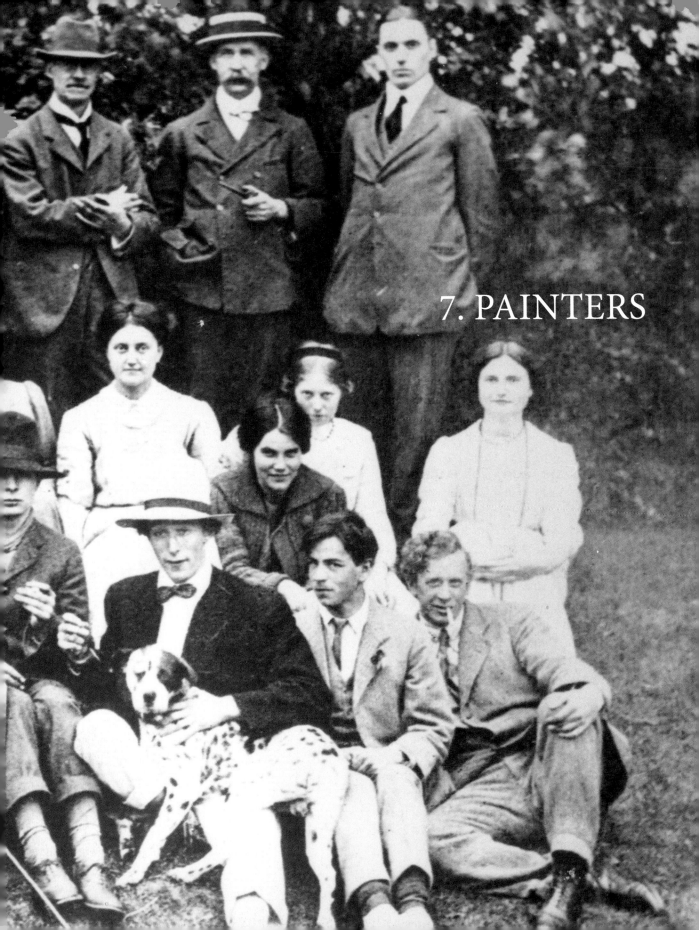

7. PAINTERS

7. Painters

I F THE GEORGIAN POETS, despite their best intentions, are now seen as
backward-looking celebrants of an agrarian, rural Britain that was fast
disappearing by 1914, there were other artists at work – chiefly in media
other than words – whose vision was the diametric opposite of the group
who gathered around Dymock that year.

December 1910, according to no less an authority than Virginia Woolf,
was the month when 'human nature changed'. If there was indeed such
a change – a fundamental alteration in the culture, consciousness and
style of modern humankind, even in an England thought of as stuffy,
predictable and conservative in the most hidebound way – then one of the
makers of that change was an Italian, Filippo Tommaso Marinetti, who
made his first visit to the country in the month that Virginia Woolf fixed
on as the moment at which the transformation occurred.

FUTURISM: MANIA FOR MACHINES

Son of a wealthy family and brought up largely in Egypt, Marinetti used
his private income to promote and propagandize for the artistic movement
that he had invented virtually single-handed – Futurism. Not an artist
himself but a publicist of genius, Marinetti cut a *bella figura*, 'adorned with
gold rings, gold chains and hundreds of flashing white teeth'. Exuberantly
moustachioed, he dressed like a dapper man about town, all spats, bowler
hats and striped turned-up trousers. But his ideas, as proclaimed to a
surprised London audience in his first Futurist Manifesto, were far from the
bourgeois conformism that this uniform suggested:

> We wish to exalt the aggressive movement, the feverish insomnia,
> running, the perilous leap, the cuff and the blow. We will destroy
> museums, libraries, and fight against moralism, feminism and all
> utilitarian cowardice. We intend to glorify the love of danger, the
> custom of energy, the strength of daring. The essential elements of
> our poetry will be courage, audacity and revolt.

In contrast to the pastoral escapism of the Georgians, the Futurists exalted
war – 'the world's only hygiene' – violence, the city, and perhaps above all

what even Rupert Brooke called 'the keen/ Unpassioned beauty of a great machine'. Marinetti's merry men were keen on machines of all sorts, and especially the engines of cars – for speed itself was one of their totems. Marinetti himself had experienced his decisive conversion to Futurism's values after crashing a car into a ditch while swerving to avoid two cyclists. It was a movement born of the twentieth century and infatuated with the new century's technologies: flight, radio communication, the internal-combustion engine, and anything that devoured distance as fast as possible. Aggressively modern, ardently masculine and proudly misogynist, the Futurists were to art what the fascists would be to politics.

It was no coincidence that Futurism was born in Italy, a land perhaps over-encumbered with the weight of the past. Growing up amid crumbling Roman statues, fallen Etruscan arches and the sheer profligacy of Italy's artistic antiquity, it is small wonder that Marinetti and his fellow Futurists – the artists Giacomo Balla, Carlo Carrà, Gino Severini and Umberto Boccioni and the architect Antonio Sant'Elia – wished to wipe out, blow up or otherwise obliterate what they saw as the dead weight of the past: a past that stifled creativity and imagination and blocked out a new world waiting to be born.

Marinetti had come to London thinking that, as the centre of the world's commerce and the capital of its greatest empire, it was 'the Futurist city par excellence' – but most Londoners had disappointed him. Their brains, he explained in a culinary metaphor, were 'heavy as steaks', while England, as he told a startled and affronted English audience, was a nation not of shopkeepers but of 'Snobs and sycophants, enslaved by old worm-eaten traditions, social conventions and romanticism'. Such a nation's art was bound to be redundant, and Marinetti recommended dragging the National Gallery's collection of Turners and Pre-Raphaelites into Trafalgar Square and burning them.

This thrilling iconoclasm was sure to strike a chord with one movement which was already perpetrating the violence that the Futurists advocated so enthusiastically. In fact, the vandalizing of the National Gallery's *Rokeby Venus*, carried out in March 1914 by a suffragette at least partly motivated by aesthetic as well as political grievances, was putting into violent practice what the Futurists merely talked about. Even a moderate suffragette like the journalist Margaret Nevinson, a member of the Women's Freedom League rather than the Pankhursts' militant Women's Social and Political Union, was impressed, telling readers of the WFL's organ *Vote*:

[The Futurists] are young men in revolt at the worship of the past.

They are determined to destroy it and erect upon its ashes the Temple of the future. War seems to be the tenet in the gospel of Futurism: war upon the classical in art, literature and music.

Mrs Nevinson was soon to have the opportunity of studying Futurism closer to home when her own wayward son Richard – the artist C. R. W. Nevinson – became the doctrine's leading English convert and practitioner.

POST-IMPRESSIONISM: THE SHOCK OF THE NEW

Marinetti had returned to London in March 1912 to attend the opening of the city's first Futurist exhibition at the Sackville Gallery. The capital's art establishment had still not recovered from the shock administered to it just two years before when, in November 1910, the critic Roger Fry, a leading light of the Bloomsbury Set, had organized a show of what he dubbed the 'Post-Impressionists' at Mayfair's Grafton Galleries.

Though most of the artists represented – Manet, Van Gogh, Cézanne, Gauguin, Matisse and even early Picasso – were already rather passé across the Channel, in Britain exposure to their gaudy colours and often unnaturalistic forms caused something of a collective coronary in the unprepared public. The critic of W. T. Stead's *Pall Mall Gazette* called the show 'the outpourings of a lunatic asylum'. Eschewing the use of words, the *Daily Telegraph* critic Sir Claude Phillips expressed his disgust rather Futuristically when he threw down the exhibition catalogue and stamped on it. His colleague from *The Times*, meanwhile, opined that the artists on show had torn up all the lessons of the past and wiped the slate clean – only they had 'stopped where a child would stop'.

If such exaggeratedly hostile responses to what was, after all, merely a collection of pictures hung on the walls of an exclusive West End gallery and seen only by the favoured few seem quite extreme, the context in which the exhibition was held must be recalled. On the same day that Fry's show opened, there was a riot in the South Wales coal-mining village of Tonypandy in which shops were looted and one miner killed. The next day the home secretary, Winston Churchill, sent troops to reinforce the local police in restoring order – giving rise to the legend that he had shot down striking miners (although no shots were fired). As well as the growing violence of the suffragettes and the simmering menace of the Ulster conundrum, politically the country was still convulsed by the repercussions of Lloyd George's radical People's Budget the previous year, and the year 1910 saw two general elections as the government battled to overcome furious opposition to its radicalism in the Tory-dominated House of Lords.

THE SHOCK OF THE NEW: the artist and art critic Roger Fry, here photographed in 1913, played a key role in raising awareness of modern art in Britain.

To many among the conservative, property-owning classes, it seemed that their economic, social and political power was under attack from all directions, and Fry's little pictures must have seemed like the cherry on a particularly unpalatable cake. To the mild-mannered Fry's astonishment and alarm, his critics viewed his show as something more subversive than 'just' an art exhibition. The poet and diplomat Wilfrid Scawen Blunt referred to its 'Works of idleness and impotent stupidity' and called it a 'pornographic show', while another critic, J. Comyns Carr, thought the pictures represented 'a wave of disease… absolute madness… the whole product seems to breathe not ineptitude merely but corruption'.

If this storm of Philistine vituperation had greeted works that, however unfamiliar, were still in the mainstream of the European tradition, what hope did the outrageous and violence-espousing Futurists have of reaching a wide public? That, of course, was not the future fascist Marinetti's aim. Avowedly anti-egalitarian, he wanted to teach the English elite, and in that goal he succeeded to a surprising degree.

NEVINSON: REBELLIOUS CHILD OF THE ELITE

Marinetti's main agent, as he bored deep into the guts of the soft, complacent, liberal and enlightened social elite, was a quintessential child of that elite, Richard Nevinson.

Nevinson's parents were typical scions of the intellectual caste that came of age with the arrival of the twentieth century. His father, Henry Nevinson, was probably the best-known radical journalist of the age. Writing for the *Daily Chronicle* and *Manchester Guardian*, he was a pioneer war correspondent, travelling to conflicts around the world from South Africa to Gallipoli. A Fabian socialist, Nevinson was, like his wife Margaret, an ardent campaigner for women's suffrage. He was also an ardent womanizer and was often absent from the family home for private, as well as professional, reasons.

Befitting a family with such earnest radical opinions, the Nevinsons' first married home was in the slums of Whitechapel in the East End, where they worked for the Toynbee Hall social centre, striving to ameliorate the conditions of dire poverty and deprivation around them. Tiring of this Sisyphian task, they moved up to the gentler climes of Hampstead – then, as now, the ultimate Mecca for London's well-heeled left-wing intelligentsia. It was not, however, a happy home. Margaret, once she had given birth to two children, became frustrated and depressed by the constraints and limitations imposed on Victorian and Edwardian women – even progressive ones. This, coupled with her husband's absences and

CLEANSING DOUCHE: *The Mudbath* (1914) by David Bomberg is an archetypal Vorticist work, reducing the human form to its angular essence. It is based on Jewish public baths near Bomberg's home in London's East End.

blatant infidelities, soured the atmosphere of the family home.

Richard inherited his mother's depressive and anxious personality, and the dark clouds hanging permanently over their corner of Hampstead hardly set his mind at rest. Sent away to a loathed Midlands public school, Uppingham, he became a moody, rebellious, permanently discontented loner only interested in, and showing an evident talent for, art – much to his parents' disapproval.

Richard Nevinson wound up at the Slade School of Art, a branch of London University. Under an exacting, conservative but inspiring professor named Henry Tonks, the Slade witnessed a flowering in the Edwardian era never matched before or since by any British art school. Augustus and Gwen John, Percy Wyndham Lewis, Stanley and Gilbert Spencer, Paul Nash, Dora Carrington, Mark Gertler, Isaac Rosenberg, Edward Wadsworth and David Bomberg all studied at the Slade. Though Tonks tried to hold his students to his own strongly classical tradition, encouraging them to copy the Old Masters with painstaking exactitude and to study the Greek statues in the nearby British Museum, the ferment that was abroad in society inevitably influenced and infected their art, causing them to swing out along by-ways that may have distressed their teacher but seeded a crop of productive fertility rich in both promise and achievement.

AUGUSTUS JOHN: THE BEARDED BOHEMIAN

Nevinson's earliest influence was the outstandingly flamboyant figure of Augustus John. A student, then a teacher, of drawing at the Slade, the bearded Welshman forged the public image of what an artist should look and behave like, with his flashing eyes and long hair and his uniform of wide-brimmed hats, cloaks and earrings. The popular press – to whom John was a gift that kept on giving for another half-century – reported with lip-smacking prurience the artist's very public 'private' life. John toured the country in a gypsy caravan, with his wife Ida and mistress Dora in tow and accompanied by an ever-growing tribe of children.

In 1910 Rupert Brooke, who had purchased two John drawings and admired the artist from afar for pursuing a free and easy way of life that Brooke himself envied but did not dare emulate, gave a vivid and charming description of the John tribe when they briefly came to rest near his home at Grantchester, outside Cambridge:

> Augustus John, the greatest painter, with two wives and seven children (all male, between 3 and 7 years) with their two caravans and a gypsy tent, are encamped by the river… I go to see them sometimes and they come here to meals… the chief wife is a very beautiful woman. And the children are lovely brown wild bare people dressed, if at all, in lovely red, yellow or brown garments of John's own choosing.

In fact, for all his Bohemian airs and scandalous flouting of convention, Augustus was resolutely conservative and respectable in style and in his later years became almost a mascot of the Establishment. He was allowed leeway and a licence to misbehave because he was an artist with a capital 'A'. The portraits of the leading personalities of his era for which he became

EVIL GENIUS? Wyndham Lewis was the aggressive arbiter of modernism in British art. But the only begetter of Vorticism alienated many with his persona as 'the Enemy'.

famous are representational, and he displayed a lordly disdain for Futurism, Vorticism, Cubism and Abstraction – the movements that would shatter his style of figurative art.

WYNDHAM LEWIS: REBEL AND OUTSIDER

A more revolutionary and subversive figure would follow John to the Slade (until his expulsion for defiantly smoking in front of his professor) and would, with Nevinson, shake British art to its foundations in a way that Roger Fry could merely dream of. Wyndham Lewis (he made haste to drop his given name of 'Percy') had mysterious origins which he deliberately made more mysterious still. Born in Nova Scotia (he claimed on a boat) with an American father (who soon disappeared from his life) and an English mother, Lewis was brought to England and endured the same misery as Nevinson of being sent to an English Midlands public school (Rugby, where he was taught by Rupert Brooke's father).

Branded a 'Frightful Artist' and asked to leave Rugby, before he was similarly expelled from the Slade, Wyndham Lewis exercised an influence on the slightly younger generations who followed him to the Slade because, unlike Augustus John, he really was a revolutionary. After being slung out of the Slade, Lewis travelled widely in Europe, where he was exposed to the exciting currents in art and literature exercising continental minds. In Paris he read the vitalist philosophy of Bergson, Nietzsche and Sorel, mixed with painters like Picasso and Modigliani, lived the Bohemian life, and returned to London in 1908 fizzing and crackling with daring ideas and a desire not just to shock but to change a country he regarded as impossibly stodgy, complacent and hidebound.

Lewis's early works were influenced by the Cubism practised by Picasso and Braque that was à la mode in the French capital, all angular shapes and jagged forms carved like a sculptor out of paint. He attended and welcomed the assault on London of Marinetti and the Futurists in 1912, but declined the Italian's invitation to put himself at the head of the British branch of the movement. He thought the Futurists' worship of early-twentieth-century objects and inventions – cars, planes, trains and skyscrapers – was altogether too obvious, vulgar and passé, and preferred his own style of inventing hardly human figures and investing them with mysterious qualities of menace and unease.

TWO EGOS AND A TOILET

The two men came into direct collision in 1914 when Marinetti confronted his reluctant disciple in the appropriate surroundings of a public toilet, where the Italian was washing after literally working himself into a lather at one of his frenetic public lectures. According to Lewis's autobiography, their confrontation went like this:

> 'You are a Futurist, Lewis!' Marinetti insisted.
> 'No, I'm not,' responded Lewis.
> 'Why don't you announce that you are a Futurist?'
> 'Because I'm not one.'
> 'Yes, but what's it matter?'
> 'It's most important.'
> 'Not at all. Futurism is good. It is all right.'
> 'Not bad. It has its points. But you Wops insist too much on the Machine. You're always on about these driving belts, you are always exploding about internal combustion. We've had machines here in England for donkeys' years. They're no novelty to *us*.'

However imperfectly remembered, the exchange gives a fine flavour of the differences between the two men. In essence, however, Lewis was – or wanted to be – a leader himself. A supreme individualist, he would never be a 'me too' passenger in anyone else's train. By 1913 he was ready to strike out on his own and form the new movement with which he hoped to transform not only art but the whole culture of England itself.

Following up his Post-Impressionist exhibitions, Roger Fry had created a commercial enterprise, the Omega Workshops, to market and sell the work of young artists that he favoured. In the wake of the Arts and Crafts movement initiated in the late-Victorian period by the idiosyncratic socialist William Morris, Fry's aim was not only to provide much needed income for his favoured stable of artists, but also to spread their own designs and ideas into the mainstream. Lewis was suitably scornful of the Workshops, dubbing them 'Fry's pincushion factory', but he was not above co-operating with them and having his work displayed and sold via Fry – until a mighty row sundered Lewis from Bloomsbury and its denizens, and changed the whole direction of British art.

TWO EGOS AND A COMMISSION

It says something about the rapidity with which modern ideas about art were entering the mainstream that the *Daily Mail* – then as now the leading organ of middlebrow, middle-class British taste and opinion – asked Roger Fry, the very man whose exhibitions had shocked the nation, to design a Post-Impressionist room for the newspaper's 1913 Ideal Home Exhibition, an event to which the aspirational suburban masses flocked annually to imbibe ideas for the designs and décor of their own homes. Lewis had already had experience designing large wall panels of the sort required by the *Mail*, as the previous year he had been commissioned to do the décor for London's first nightclub – the Cave of the Golden Calf in Heddon Street – opened by the Austrian-born Madame Frida Strindberg, second wife of the late, great Swedish dramatist.

With that commission under his belt, Lewis arrogantly assumed that Fry would choose him for the task, and when that proved not to be the case, he felt both personally and artistically slighted. He circulated a round-robin angrily accusing Fry of all manner of underhand deviousness. His intention now was clear: in inviting his own group of friends and disciples to sign it and join him, he was breaking away from the Bloomsberries and their parlour-pink, milk-and-water modernism and starting something altogether more daring.

Meanwhile, in November 1913, Marinetti had once again descended on London, with Richard Nevinson acting as his chief cheerleader and keeper of the Futurist flame in England. Nevinson had followed Lewis over to Paris, but the younger man's experience in the French capital had been altogether more dispiriting – despite, or because of, the fact that he was often mistaken for a Russian and even rubbed shoulders with Lenin. On his return to England, Nevinson suffered a full-blown nervous breakdown, exacerbated by his unrequited love for his fellow Slade student, Dora Carrington. His feelings of rejection intensified, and he began to suffer the delusion that the whole world was conspiring to defeat him and stifle his talent.

Nevinson's reaction was defiance. He bought a motor-bike and raced around London on it, fully embracing the Futurist worship of speed and machines. He was ready, when Lewis's call came, to join his mentor in lighting the flame of revolt under the dusty drapes of the art establishment.

In March 1914 Lewis, with his current girlfriend, an art graduate called Kate Lechmere, opened what they boldly dubbed the Rebel Art Centre at 38 Great Ormond Street, in central London. Funded by a successful commission to paint frescoes for the salon of Lady Drogheda, a fashionable London hostess, and also financed by Kate, who found herself in the traditional female role of making tea and cakes for the other artists, Lewis set up shop in the first-floor offices, with his flat behind it.

Here he assembled the rebel band who would become the Vorticists: the painters David Bomberg, Frederick Etchells, Edward Wadsworth and William Roberts, and the sculptors Henri Gaudier-Brzeska and Jacob

Epstein. Nevinson was a rebel too – but would never join the Vorticists. Offering a caustic but supportive eye was the startlingly original critic, philosopher and poet Thomas Ernest Hulme. But the ringmaster of the rebels' revels was the poet and publicist Ezra Loomis Pound.

EZRA POUND: THE AMERICAN ANTI-ROMANTIC

Like his friends and fellow American poets T. S. Eliot, Conrad Aiken and Robert Frost, Pound came to pre-1914 London from a still-provincial America because it was the vibrant world capital of English-speaking culture. Pound arrived in 1908 and instantly made an impression, not least because of the uniform he cultivated, consisting, according to his friend, the writer Ford Madox Ford, of a flourished cane, trousers made of green billiard-table cloth, pink coat, blue shirt, hand-painted Japanese tie, an immense sombrero hat, a flaming-red beard cut to a point, and a single blue earring borrowed from a lady friend. Pound's efforts to penetrate literary and artistic London were equally attention-seeking: he set his sombrero straight at W. B. Yeats.

The great Irish poet, living at the time in Woburn Buildings, London, and already recognized by his peers as first among equals, responded like a stroked cat to the young American's shameless flattery and soon came to accept – as would many others – the brash interloper's word as law when it came to criticism of his verse. Acting as Yeats's self-appointed secretary, Pound bore him away to Ashdown Forest in Sussex, where they shared a remote cottage over three winters. He cemented the relationship by taking up with Dorothy Shakespear, daughter of Yeats's mistress Olivia Shakespear, and, in April 1914, marrying her in Kensington's St Mary Abbots Church, a few steps away from Pound's mews house. Crucially for the development of Yeats's genius, Pound turned his interest away from the Celtic mysticism of his youth and to the poetic forms of Japan and China. Pound was the arch anti-romantic who demanded hardness, classical clarity and lean, mean modern forms in poetry. He also shared Marinetti's genius for publicity, inventing and bestowing the names on the Imagist movement in verse and on Vorticism in art.

Pound's powerful, uncompromising personality impressed itself – for good or ill – on all who met him, and few questioned his self-made claim to be the absolute arbiter on what was good or bad in modern art and poetry. It was a claim that he staked in public early in 1914, when he delivered a lecture on Imagism – and read examples of what he considered Imagist poetry – at a public meeting in Kensington Town Hall, sharing the stage with Lewis and the combative critic T. E. Hulme. Pound, clad in velvet jacket and floppy hat, boomed out the verse in his Midwestern twang. Lewis, recognizing both Pound and Hulme as rivals, mocked the American's reading as 'rather a joke' and poked snobbish fun at Hulme's 'nagging, nasal, North-country accent'. When it came to his own turn to read, however, Lewis buried his face in his notes and was reported to be inaudible.

The control-freak elements in Lewis's character eventually caused him to fall out with almost everybody – he would rejoice in the name 'the Enemy' – most notoriously with his Bloomsbury foes, but also with his own friends and allies. An early quarrel, and one in which the combative and prickly Lewis certainly came off worse, was with Hulme, who was as much of a fighter as Lewis himself – but much tougher too.

HULME: THE ANTI-IDEALIST BRUISER

A hard-nosed product of a wealthy Staffordshire Midlands family, the arrogant and opinionated Hulme had the distinction of being expelled from Cambridge University not once but twice: once for rowdyism, when he heckled a theatre performance, and again for attempting to seduce a don's daughter. Both activities were typical of Hulme, a hard-bitten customer and obsessive womanizer, who carried a bespoke brass knuckle-duster, designed for him by the sculptor Henri Gaudier-Brzeska and made in the shape of a woman with her legs apart. Austerely intellectual, Hulme, like Lewis, absorbed the influence of Bergson and Sorel in Paris, and set his face like flint against any hints of lushness, romanticism or idealism in art or literature, calling for modern forms which recognized the 'cindery' nature of reality and a Tory philosophy which recognized the sadly fallen state of humankind.

After Hulme had been blown to bits by a shell in 1917, Lewis would remember him kindly as 'a very large and imposing man, well over six foot, broad shouldered and with legs like a racing cyclist… He was a very talkative jolly giant, arrogantly argumentative, but a great laugher… He was very fond of the girls. His conversation mostly bore on that subject.'

Like Pound, Hulme lectured at Lewis's Rebel Art Centre in 1914, but such amity would not last long. As attracted to and attractive to women as Hulme, Lewis, with his saturnine, moustachioed good looks, was in the spring of 1914 involved with the wealthy Kate Lechmere, a cheerful former art student who was as gleefully erotic and free with her favours as her suitors. Lewis, smitten, wrote to her: 'I have as many kisses as the envelope will hold. The rest I keep in my mouth for you.' Kate responded with avidity, finding her lover witty and exciting. But then he made the mistake of letting her meet Hulme, and the attraction between the two was instant – and lasting. Indeed, Hulme was to become the love of Lechmere's life.

LARGER THAN LIFE: the pugnacious English modernist critic and poet Thomas Ernest Hulme volunteered as an artilleryman in 1914. Hulme's short, but intellectually productive, life was ended by a direct hit from a German shell in West Flanders in 1917.

Lewis feared that he would lose not only his lover but her financial support for the Rebel Art Centre and his leadership of the nation's intellectual avant-garde into the bargain, especially as Hulme favoured – and publicly praised – the sculptors Epstein and Gaudier-Brzeska and the painter David Bomberg rather than his own works.

In June 1914 Lechmere's growing attraction to Hulme sparked a final confrontation between the pair. Lewis stormed round to a house in Soho's Frith Street where Hulme was living with another woman, demanded that he leave Lechmere alone – and seized him by the throat. But he had picked on the wrong man.

The massive Hulme seized Lewis in his turn, removed him bodily from the house, and hung him upside down from his trouser turn-ups on the railings in Soho Square. 'I never see the summer house in the centre [of the square],' recalled Lewis, 'without remembering how I saw it upside down.' So, humiliatingly, ended the brief life of the Rebel Art Centre after just four months. Ending their relationship, Lechmere informed Lewis that she would not pay the next quarter's rent for the centre, and its contents were stripped out and the rooms abandoned. But from this death the most exciting native-born British art movement of the early twentieth century – Vorticism – was born.

THE VORTICIST MANIFESTO

Hostility between Lewis's rebels and their artistic rivals was not confined just to verbal and printed fisticuffs. As the violent quarrel with Hulme had proved, Lewis was quite prepared to translate artistic disagreements into actual physical show-downs.

When Marinetti made his last drum-rolling visit to London late in 1913, his disciple Nevinson, who had organized the visit, and Lewis were still allies in the front rank of modernism.

At a welcome dinner given at the Florence restaurant in Rupert Street – inevitably located in Soho, where most scenes of the Futurist/Vorticist revolution were played out – while Nevinson pounded the drums to provide the necessary percussion, the Italian declaimed a poem which Lewis later compared to an artillery bombardment on the Western Front. In the poem Marinetti attempted to reproduce phonetically the sounds of a modern battle by shrieking in a variety of pitches:

Zang – tumb – zang – tuuuuubb – tatatatata –
picpacpampacpampicpampicpacuuuuuuuu
ZANG-TUMB-TUMB-TUUUUM…

'IL MIGLIOR FABBRO':*
Like Wyndham Lewis, poet and critic Ezra Pound brought a bracing Atlantic gale to the staid world of Britain's arts. Pound is here photographed at his Kensington home in October 1913.

* In a 1925 edition of his long poem *The Waste Land*, T. S. Eliot included the dedication 'For Ezra Pound: *il miglior fabbro*', quoting line 117 of Canto XXVI of Dante's *Purgatorio*, in which Dante defined the twelfth-century troubadour Arnaut Daniel as 'the better craftsman'.

In June 1914, Marinetti was back, but this time Lewis was his enemy and prepared to do battle. Provoked by a Futurist Manifesto published in the *Observer*, which quite wrongly identified Bomberg, Epstein, Etchells, Wadsworth and Lewis himself as Futurists under Nevinson's leadership, Lewis assembled a shock troop of his friends in Soho's Greek Street. The *combattimenti* included Lewis himself, Hulme (this was a few days before their break-up over Kate), Gaudier-Brzeska and the no-nonsense Yorkshireman Edward Wadsworth.

The group shouldered their way into the Doré Gallery in New Bond Street, where Nevinson was delivering a lecture. Here, for the first time in public, Lewis proclaimed that he and his friends were Vorticists, not Futurists. He heckled the meeting, which broke up in disorder after someone let off a firecracker.

It was in this same momentous month of June, just as the world heard the ominous news of the shots in Sarajevo, that a large broadsheet magazine entitled *BLAST* was published, with the title set diagonally in bold black across the eye-catching shocking-pink cover. British graphic art had never known anything like it. Distribution was delayed at the last minute as the publisher, John Lane, insisted that two 'obscenities' – the word 'testicles' in a poem by Pound and a description of an orgasm – were laboriously inked out by hand: a chore naturally delegated by the chauvinist male Vorticists to two female camp-followers.

The Vorticist manifesto was signed by eleven prominent young artists and writers, including Lewis, Wadsworth, Gaudier-Brzeska, Roberts and Pound – though notably not Hulme, who had been excluded at the last moment after his spat with Lewis.

Its principal feature, drawn up by Lewis and Pound and similarly printed in anarchic bold lettering, 'blasted' people and things they disliked and 'blessed' those of which they approved. Among those blasted were whole nations – England and France – humour, Aestheticism and the Victorian era. Beyond the roars and shouting, however, the 160-page publication was a compendium of the cutting edge of English art and letters, including stories by Ford Madox Ford and Rebecca West, poems by Pound, and a play, *Enemy of the Stars*, by Lewis, who was as proud of his modernist ways with words as he was of his art.

The magazine's art, influenced by Cubism as well as Futurism, put Roger Fry's pallid Post-Impressionism to shame with its imagined, robotic figures and angular, aggressive lines with their sharp spear-points. Vorticism, despite later claims to the contrary by some of his followers, was the creation of Lewis and bore his hallmarks of originality, innovation – and provocation. His manifesto concluded:

Our Vortex is proud of its polished sides.
Our Vortex will not hear of anything but its disastrous polished dance.
Our Vortex desires the immobile rhythm of its swiftness.
Our Vortex rushes out like an angry dog at your Impressionistic fuss.
Our Vortex is white and abstract with its red-hot swiftness.

Richard Aldington, editor of a rival arts magazine, the *Egotist*, who had also signed the Vorticist manifesto, proclaimed *BLAST* 'the most amazing, energetic, stimulating production I have ever seen'. But the shots that would kill the movement – just a year after its birth – had already been fired.

BLASTED: the first section of Wyndham Lewis's coruscating manifesto, *Blast 1*, 1914; a declaration of war that came just before the real thing.

BLAST First (from politeness) **ENGLAND**

CURSE ITS CLIMATE FOR ITS SINS AND INFECTIONS

DISMAL SYMBOL, SET round our bodies,
of effeminate lout within.
VICTORIAN VAMPIRE, the **LONDON** cloud sucks
the **TOWN'S** heart.

A 1000 MILE LONG, 2 KILOMETER Deep

BODY OF WATER even, is pushed against us
from the Floridas, **TO MAKE US MILD.**

OFFICIOUS MOUNTAINS keep back **DRASTIC WINDS**

SO MUCH VAST MACHINERY TO PRODUCE

THE CURATE of "Eltham"
BRITANNIC ÆSTHETE
WILD NATURE CRANK
DOMESTICATED
                        POLICEMAN
LONDON COLISEUM
  SOCIALIST-PLAYWRIGHT
DALY'S MUSICAL COMEDY
GAIETY CHORUS GIRL
TONKS

11

8. CLUBS AND COTERIES

CALF LOVE: Spencer Gore's Gauguinesque study for a mural decoration intended for the Cave of the Golden Calf, the nightclub run by Frida Strindberg off London's Regent Street.

8. Clubs and Coteries

THE ESTABLISHMENT RECOGNIZED as London's first ever nightclub, the extravagantly named Cave of the Golden Calf – in reality a basement beneath the warehouse of a draper specializing in Scottish tweed at 9 Heddon Street, a cul-de-sac off Regent Street – closed its doors and declared itself bankrupt in February 1914. Eight months later, as Europe swirled down the vortex leading it into world war, the club's founder and moving spirit, Madame Frida Strindberg, departed for America on the liner *Campania*. It was, in more than one sense, the end of an era.

Madame Strindberg – the Austrian-born second wife of the great Swedish dramatist and hater of womankind, August Strindberg – had arrived in England in 1908, as part of the same artistic influx that saw Pound, Eliot and Marinetti migrate to a London that rivalled New York and Vienna as a cultural magnet. Frida, appropriately for a Viennese of the Freud–Schnitzler era, was an overwrought, emotional, sensual woman nearing forty, but she was also a high achiever in the arts who made money by successfully dealing in modern painting, sometimes buying and selling pictures that were not actually for sale. Within two years of her arrival she had met and, inevitably, been seduced by Augustus John.

The seduction had not proved a problem for the flamboyant Welshman as Frida – like her Austrian compatriot and contemporary Alma Mahler – made something of a speciality of collecting lovers whom she perceived to be possessed by genius. Her stormy marriage to Strindberg had ended when the experimental German dramatist Frank Wedekind had made her pregnant, and her first meeting with John, which had concluded with him bedding her, had taken place when she had actually been chasing Wyndham Lewis. Now, Augustus John swiftly moved from the role of pursuing hunter to that of pursued prey.

THE HELL-BITCH OF THE WESTERN WORLD

Convinced that only under her guidance could John bring his talent to its fullest fruition, Frida embarked on an attempt to take over his life that began with him amusedly describing her to friends as 'the mad Austrian' but ended with him fleeing in terror from a foul fiend whom he characterized as 'the walking hell-bitch of the western world'. He added: 'She seems to have a lust for power and sticks at nothing to bring people under her sway. She's a dealer in works of art and a would-be appropriator of the bodies and souls of those that make them.'

Always superstitious, John became convinced that Madame Strindberg had the power of second sight – a belief confirmed, in his eyes, when, attempting to escape her by taking the boat train to Paris without telling anyone his destination, she turned up on the platform at Victoria brandishing a revolver. It is more likely, in fact, that Madame Strindberg paid private detectives to trail her quarry. So ardent did her stalking of the artist become that she followed him to his hotel in Paris, where she melodramatically attempted suicide by swallowing veronal.

Rebuffed, she then reportedly paid thugs to beat John up (they attacked the wrong man) and on another occasion lobbed full champagne bottles at his head as a punishment for failing to acknowledge her. In something of an understatement, an understandably paranoid John, who normally took the dominant role in his love affairs, acknowledged: 'I admit that the sight of Mme Strindberg bearing down on me in an open taxi-cab, a glad smile of greeting on her face, shaded with a hat turned up behind and bearing a luxuriant outcrop of sweet peas – this sight, I confess, unnerved me.' Such was the outlandishly colourful and curious figure who in 1914 became one of the chief arbiters of London's avant-garde.

IN THE CAVE OF THE GOLDEN CALF

It was, in fact, John's artistic rival, Wyndham Lewis, whom Frida chose to execute the wall decorations of the Cave when she opened the club in 1912. (John himself resolutely refused to set foot in the place.) The germ of the idea for the club had lodged in her fertile brain in 1911, when J. T. Grein, drama critic of the *Sunday Times*, complained of the dullness of London's night life. What the capital lacked, Grein lamented, was a cabaret on the lines of Paris's Folies Bergères, where 'Poets, dramatists, singers… recite and create their fancies.' Frida read Grein's column and resolved to create just such a cabaret. Flush with funds from the sale of one of John's paintings and influenced by Roger Fry's second Post-Impressionist exhibition at the Grafton Galleries, which had showcased their work, she commissioned Lewis, Charles Ginner and another painter called Spencer Gore (who would die of pneumonia in March 1914), along with the sculptors Jacob Epstein and Eric Gill, to provide the new club's décor. She chose as her theme the cult of the golden calf – the phallic bull worshipped by pagans – a symbol of the wild hedonism she hoped the cabaret would encourage.

In April 1912 – the ominous month in which the *Titanic* foundered – a

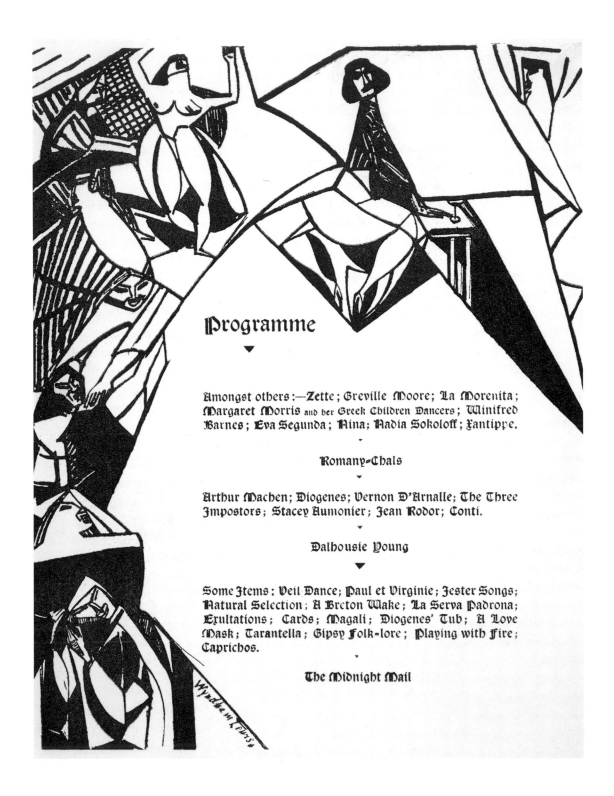

prospectus for the club promised that it would 'do away with the necessity of crossing the Channel to laugh freely and to sit up after nursery hours'. It was the recently deceased king, Edward VII, who had first loosened the whalebone stays of his mother Victoria's sternly puritanical public morality by beating a lascivious path to Paris, followed by many other philandering Englishmen. Here, as a by-product of his pleasure-seeking, Edward had been instrumental in paving the way for the 1904 Entente Cordiale, destined to bear such bloody fruit ten years later. Now, Frida was proposing to bring to London the Parisian Moulin Rouge style, with its Bohemian combination of decadence and the cutting edge of the artistic revolution. England, in which the plush velvet seats and private rooms of the Café Royal had previously seemed the last word in shocking, daring decadence, would never be its staid, stuffy self again.

Specifically, Frida's Cave promised 'Gaiety... but gaiety stimulating thought'. Wyndham Lewis grabbed Frida's commission to design the club's menus and programmes, as well as to paint the pictures on its walls, with both hands, confessing later that he would have done the work for nothing. Frida, Lewis and Epstein were all foreign-born, and the club's ethos was defiantly international and un- (or even anti-) English. The writer Osbert Sitwell noted his fellow Guards officers at the Cave, drinking with Bohemian artists 'in a super-heated Vorticist garden of gesticulating figures, dancing and talking while the primitive forms of ragtime throbbed through the wide room'.

As Sitwell noted, the London atmosphere among the crumbling upper crust, as the Cave opened, was rotten ripe and ready for almost any decadent extravagance, as though, unconsciously, the party-goers and revellers were aware of the chasm opening beneath their feet. 'Night by night, during the summer of 1913 and 1914,' he wrote,

> The entertainments grew in number and magnificence. One band was no longer enough, there must be two, three even. Electric fans whirled on top of enormous blocks of ice, buried in banks of hydrangeas... Never had there been such displays of flowers... mounds of peaches, figs, nectarines and strawberries at all seasons, brought from their steamy tents of glass. Champagne bottles stood stacked on the sideboards... And to the rich the show was free.

To encourage the atmosphere of frenzied pleasure-seeking, Lewis's trademark angular figures had mask-like faces and intertwined limbs. The sculptors Epstein and Gill, for their part, added the creatures – tigers,

CLUBBING: programme for the Cabaret Theatre Club at the Cave of the Golden Calf. Opened in 1912, the nightclub closed in 1914 on the eve of war.

monkeys and a representation of the golden calf itself, suggesting a frenetic, jungle-like atmosphere of unbridled animal lusts. Beneath the ceiling painted green and white, Epstein transformed the cellar's pillars into white caryatid totem-poles, with heads of hawks, cats and camels painted a lurid red. Gill – who combined fervent Catholicism with a private 'religion' of omnisexuality, in which he abused his own daughters as well as the family dog – carved the club's eponymous calf as a rampant beast with a prominent phallus.

CHAOS AT THE CALF

Despite such elaborate arrangements, the harum-scarum Frida prepared for opening night sloppily, with typical Austrian *schlamperei*, recruiting a mistress of ceremonies, Bokken Lasson, who happened to be passing through London, only at the very last minute. Lasson described the chaos on the eve of the Cave's birth:

> [The Cave] was naked and cold with no tables or chairs, with mortar and limestone dust everywhere. It looked like a construction site or a ruin. I could not imagine how this space could be ready to host a critical audience full of expectations the following evening. And even though I knew from my own experience that miracles could be done in twenty-four hours, I was quite nervous on behalf of Madame Strindberg. She hurried around among the craftsmen, talked seductively with them, gave instructions left and right, turned away unpleasant bills and had a fight with a furniture company in order to convince them to deliver chairs and tables in time, without cash payment.

Somehow, order emerged from the confusion, although the drop curtain in front of the club's stage – painted by Lewis at literally the last moment with a composition of chunky orange nudes and horses on a beach – had not yet dried. So, when the public was admitted to the Cave on the sultry night of 26 June, descending through what *The Times* described as 'a sort of manhole', they found themselves seated at a ring of tables around a low stage amid the garish and primitive imaginings of Lewis, Gore, Ginner, Gill and Epstein, which the *Times* critic sniffily described as 'infantile and not funny imitations of what one sees across the water'. Defying the heat of the night, Madame Strindberg, caked in chalk-white slap, greeted her guests in a heavy fur coat.

The programme that first evening included Bokken Lasson accompanying herself on guitar to songs by Grieg from her native Norway, a reading of Scandinavian fairy tales, a Miss Margaret Morris executing a barefoot dance, a Spanish flamenco dancer, and a recitation of Wilde's fable 'The Happy Prince', read by 'a young actor with a beautiful voice'. To close, a young Cockney delivered a 'serio-comic' homily about the Cave, and in true cabaret fashion mocked the audience by reminding everyone – shock, horror – that resident artist Spencer Gore was the nephew of a bishop.

The Cave soon became the haunt of fashionable London, which was drawn by gypsy music, dance bands playing music for the latest crazes, including the turkey trot and the bunny hug, and cabaret turns – along with a 50 per cent discount on the entrance fee offered by Frida as bait to attract the impecunious but talented glitterati. Among artists and writers who patronized the place, and even performed there, were Ezra Pound, Ford Madox Ford, Henri Gaudier-Brzeska and Katherine Mansfield. A hangover from the Wildean era, the journalist and boastful libertine Frank Harris entertained the audience with a recitation of Russian stories.

The more daring sections of the press gave cautious approval. In January 1914 *The Sketch* noted that the Cave had set the pace for 'another new movement' in London, observing that three more late-night clubs – the Four Hundred, Murray's and the Lotus – had followed down the path the Cave had first trodden. Not all the new clubs had the same artistic agenda as the Cave, according to one Captain Ernest Schiff, who wrote disapprovingly to a future Liberal home secretary, Sir John Simon:

> A very bad fellow, Jack Mays, is the proprietor of Murray's Club in Beak Street – quite an amusing place. But for vice or money or both he induces girls to smoke opium in some foul place. He is an American, and does a good deal of harm.

In setting such a social trend, Madame Strindberg had put in motion a movement that would only reach full fruition a decade later in the 'roaring Twenties', in the wake of the great bloodletting of 1914–18, when free and easy sexual behaviour, routine drug-taking, and nightclub life became the norm for the smarter, faster post-war generation. But as a pioneer, she paid the price – quite literally. Within a month of *The Sketch*'s praise, the Cave of the Golden Calf went bust and shut its doors for good.

As with so many artistic entrepreneurs, Madame Strindberg's accounts never quite added up. Despite the money she made from wheeling and dealing in pictures, a substantial inheritance, and the Cave's entry fees, there was never quite enough cash to go around. Spencer Gore was paid for his work in decorating the club not with money but with drawings by Augustus John. The other artists – apart from Lewis, who, true to his tough-guy image, ensured that Madame Strindberg paid his £60 fee and even raided the till for his final instalment – were never paid at all. What little cash there was, Frida spent. For its second season in 1913 she renovated the Cave and reconstructed its stage. Obsessed with the latest dance craze – the Argentine tango – she instituted 'tango nights' and 'tango teas', which were washed down with champagne to make the party go with a fizz, and spent a small fortune importing a tango teacher from Paris.

The notoriety of the club – especially after Marinetti staged his Futurist evening there – attracted the unwelcome attention of the authorities, and the police raided the premises more than once. Taking advantage of Frida's inattention to the accounts, waiters began to pocket more than their tips, and more money was wasted when Frida hired private eyes in an attempt to spy on the malefactors. The remaining cash having run out, Frida was forced to declare the Cave bankrupt and it shut its doors for the last time in 1914. Stripping the club of anything of value that she could sell, she made preparations to sail for the New World, writing a fond farewell to Augustus John as she went:

I'm leaving the Cabaret. Dreams are sweeter than reality.
We shall never meet again now. Goodbye John, I don't know
whether you know at the bottom of your heart how awfully
good you are…

Something of the Cave's anarchic spirit, however, survived Madame Strindberg's departure – in Lewis's short-lived Rebel Art Centre and, just as briefly, in a pale imitation of the club he had never deigned to enter, an establishment that Augustus John himself founded: the Crabtree Club, in Soho's Greek Street. Intended, according to John, to be the haunt of 'artists, poets and musicians', the Crabtree in practice attracted artists' models 'wearing black hats and throwing bottles'. The atmosphere was more muscular than the Cave's had been, with boxing matches staged alongside its more arty offerings. Real artists, however, were scornful: 'A most disgusting place!' was the opinion of Paul Nash, official war artist in both world wars. Where only the very lowest city Jews and the most pinched harlots attend. A place of utter coarseness and dull, unrelieved monotony. John alone, a great, pathetic muzzy god, a sort of Silenus – but alas no nymphs, satyrs and leopards to complete the picture.'

THE CORRUPT COTERIE

Among the most enthusiastic patrons of the Cave of the Golden Calf were the members of the social set who called themselves the 'Corrupt Coterie'. The Coterie were themselves the sons and daughters of a late Victorian and early Edwardian high-society clique called 'the Souls'. The Souls, hugely influential in the world of politics and the country-house weekends that characterized the last flowering of the British aristocracy, included among their more prominent members George Nathaniel Curzon, sometime foreign secretary and viceroy of India; his fellow Tory grandee, Arthur Balfour, prime minister before he was ousted in the 1906 Liberal landslide; and the great hostesses, Lady Elcho, Ettie Grenfell and the duchess of Rutland.

Although discreet, corridor-creeping adultery in country houses was part and parcel of the Souls' way of life. Understandably, it led to confusion over the paternity of some of their progeny, and the Souls largely kept their affairs of the heart to each other, confiding their secrets only to those with a need to know – and often not even to them. The attitude of the second generation of Souls, the Corrupt Coterie, was very different. All brought up as the sons and daughters of privilege, if not of their 'official' parents, they took their position at the centre of English high society for granted.

The Coterie were not unduly exercised by the extreme social inequalities of the Edwardian era in which they had been raised, acting out their luxurious lifestyles free of guilt as part of the natural order of things. Raised in the long shadows of their overachieving parents, the Coterie's principal purpose was the pursuit of pleasure; their default attitude one of cynical heartlessness, touching, on occasion, on downright cruelty.

Raised with the legacy of their parents' sexual hypocrisy, the Coterie scorned the outward conventions which the older generation maintained. Their leading members – the undisputed golden couple, although they were not actually paired in love – were Lady Diana Manners, youngest daughter of the duke and duchess of Rutland (although her real father was Henry Cust, a caddish sporting Soul), and Raymond Asquith, eldest son of the prime minister, Herbert Henry Asquith. Diana was the radiantly lovely reigning society beauty of the seasons just before the outbreak of war, while Raymond, who had carved a swathe eclipsing all his contemporaries at Winchester, Balliol College, Oxford and the bar, provided the Coterie with their intellectual input.

Both gave their own takes on their set. 'I do not know how it came to be called the Coterie – the Corrupt Coterie to give it its full title,' recalled Diana. 'As a name, I am a little ashamed of it, as my mother was of the "Souls". There was among us a reverberation of the Yellow Book and Aubrey Beardsley, Ernest Dowson, Baudelaire and Max Beerbohm. Swinburne often got recited. Our pride was to be unafraid of words, unshocked by drink, and unashamed of decadence and gambling – Unlike-Other-People, I'm afraid.'

While Diana appeared slightly shame-faced at her peers' snobbery and unabashed social elitism, the arrogant Raymond, who followed his father into Liberal politics, positively gloried in it. 'Eighteenth-century methods worked well enough when we had a talented aristocracy, but we can't afford nowadays to limit our choice of Ministers to a few stuffy families with ugly faces, bad manners and a belief in the Nicene Creed,' he loftily proclaimed. 'The day of the clever Cad is at hand… a gentleman may make a large fortune but only a cad can look after it.'

As his reference to the Nicene Creed shows, Raymond's particular bugbear was the organized religion of Anglican Christianity, still outwardly conformed to – if secretly disbelieved in – by the Souls' generation. Arthur Balfour, elder statesman and the epitome of the Souls, had written an elegant apologia for agnosticism, *A Defence of Philosophic Doubt*, and opined that 'Few things matter very much – and most things don't matter at all,' but Raymond carried this casual cynicism much further, scornfully telling Diana that if Christ had been clean-shaven, the Virgin worn rouge, and the Holy Ghost an eagle rather than a dove, then Christianity might have had more meaning. 'But no. God played his cards badly from beginning to end.'

The Coterie's high jinks may seem tame by modern standards but were deeply shocking to their elders – a fact which brought a delicious frisson of delight to the young people. Where their parents had quaffed champagne, they injected morphine, smoked opium, snorted cocaine and breathed in chloroform ('cholers') or ether. They 'spooned' in hansom cabs, preferred the tango or the turkey trot to the staid waltz, and kissed and canoodled in public where their parents had merely flirted.

It was not, however, what their children did with their bodies that shocked their parents the most, but the mental outlook revealed by their antics. Margot Asquith, an original Soul and Raymond's stepmother, was 'Never more shocked in my life' than when her daughter Violet revealed the nature of a game she had learned at Stanway, one of the great country houses frequented by the Coterie. Called 'Breaking the News', players of the game, in a satire on the charades favoured by the Souls, had to act out telling a parent that a beloved child had died. 'A more terrible game I could never imagine,' Margot Asquith opined, 'Heartless and Brutal.'

But heartlessness and brutality lay at the core of the Coterie, at least

FRAGILE BEAUTY: the socialite Diana Manners, youngest daughter of the duchess of Rutland, epitomized the aristocratic set called the Corrupt Coterie. Almost all her suitors were killed in the Great War.

according to Lady Cynthia Asquith, the wife of another of Asquith's sons, Herbert ('Beb'). Herself a member of the Coterie, Cynthia judged that 'there is an insidiously corruptive poison in their minds – brilliantly distilled by their inspiration, Raymond. I don't care a damn about their morals and manners, but I do think what – for want of a better word – I call their anti-cant is really suicidal to happiness.'

LOST SOULS, LOST SOULS

Little did Lady Cynthia know that something even deadlier and more murderous to happiness than the Coterie's flippant cynicism lay just around the corner for many of them. Of the Coterie's major members, Raymond Asquith would die on the Somme in September 1916, shot while leading his men into action. He is buried in the same cemetery as his distant cousin Edward 'Bim' Tennant, who died in the same action attacking the German-held hamlet of Ginchy.

In the same battle, a young Grenadier Guardsman, Harold Macmillan, shot and grievously wounded, fell into a shell-hole and spent the day reading the plays of Aeschylus, which he kept in the breast pocket of his tunic. He stayed alive by playing dead when a prowling German crept around to loot the corpses. Such scenes were hardly imaginable to Macmillan in the Lent term of 1914 when, having gained a First in Classical Moderations at Oxford, he could afford to sit back and enjoy 'Eight weeks of bliss':

> 1914… was a glorious summer – day after day, week after week, of cloudless atmosphere with soft voluptuous breezes and a Mediterranean sky. There were two years and more before Greats. There was little to be done but collect our books, to go – for form's sake – to a few lectures and to enjoy ourselves.

Macmillan and his friends

> played tennis and cricket, we punted, we bathed. We had luncheon and dinner parties. We lazed in the quad reading Dostoyevsky. Occasionally we went to London, to the Russian opera and ballet…

At last it came to an end. But pleasure was only postponed. I had arranged to go again, with other friends to a chalet [in the Haute-Savoie] in the first week in August. Everything was prepared… Then the storm broke; the axe fell.

The Great War would scythe down the scions of the British aristocracy like sheaves of golden corn. The same catastrophe swallowed up the brothers Julian and Billy Grenfell, Coterie members and handsome, curly-headed sons of the leading Soul hostess, Lady Ettie Desborough. In 1913 Ettie inherited Panshanger, a huge stately pile in Hertfordshire which she promptly set about modernizing, installing new-fangled central heating and selling a Raphael for £70,000 to pay the bills. Ettie was so grand and rich that, when she married Willy Grenfell, an athletic, sporting former Tory MP (he had swum the Niagara rapids and rowed across the Channel), who was ennobled as Lord Desborough by his friend and fellow Soul, Arthur Balfour, her family thought her husband beneath her.

Julian – a professional soldier, pig-sticker, boxer and poet (though of a distinctly un-pacifist sort) and heir to his father's Taplow Court, a vast house surrounded by 3,000 acres of prime Thames-side land near Maidenhead – was a natural warrior who loved war. He would steal out at night into No Man's Land between the trenches, fix the sights of his rifle on a gap in the German wire, and shoot any unfortunate who happened to be passing. In October 1914 he wrote home from the front: 'I adore war. It has all the fun of a picnic without the objectlessness of it. I have never been so well or so happy.' Grenfell died after being struck in the head with a shell splinter in 1915. The next day *The Times* printed his poem 'Into Battle':

> And Life is Colour and Warmth and Light,
> And a striving evermore for these;
> And he is dead who will not fight;
> And who dies fighting has increase.

Two more brothers – Hugo and Yvo Charteris, the sons of Lady Elcho, chatelaine of Stanway – also died. Other Coterie members who perished included the 'shooting star' of the group, Patrick Shaw-Stewart, a Barings banker and young lover of Lady Desborough, killed by a shell on 31 December 1917; Charles Lister – a self-styled upper-class socialist (the son of Lord Ribblesdale, he had converted to socialism while at Eton) – who accompanied Rupert Brooke on the way to Gallipoli and survived the carnage there, only to die on the Somme the following year; and Edward Horner, a

FUTURE PRIME MINISTER Harold Macmillan (second from left in the front row, sitting at the feet of the Tory politician Austen Chamberlain) at Oxford, 1914. His university career was about to be rudely interrupted by the war.

laughing giant and brother to Raymond Asquith's wife Katharine, killed at Cambrai in 1917. With him, wrote his devastated mother, 'Perished the last hope of direct male succession in an ancient and honourable English house. And there passed too a gay, sunny and adorable nature, the love of which made life sweeter…'

Three of Prime Minister Asquith's own sons – Raymond, Arthur ('Oc') and Herbert ('Beb') – volunteered to fight at the front. Raymond was killed; Oc – who also accompanied Brooke on the Gallipoli expedition and rose

from subaltern to become the youngest general in the British Army – lost a leg; and Beb's nerves were permanently shattered by his experiences as a gunner on the Western Front. Before he died, the acid-tongued Raymond made it very clear what he thought of the war that his father had led the nation into and was incompetently presiding over:

> A blind God butts about the world with a pair of delicately malignant antennae to detect whatever is fit to live, and an iron hoof to stamp it into the dust when found… One's instinct that the world (as we know it) is governed by chance is almost shaken by the accumulating evidence that it is the best which is picked out for destruction… I agree about the utter senselessness of war… The suggestion that it elevates the character is hideous. Burglary, assassination and picking oakum would do as much for anyone.

The war's end left both the Souls and the Coterie hollowed out, devastated and bereaved. Their class had lost its power, their caste its moral code and its previously unquestioned authority, and their former joie de vivre lay buried in the torn earth of France and Flanders. Now, ageing, childless and alone, it was the women, who had lost husbands, brothers, sons and lovers, who were left to pick up the broken shards of their previously perfectly formed existence and piece them together as best they could. The houses where they had fucked and frolicked – Mells, Clouds, Stanway, Taplow – were now echoing, empty mausoleums, peopled only by wraiths and ghosts. The dances that had once filled them had been but – as a Coterie party in August 1914 was actually themed and titled – dances of death.

9. THE LAST SEASON

LAST HURRAH for the old aristocratic order: Sir Maurice and Lady FitzGerald and their party arrive at the Cowes Regatta, 1910.

9. The Last Season

IT IS TEMPTING TO BELIEVE that the shenanigans of upper-caste social sets such as the Souls and their children of the Coterie – frivolous, charming and brittle as they appear in hindsight – had little relevance to the mass of the country's people: nothing could be further from the truth. The first fourteen years of the twentieth century were an era when a tiny social elite held the threads of social, economic and political power firmly in their grasp. They were educated at the same schools and universities; belonged to the same clubs (including the most exclusive club of all, the Houses of Parliament); dined and partied in one another's grand London houses; and spent their long weekends playing, hunting, shooting and fishing in the same even grander country houses. In the summer they rowed in the Henley Regatta; attended Ascot race week and watched the tennis tournaments at Wimbledon; yachted in the Solent; played cricket at Lord's and the Oval; and went on long holidays in resorts such as Biarritz and Marienbad.

Despite the fierce political differences over budgets and Ulster, Tories and Liberals came from the same upper-crust elite, sharing the same assumptions and participating in the same seasonal social round. The two tribes even intermarried. Before the shadows of war, like blue-black thunderheads, began to steal across the long summer lawns of 1914, the season that year appeared like any other: cricket and tennis whites; boating on the Thames at Henley and Maidenhead; public-school speech days. Secure in the knowledge that their kind were the proud owners of 99 per cent of Britain's land, the aristocratic elite basked in the warm sunshine of that season, apparently oblivious of the gathering storm that would shatter their garden parties for good.

BORN TO PRIVILEGE AND POWER

The Coterie members, observing that year their elders' rituals with their usual caustic eyes, were well aware of the statistics. At Belvoir Castle, the Midlands Gothic folly home of Diana Manners's 'official' father, the duke of Rutland, rents from the duke's tenants totalled almost £100,000 at a time when those same tenants earned around a pound a week. In the Upstairs/Downstairs world of the castle, fifty servants, all jostling for petty advantage

NEARLY GONE: boaters and
muslin dresses at the
Henley Regatta, July 1914 –
the last major social event of
the summer season and the
end of an era.

in their hierarchy, served the duke and duchess, their three daughters and guests. One of the latter, visiting in 1914, described the castle as 'Absurd… a pantomime scene'.

'The golden summer of 1914 for the few,' as one modern writer has noted, 'was guaranteed by the servitude of the many.' An army of half a million men and women – butlers, cooks, lady's maids, chambermaids, chauffeurs, grooms, pantry boys and boot blacks – served this tiny caste as domestic servants. In April 1914, when King George V and Queen Mary stayed with the earl of Derby, 'the uncrowned king of Lancashire', to watch the Grand National at Aintree, their needs were met by no fewer than 151 servants.

The following month, horse-racing was the focus of southern high society too, when the season opened in May at Hawthorn Hill in Berkshire with the Household Brigade's Steeplechases held in a burst of golden spring sunshine. As the cavalrymen who would soon be taking their mounts to war in France competed to hurl themselves over the hedges, members of the Coterie assembled at Lord and Lady Desborough's nearby sprawling folly of a home at Taplow. Their aim was to see – and if possible to fly – with one of the season's sensations, the daring aviator Gustav Hamel.

Despite his German-sounding name, Hamel, like the contemporary composer Gustav Holst, was impeccably English. Educated at Westminster School, he had found fame by such stunts as delivering the first airmail in Britain and perfecting his party piece, looping the loop. In January 1914 Hamel had taken a society lady, Miss Trehawke Davis, aloft and looped the loop with her – she thus became the first woman in aviation history to experience the manoeuvre. Now, at Maidenhead, he took another brave Coterie member, Sybil Hart-Davis, up to repeat the trick. Lady Diana Manners, forbidden by her father to fly, could only watch from the ground as her friend, secured by a pair of shoulder straps, whirled aloft in the gravity-defying feat. After landing safely, Hamel took Sybil up again: this time she was clutching a pair of piglets to prove – in a typically waggish Coterie in-joke – that 'pigs could fly'.

A few days later, Hamel was dead. On 23 May, returning across the Channel after picking up a new aircraft in France, he vanished into thin air. His body was never found, though a corpse fitting his description was spotted floating in the Channel by some fishermen in July. Hamel thus became the first airman to die in the deceptively narrow strip of water that had become narrower still a few short years before – in 1909, when the Frenchman Louis Blériot became the first man to traverse *La Manche* by air, landing outside the walls of Dover Castle and claiming a £1,000 prize offered by the *Daily Mail*.

STUNT MAN: the pioneer pilot Gustav Hamel with his aeroplane. His daring aerial antics ended when he disappeared over the Channel in May 1914.

Ignoring the ominous tragedy of Hamel's death, the ladies who had flown with him continued the summer season at full tilt. Famous society hostesses, the likes of Ladies Cunard, Curzon, Clifton and Dalkeith and – most magnificent of all – Lady Londonderry, vied with each other to throw the most lavish parties and receptions, the most elaborate costumed balls. Racing at Newmarket alternated with polo on Leopold de Rothschild's Gunnersbury Park ground. An American team was scratched together to play this most English of games, but even so the numbers didn't quite add up, so Julian and Billy Grenfell sportingly volunteered to play alongside their American cousins.

TROUBLE IN PARADISE

As brilliantly shining summer day succeeded luminously blue day, it seemed as if the weather itself was conspiring with the calendar to make this season the most gorgeous of them all, as if every last drop of juice was being squeezed out of the fruit before the fall into rottenness. The language of politics, too, reflected the uneasy atmosphere of frenzied pleasure-seeking while the sun still shone before impending doom closed in. As Ulster rolled closer towards a seemingly inevitable cataclysm, from either side of the battle lines the talk was of conflict, not peace. Speaking to a Belfast rally, Sir Edward Carson bellowed that he wanted a 'clean war, [and] a clean fight', while, from the other side of the barricades, an ever-belligerent Winston Churchill told an audience that 'Bloodshed no doubt is lamentable… but there are worse things than bloodshed, even on an extensive scale.'

Words of war come easily to politicians who will not have to fight. It is strange, though, to find them, in this last season of 1914, also flowing from the mouths of women, the source and nurturers of life, with Emmeline and Christabel Pankhurst calling for an intensification of the violent suffragette struggle, a campaign that they called the 'women's war'.

It was not only the militant women's movement that sensed, almost scented the stench of the coming catastrophe. Writing retrospectively, the writer J. B. Priestley said of the summer before the war:

My drifting and planless state of mind was far from uncommon… other people, in situations very different from mine, did not know where they were going or what they wanted to do in the near future. If they were not aware of this blank, this emptiness never flashing the signal WAR, then they were haunted during these months by the idea of something going, something being lost.

The dreaded word 'war' was of course a commonplace to the artists and writers of the avant-garde. Ezra Pound admiringly called his friend Wyndham Lewis 'A man of war', while Lewis himself, in his *BLAST* manifesto, used extravagantly violent language and illustrations adorned with titles such as 'Plan of War' and 'Slow Attack'. In a spirit of making his readers' flesh creep, Lewis declared: 'Killing somebody must be the greatest pleasure in existence: either like killing yourself without being interfered with by the instinct of self-preservation – or exterminating the instinct of self-preservation itself!'

Not everyone was pleased with the pronouncements of the painter spearheading the cutting edge of modern art. Speaking at the banquet marking the opening of the Royal Academy's annual summer show in early May, a royal personage, Prince Arthur of Connaught, made an outspoken attack on what he called the 'perverted' values of modern art. Contemporary painting, he fulminated, was full of unbecoming aggression and violence. As if to bear out his words, violence attended the exhibition itself when, in a copy-cat echo of Mary Richardson's assault on the *Rokeby Venus*, an elderly unidentified suffragette, though described as being of 'peaceable appearance', nonetheless produced a meat cleaver and attacked one of the stars of the show: the era's most fashionable portrait painter John Singer Sargent's painting of his fellow expatriate American, the novelist Henry James.

The portrait of 'the Master', resembling a large lump of Edam cheese in a striped waistcoat, was protected by glass and suffered only superficial damage, soon made good by the artist himself. Before magistrates the next day, the attacker explained that her motive had been to protest against the sexist neglect of women artists by the Academy's hanging committee, and the high monetary value (between £100 and £200) put on the representation of the elderly writer. The latest attack was not the only manifestation of cultural vandalism that summer: a case of priceless porcelain at the British Museum was smashed and an attempt made to burn down Westminster Abbey. It was going to be – literally – a long, hot summer.

Arthur of Connaught was not the only member of the royal family exhibiting Philistine tendencies that summer. King George V's eldest son, the Prince of Wales (known to his intimates as 'the Pragga Wagga') had just returned to Magdalen College, Oxford – one of a long line of royal duffers admitted to Britain's most prestigious universities, Oxford and Cambridge, because of their status rather than their intellect. Even the prince's mentor at Magdalen, the college's president, Sir Herbert Warren, admitted to *The Times* of his protégé that 'Bookish he will never be'.

Instead of his books, the prince occupied his time with golf, beagling and rowing – or at least watching from the river bank, as his own puny physique was not sufficiently muscular. It must have come as some relief when war broke out in August and he was able to swap the pretence of his studies for a life behind the lines as an (equally fake) officer in the Grenadier Guards. Here, he would be kept far from the dangerous front, having to borrow a bicycle whenever he wanted to escape the restraining hands of his minder officers.

A DAY AT THE RACES

The merry month of May reached its social apex on the 27th with Derby Day on the Epsom Downs. The previous year, the famous flat race had been tragically disrupted when a militant suffragette, Emily Wilding Davison, had darted under the railings to bring down King George V's horse, Anmer. As it fell, the horse's flailing hooves had fractured Emily's skull, causing injuries from which she died four days later. Race-goers from the king and queen down did not let the memory of Davison's martyrdom deter them from enjoying their sport, as half a million of them – the men attired in toppers, trilbies, boaters or flat caps depending on their class; the ladies in white muslin and wide-brimmed hats bestrewn with floral colour – converged on Epsom by coach, car, rail and on foot. The king and Queen Mary were present in person, their hopes resting this year on their horse Black Jester – a hot favourite. In the event, the royals were foiled again. Not, this time, by a suffragette, but by the French-bred Durbar II, a 20–1 outsider owned by an American, H. B. Duryea, which romped home.

Winners and losers celebrated their success or drowned their sorrows in contrasting styles. Mr Duryea threw a lavish party in the Berkeley grill-room, the tables of which were decorated in his green and white racing colours. The king and queen, for their part, hosted a traditional Derby Night dinner for the Jockey Club at Buckingham Palace. Afterwards, many of the diners drove to Devonshire House, the London home of the duke and duchess of Devonshire, freshly decorated with flowers specially brought from their Chatsworth estate in Derbyshire. The duchess stood erect at the head of the grand staircase to receive her guests. In the gold and white ballroom the king and queen watched from two thrones in a wall niche, nibbling canapés from a solid-gold plate before leaving. After their departure, the younger guests let their hair down and the sedate waltz gave way to wilder dances – like the openly erotic tango, the turkey trot, the bunny hug and the fish walk – imported from across the Atlantic. It was not yet clear that the dance was being held on the edge of a volcano.

'NEVER SUCH INNOCENCE AGAIN': well-heeled picnickers take luncheon at the Bath Horse Show, c. 1910.

THE RUSSIANS ARE COMING...

Another kind of dancing still held London in thrall: the Russian ballet first brought to Britain in 1911 by its creator, the impresario of genius Sergei Diaghilev. Working with composers including Rimsky-Korsakov, Debussy and Stravinsky, Diaghilev pioneered a daringly contemporary style, combining primitive, overtly sexual motifs with lavish and extravagant sets and décor. The ethos of the ballet was exemplified by its troubled star, the choreographer and principal dancer Vaslav Nijinsky, whose fantastic leaps and quivering, sexually explicit gestures both scandalized and fascinated the high-society clientele who flocked to watch him. Rupert Brooke was one of those dazzled by the experience, writing in 1912 of the Russians: 'They, if anything, can redeem our civilization.'

With each season, Diaghilev became more daring and more outrageous. In 1912 a ballet entitled *L'Après-midi d'un faune*, a tale of woodland romance between a faun and a nymph – inspired by a Stéphane Mallarmé poem and using music by Claude Debussy as its score – had featured the muscular Nijinsky, clad in a skin-tight leotard that left little to the imagination as he shiveringly simulated an orgasm. Though the shocked audience remained hushed on the opening night of this 'offence against good taste', as one admirer called it, the Paris press was apocalyptic in its outrage. Gaston Calmette, editor of the conservative *Le Figaro*, refused to print his own critic's review of the piece, instead penning his own foaming denunciation of its 'filthy and bestial movements… as crude as they are indecent'.

Calmette – the dedicatee of his friend Proust's *À la recherche du temps perdu* – would face something even more dangerous than a controversial ballet in March 1914, when he found himself looking down the barrel of a pistol held by Madame Henriette Caillaux, wife of France's finance minister Joseph Caillaux. Calmette had been using Caillaux's purloined love letters in a ruthless campaign against the radical politician, accusing him of treasonous collusion with France's German enemy. Madame Caillaux, newly purchased pistol in hand, confronted the pugnacious editor in his office to defend her and her husband's honour, and pumped four bullets into him. As Europe tipped down the slope towards war, it was not the galloping crisis that monopolized the attention of the French press and public that summer but Madame Caillaux's trial for Calmette's killing. Naturally, a gallant Gallic jury found her act a crime of passion – and acquitted her.

Back in 1913, undeterred by Calmette's criticism of *L'Après-midi*, Diaghilev pushed the envelope of the acceptable even further, in fact tore it apart, when he staged the première of Stravinsky's revolutionary *Rite of Spring* in the new Champs-Élysées theatre. The ballet, with its discordant

LEAP INTO THE DARK: Vaslav Nijinsky, the brilliant but troubled star of Diaghilev's Ballets Russes, who dazzled London and all Europe before the war.

chords, strange, jerky rhythms and strangulated bassoons, was controversial enough, but the theme – human sacrifice in a pagan, primitive Russia – was even more shocking, with a girl literally dancing herself to death. Diaghilev had carefully primed the pumps of outrage in the press, with a pre-première interview in which he predicted a riot – and a riot duly transpired. Or at least there was a lot of noise. Hardly had Stravinsky's overture opened when the hissing and booing – countered by the cheers of the ballet's backers – began. The cacophony continued until the composer, accompanied by Diaghilev and Nijinsky, took their bows.

In stark contrast to its rough ride in Paris, London received *The Rite of Spring*, when Diaghilev brought it to Covent Garden in the same season, with 'polite amazement'. The acclaim with which high society received the Russian ballet morphed into a fashionable wave of enthusiasm for all things Russian. Women, led by the aristocratic Lady Ripon, wife of the best shot in England, who was of Russian descent and Diaghilev's hostess in Britain, sported Russian-style turbans; astrakhan fur was de rigueur, Russian tea-rooms opened and vodka became the drink of choice.

There were other, less elevated entertainments on offer in London that summer for the capital's well-heeled young men – known in the parlance of the day as 'Nuts' – to squire their lady friends along to. In April the Palace Theatre presented *The Passing Show of 1914*, a musical revue whose signature song, warbled by the handsome, deep-brown-voiced Basil Hallam, was 'Gilbert the Filbert':

I'm Gilbert the Filbert, the Nut with the K,
The pride of Piccadilly, the blasé roué.
Oh, Hades, the ladies all leave their wooden huts
For Gilbert the Filbert, the Colonel of the Nuts.

Hallam, moustachioed, elegant and dapper, would join the infant Royal Flying Corps in 1915, but was destined to die on the Somme in August 1916 when he fell thousands of feet from an observation balloon as it drifted towards enemy lines.

The same month that *The Passing Show* opened, a more permanent addition to the theatrical repertory was born with the London première of George Bernard Shaw's *Pygmalion*, starring his favourite actors Sir Herbert Beerbohm Tree as the pompous philologist Henry Higgins and Mrs Patrick Campbell as his Cockney flower-girl protégé Eliza Doolittle. Directed by the Irish windbag personally, the wordy five-act show stood out, not so much for its satire of England's still rampant class-consciousness, but for one word in particular – the epithet 'bloody', all the more thrillingly shocking as it emanated from the mouth of a lady, as Eliza declared 'Not bloody likely!' It says much for the changes wrought by the Great War that blood – the real stuff – which would flow in torrents before the year was out would be less shocking to a theatre audience than that one iconic little word.

PARTYING ON A PRECIPICE

As June climbed towards midsummer, with no break in the fine weather, the party rolled remorselessly on. 'Dances are nicer as well as longer,' a letter writer claimed in that month's edition of the society magazine *The Tatler*:

> Most of 'em begin with dinner… And without the five o'clock kippers, kidneys and beer, whose succulent savour rouses even the sleepy chaperone from her secret slumbers, no really smart dance is counted as done tophole.

Another *Tatler* columnist aped an invitation from a society hostess: 'You'll come to my little party? And when you do go along you find a marquee in the garden, Cassano's band busy and tom tits' toes on toast with the Bollinger for supper.'

The background grumbling of politics and distant rumours of war were the mood music behind the partying of the 1914 summer season. But it was not, at first, the echoes of the distant shots at Sarajevo that disturbed the party atmosphere but a crisis far closer to home: Ulster. On 21 May the House of Commons belatedly gave a final third reading to the long-awaited and bitterly contested Irish Home Rule Bill. However, behind the scenes, Prime Minister Asquith had been holding secret talks with both the Tory and the Ulster Unionist leaders, Bonar Law and Edward Carson, in a bid to wriggle off the painful hook that his government had impaled itself upon.

Asquith had agreed that any Ulster county that wished to opt out of Home Rule could do so – at least for six years – provided that a majority in local referendums voted in favour. This proposal formed the basis of a series of conferences – called at the suggestion of the king, who was desperate to prevent part of his realm from descending into open conflict – between the Liberal government and its Irish Parliamentary Party allies on one side, and the Tories and their Ulster Unionist friends on the other. With the shadow of the shots at Sarajevo looming ever more menacingly over the deliberations, the conference, held between 21 and 24 July and presided over by the neutral Speaker of the House of Commons, never got, in Churchill's contemptuous phrase, beyond 'the muddy by-ways of Fermanagh and Tyrone' – two Ulster counties whose mixed populations made it doubtful whether they would opt in or out of Home Rule.

Despite these tentative and ultimately futile peace moves, Ulster succeeded in disrupting the smooth running of the social season. While the Souls had socialized, met, mingled and even married across party lines, the divisions over Ulster opened fissures among the ruling elite that became yawning chasms. The Conservative Lady Theresa Londonderry, president of the Ulster Unionist Women's Council, whose grand Londonderry House on Park Lane was one of the hubs of the high-society season, flatly refused even to enter a house if she suspected that a Liberal might be present. Asquith's customary invitation to the Tory Lord Curzon's summer ball went unaccountably missing, while his wife Margot found herself being cut stone-dead by Tory ladies in the Speakers' Gallery of the Commons.

Nervousness about the impending atmosphere of violence caused a tightening of security at Buckingham Palace itself. Those attending court balls and levees found themselves being asked to show their tickets – an unheard-of affront to English notions of privacy and liberty.

On 4 June, the 'Glorious Fourth', the most important date in the calendar at Eton, England's most exclusive and expensive public school, the king's eldest child, Princess Mary, came to the college, along with other notables such as Lady Desborough, to visit her brother, Prince Henry, the king's third son, a young Etonian.

The scene was a sea of 'silk hats and sunshine. Muslin, chiffon, parasols and lace as waves of visitors swept into the college's Chapel; to School Yard; to hear speeches in Latin; to watch cricket on Agar's Plough.' After luncheon, amidst more sunshine, strawberries were consumed as the multitudes awaited the day's highlight: a procession of flower-bedecked boats passing along the Thames with their crews in fancy dress against a background of exploding fireworks. Within weeks of this lavish display, the first of the 1,157 former Etonians who would die in the Great War – one-fifth of those who fought – had been killed.

The topmost peak of the 1914 season had not yet been scaled. That came in mid-June, with Ascot week, the premier racing event at which the costumes racegoers donned attracted more attention than the performance of the horses on the track. Then, as now, there was a Darwinian struggle among the socialites to obtain entrance to the exclusive Royal Enclosure. Then, as now, actresses vied with aristocrats to wear the most eye-catching, outrageous or near-absurd clothes. On the first day of the meeting, there was an ominous chill in the air – the first sign of a break in the hot weather since May. Fur coats and capes were much in evidence, which caused a headache for the nervously security-conscious staff inside the Enclosure. 'All our poor little wraps and things,' complained one racegoer, 'were bundled off by police. Will the Suffragettes, one wonders, still be keeping… Society on tenter-hooks, say in the Season of 1917?' In the event, of course, other and very different concerns would be preoccupying society in the season of 1917.

Another great sporting summit – the Wimbledon lawn tennis championships, already in their fourth decade – began on 22 June. The men's final was an all-Antipodean affair with New Zealand's 's reigning champion, the flamboyant and energetic Tony Wilding – who had been the first man to ride a motorcycle from Land's End in Cornwall to John O'Groats at Scotland's northern tip – expected to win the title for the fifth year in succession. But, in a fiercely fought match, he was narrowly beaten by Australia's Norman Brookes. Within a year, Wilding was dead: enlisting on Winston Churchill's advice in the Royal Marines, he was commanding a squadron of armoured Rolls-Royces when he was killed by a shell landing on the roof of his dug-out during the Battle of Aubers Ridge in May 1915.

THE SHOT HEARD AROUND THE WORLD
Halfway through Wimbledon week came the shot on a distant frontier that would ultimately kill Tony Wilding – and up to ten million more young and not-so-young men. A group of Bosnian Serb revolutionaries, sponsored and trained in Belgrade by a nationalist secret society rejoicing in the conspiratorial name the Black Hand, successfully assassinated the heir to the throne of Austria-Hungary, Archduke Franz Ferdinand, and his wife Sophie, while they were visiting Sarajevo, the capital of Bosnia, the province that Austria had recently annexed. At first reaction in Britain to this alarming news was muted: people were used to violence in the Balkans, the scene of two full-scale wars and numerous assassinations in the first years of the century. Why, many wondered, should this be any different? For the moment, the ball went on.

The season was ending, in fact, in a whole welter of balls and dances. Most ironically titled of all was the Anglo-American Peace Centenary Ball, held at the Albert Hall to celebrate one hundred years of peace between the two great English-speaking powers since the war of 1814 had seen British troops occupy Washington and burn the White House. 'In celebrating the centenary of Peace,' read the ball's brochure, 'the countries that have given birth to Shakespeare and Lincoln, Milton and Penn… are setting a magnificent example to the rest of the civilized world.'

LAID BACK: former premier and sporting elder statesman Lord (Arthur) Balfour at Wimbledon, 1914, with New Zealand tennis player A. F. 'Tony' Wilding, Wimbledon men's singles champion, 1910–13.

One ball – the Cavalry Ball – held at Knightsbridge Barracks, was graced by a warrior who was very much a man of war, rather than of peace. Horatio Herbert Kitchener, the magnificently moustached 'K', who had crushed Sudan's Dervishes at Omdurman in 1898 and then South Africa's Boers – using methods very far from the gentlest – was not known as a man for the ladies. But there he sat, 'holding court like a king,' observed Osbert Sitwell, 'In a bower of wreaths and flowers'. The stern-faced general's unsmiling features, recalled Sitwell, burnished by the unforgiving suns of Africa, 'Seemed tawny beyond sunburn and pertained to the planet Mars'. Within weeks, the warlord, appointed secretary of state for war by a pacifically inclined Liberal government, would, in the conflict's most famous poster, be drawing millions towards the trenches with his dramatically pointing finger and his stern injunction: 'Your country needs you!'

There was a Midnight Ball to benefit the blind at the Savoy Hotel at which gypsies, Futurists, pierrots and Apaches brought over from Paris provided the entertainment; and a Daimler car and an aeroplane flight for two were among the prizes in the raffle. London's large and rich American community, who had energized the British aristocracy's etiolated blood with their genes and refilled their depleted coffers with their dollars, were prominent at these balls, foremost among them the Astors, owners of two stately homes at Cliveden and Hever Castle and one-time proprietors of that embodiment of Englishness, *The Times*.

The Astors held their own private dance, at which the clothes were said to rival in sheer gaudy gorgeousness the costumes of the Russian ballet. It was on the same June night as the Countess of Huntingdon's 'Pink Party' held at Claridge's Hotel, at which the only dress code was shocking pink. All obediently turned up rose-hued, apart from the Duchess of Marlborough, who appeared in shimmering white and ropes of creamy pearls. She was forgiven this solecism, first, because she was American, and second, because she was, after all, a duchess.

There was going to be one more ball – the grandest of all – to crown the season. It was to have been held on 29 June but was postponed while the court mourned the death of Franz Ferdinand the day before in Sarajevo. By the end of that ominous month, wrote Osbert Sitwell, an observant young Guards officer surveying the social scene from his base in London's Wellington Barracks, 'the birds of prey were assembling, hovering, watching; the politicians would supply the carrion, though not in their own person'.

'THE HUN IS AT THE GATE': field-grey-clad German soldiers sweep across the fields of Flanders, August 1914.

10. DESCENT INTO THE DARK

10. Descent into the Dark

THE ATTENTION OF PRIME MINISTER H. H. Asquith, in the month between the assassination of Archduke Franz Ferdinand in Sarajevo and the final week of crisis preceding the actual outbreak of war, was almost entirely on other things. Asquith was not very interested in foreign affairs at the best of times, choosing to delegate such matters to his foreign secretary, Sir Edward Grey. Even Grey was not particularly interested. Throughout his eleven-year tenure in office he went abroad just once. He preferred to spend his weekends angling on the River Test at his tumbledown cottage in Hampshire, casting for salmon and tickling trout rather than fishing in his red boxes for diplomatic dispatches.

As June ticked into July and the long simmering summer reached its boiling point, Asquith and his government remained wholly engrossed in the Irish crisis, seemingly oblivious to the drama brewing in the Balkans. But the prime minister was distracted even from this domestic concern by a matter that seemed yet more vital than peace and war in Ulster: his ongoing relationship with Venetia Stanley. By now the daily correspondence between the ill-matched pair had reached almost email levels, with letters flying from Asquith's pen at all moments of the day and night – notably during cabinet meetings.

AN ULTIMATUM AND A BLANK CHEQUE

Austria had waited for almost a month after the assassination without stirring its diplomatic stumps – at least on the surface. Nervous diplomats across the world – particularly in Britain, which had no appetite for a European war – dared to heave a sigh of relief and breathe again, hoping that the moment for hasty, precipitate action had passed and that the unfortunate double murder could be quietly forgotten. Beneath the calm and placid summer waters, however, Austrian officials had been busy. Their first concern had been to ensure the support of their neighbour and essential ally – Germany – for any action against Serbia. The foolish and bombastic Kaiser Wilhelm II, who had enjoyed a warm personal friendship with the murdered archduke, was only too happy for what he saw as the upstart Balkan bandit state Serbia to be taught a sharp lesson and thoroughly humiliated. Not fully realizing that the action Austria

THE SPARK THAT FIRED THE FUSE: a fanciful illustration – from the Italian weekly newspaper *La Domenica del Corriere* – of the assassination of Austrian Archduke Franz Ferdinand and his wife Sophie at Sarajevo, 28 June 1914.

was contemplating would mean at least a Balkan war, and quite possibly a general European conflagration, the Kaiser gave his consent to Austria's ultimatum to Belgrade, before hurrying off, heedless of the consequences, on a yachting cruise to the Norwegian fjords.

Armed with Germany's complacent acquiescence to do their worst – the agreement that has gone down in history as the 'blank cheque' – Austria dropped its bombshell on 23 July, almost a month after the assassination. The ultimatum was so severe that no state with any claim to independence could possibly have accepted it. Serbia would have to dissolve all organizations deemed (by the Austrians) anti-Austrian, admit its part in the assassination conspiracy, and allow Austrian officials to come to Belgrade to take charge of the investigation into the plot. Austria knew perfectly well that the outrageous demands would be refused, and its envoys in Belgrade who delivered the document had already packed their bags to leave as a prelude to a formal declaration of war.

In London, for his part, Asquith was inclined to see the justice of the Austrian case, until he learned the details of the ultimatum. On 22 July he told Venetia, with his habitual smugness, 'Happily there seems to be no reason why we should be anything more than spectators' to a war, but within a week he was changing his tune. Using the archaic spelling of Serbia, he wrote to his young mistress during the weekend of 24–26 July:

> on many if not most of the points [of the ultimatum] Austria has a good and Servia a very bad case. But the Austrians are quite the stupidest people in Europe (as the Italians are the most perfidious) and there is a brutality about their mode of procedure which will make many people think that it is a case of a big Power wantonly bullying a little one.

That same weekend saw the landing of rifles destined for the Irish Volunteers at Howth, and the subsequent shooting of three Dubliners by British soldiers attempting to seize the weapons. With Ireland on the brink of civil war it is no wonder that minds in Whitehall were still concentrated on events across the Irish Sea rather than those across the English Channel. When *The Times* thundered on Monday morning, 27 July, that 'There can no longer be the slightest doubt that the country is now confronted with one of the greatest crises in the history of the British race', the newspaper was talking about Ireland, not Europe.

EDGING TOWARDS THE BRINK

When Whitehall belatedly woke up to the gravity of the crisis – and to the fact that an all-out European war was now a certainty – there was a mad last-minute scrabble to avert it. Grey first sought to assemble the major players – Germany, Austria, Russia and France – in an emergency conference to avert the conflict even as these powers were mobilizing their armies and Austria and Serbia were actually already at war. And when, inevitably, that initiative failed, the cabinet was faced with the awesome decision of whether to intervene.

On Tuesday 28 July Asquith met with the key ministers: Grey; his friend Haldane who, though now Lord Chancellor, still took a close interest in military matters; and Churchill at the Admiralty (with Eddie Marsh anxiously dancing attendance). The next morning, Wednesday, the cabinet approved the precautionary calling of a state of military readiness. (Churchill, pugnacious and prescient as ever, had already the previous evening, on his own responsibility, ordered the fleet to sail through the Channel and take up its war stations from its base at Scapa Flow in the Orkney islands.) But – for the moment – that was as far as Britain's belligerence went. Asquith was uncomfortably aware that around half the ministers in his twenty-man cabinet – including his chancellor, Lloyd George – were potential members of a 'peace party' opposed to any involvement in a continental war. Lloyd George had even made a speech on 23 July – the very day that Austria delivered its fateful ultimatum – reinforcing his New Year message of peace. Anglo-German relations, the chancellor declared again, were better than they had been for years. If Asquith was to keep his government and party united, it was essential that German aggression should make the case for war overwhelming enough to convince even the most extreme members of this peace faction.

Germany duly obliged. According to the timetables lovingly evolved by her military planners over the previous decade and known, after their recently deceased originator Count Alfred von Schlieffen, as the Schlieffen Plan, she would, as Asquith had feared (indeed, Wednesday's cabinet had spent some time discussing the prospect), invade Belgium in an attempt to envelope the French armies with a massive wheeling offensive involving more than a million men. This would be a flagrant violation of Belgian neutrality, a status guaranteed by all the great powers when the Belgian state was established in 1830, and a clear *casus belli* for Britain. But hundreds of trains packed with soldiers in their field-grey uniforms and picturesque pointed *Pickelhaube* helmets were already rolling across the River Rhine towards the Belgian frontier.

Asquith, however, was still hoping against hope that peace could somehow be preserved. Although his pugnacious wife Margot was all for throwing out the peace party – the hated Lloyd George among them – and forming a coalition with the Tories, Asquith, true to his nature as well as his policy, was, as ever, cautious. He wished to keep his own party united, and even at this late hour believed it faintly possible that the flower of safety could be snatched from the nettle of danger. 'Of course we want to keep out of it,' he wrote on the evening of Wednesday 29 July, 'But the worst thing we could do would be to announce to the world at the present time that in no circumstances would we intervene.' Making that warning

THE LAST OLYMPIAN: H. H. Asquith, the Liberal prime minister who presided over the multiple crises of his era with magisterial calm, but whose complacent confidence was tested to destruction by war.

explicit, Grey summoned Germany's Anglophile envoy in London, Ambassador Prince Lichnowsky, to tell him that in the event of a war between Germany and France Britain would not stand idly by. Germany now knew that her hopes of keeping Britain neutral were in vain.

That night, with all lights doused, the ships of the Grand Fleet weighed anchor and sailed east through the Channel en route to war. The man who had ordered them to sea, Winston Churchill, pictured their departure in his own incomparable romantic prose:

> Scores of gigantic castles of steel wending their way across the misty, shining sea, like giants bowed in anxious thought. We may picture them again as darkness fell, eighteen miles of warships running at high speed and in absolute blackness through the Narrow Straits.

As the week wore on, the situation continued to deteriorate. On Thursday 30 July Asquith learned from Britain's ambassador in Berlin, Sir Edward Goschen, that Germany was intent on marching into France. Moreover, at a meeting with Goschen, the German chancellor Theobald von Bethmann-Hollweg, under the stress of events, inadvertently blurted out Germany's secret war plan: to invade France via neutral Belgium. Upon learning of this, Asquith commented with excessive mildness: 'There is something crude and almost childlike about German diplomacy.'

The following day, Friday 31 July, the French began to exert pressure on their ally to come at once to their aid. As the financial centres of the City of London grew increasingly nervous, Asquith still hesitated, waiting upon events. Before the violation of Belgian neutrality, opinion in his own party was overwhelmingly against British participation in a European war, and public opinion probably equally so. Then, as he sat with cabinet colleagues after dinner that evening, came the false dawn of a glimmer of hope. It came in the form of a message from Britain's Berlin embassy suggesting that the Kaiser, faced with the awful reality of where his sabre-rattling would lead, wanted to draw back from the brink. If Russia's mobilization of its millions of men could be held up, hinted the 'All Highest', then he for his part would endeavour to 'restrain' his Austrian ally.

At once Asquith set to work to draft a personal appeal from King George V to his look-alike cousin, Tsar Nicholas II of Russia, to freeze the mobilization of his masses. As the month of August began, at 1.30 a.m., Asquith called a taxi and motored around the corner from Downing Street to Buckingham Palace and summoned a sleepy monarch from what the prime minister called his 'beauty sleep'. Clad in a brown dressing gown, the king merely appended the personal greeting 'My dear Nicky' to the letter, signing it 'Georgie' before stomping back to bed. Asquith sent off the message to St Petersburg and followed suit. Just to show that Britain was still maintaining her neutrality, similar pleas for moderation were also sent to Paris and Berlin. But things were careering out of control.

A CABINET DIVIDED

On Saturday morning, in an unprecedented break with tradition, the cabinet met at 11 a.m., interrupting the sacred English weekend, with Asquith braced for resignations from the 'peace party'. Then, as now, the cause of peace at any price was championed by the ultra-Liberal *Manchester Guardian* (now *The Guardian*) and leading cabinet members followed the paper's pacific line. Battle-lines were being drawn within the cabinet, with the upholder of Gladstonian rectitude, John Morley, and Sir John Simon all for issuing a declaration that under no circumstances would Britain intervene; while in the 'war party' Grey threatened resignation if any such statement were made and Churchill orated for an hour, trying to persuade his reluctant colleagues of the need for immediate mobilization. The main target of Churchill's eloquence was his friend and rival Lloyd George, who gave the first signs that his previous pacifism might be wavering. Asquith and Haldane uneasily held the centre ground, waiting upon events. They would be quick to come. That same Saturday night Germany declared war on Russia.

Just as the realization sank in in London that a war was certain and that Britain was unlikely to be able to steer clear and keep out of it, a simultaneous realization dawned in Berlin. Clutching at straws, an unstable Kaiser, encouraged by messages from his London ambassador Lichnowsky that Britain might remain neutral if the war was confined to an eastern conflict with Russia, sent for his army commander-in-chief, Helmuth von Moltke (the younger), the architect of Germany's evolving war plans after the death of their founding father, Schlieffen. Waving Lichnowsky's optimistic telegrams at the ponderous, flabby-faced marshal, the Kaiser demanded that his armies should execute an abrupt U-turn, reverse their march towards the west and hotfoot it across the Fatherland to fight Russia. Moltke exploded. Did not the Kaiser realize that the armies were already in motion? That they were moving according to meticulously worked-out railway timetables? That the plans for hooking through Belgium into France had been developed and refined over years of painstaking planning, war games, and military rides? Putting that into reverse would be – quite literally – impossible. Besides, the armies had already crossed into the tiny neutral statelet of Luxembourg. The invasion of the west had begun.

On Sunday 2 August, with an even more unheard-of disregard for convention than on the previous day, the cabinet again met at 11 a.m. on the Sabbath, and, goaded by a declaration from the opposition Tory leaders that Britain must stand by Russia and France, took another step towards war: Grey was authorized to tell the veteran French ambassador Paul Cambon – who had been pressing for Britain's support under the Entente Cordiale he had helped negotiate, and whose brother Jules represented his country in Germany – that Britain would not allow the German fleet to make the English Channel the base for hostile operations against France. The decision was enough to prompt the first cabinet resignation by a peace party member – that of John Burns, President of the Board of Trade, its sole Labour member. After adjourning at 2 p.m. for lunch, the cabinet gathered again at 6.30. There were no definite new developments, beyond a hardening determination on behalf of the peace party's members to resign if Britain went to war, but as Asquith returned with three of his children from a dinner with his party colleagues Reginald McKenna and Edwin Montagu, he recoiled from the sight and sounds of gathering war hysteria. 'There were large crowds perambulating the streets and cheering the King at Buckingham Palace,' he told Venetia:

> One could hear the distant roaring at 1 or 1.30 in the morning. War or anything that seems likely to lead to war is always popular with the London mob. You remember Sir R. Walpole's remark: 'Now they are ringing their bells; in a few weeks they'll be wringing their hands'. How one loathes such levity.

The same day Russian troops had crossed into East Prussia and German troops into Luxembourg.

On Monday morning, having been shamed by Burns's principled walk-out into following suit, Morley and Simon also submitted letters of resignation, and when the cabinet met for the fourth day in succession, Lord Beauchamp – whose gamekeepers had caused such trouble to the Dymock poets – followed. But, crucially, an overnight development stemmed the flow of resignations and strengthened the hand of the war party. News came through that Germany had issued an ultimatum to Belgium demanding permission for its armies to march unimpeded across Belgian territory en route to invading France. Belgium had rejected the demand outright. On receiving the news Asquith ordered the mobilization of the army. This was the confirmation of the deepest hopes and fears of both party factions. The potential leader of the peace party, Lloyd George – whose resignation would almost certainly have brought down the government – his finger on the pulse of public opinion, swung decisively in favour of war, justifying the switch with the argument that Germany's weekend belligerence had changed everything. 'The war had leapt in popularity between Saturday and Monday… the threatened invasion of Belgium had set the nation on fire.'

FLIGHT OF THE DOVES

Lloyd George's always lively Welsh nationalism had also been affronted by this trampling of a small country. With all the fervour of a convert, the chancellor turned on his eloquence and successfully appealed to the gang of four peaceniks who had already resigned to stay on the government benches for the crucial parliamentary debate that had been called that afternoon. At 3 p.m. the Commons convened in Westminster. In the bright summer sunshine, members had to push their way through the crowds that had thronged the streets. It was the August bank holiday, and normally the capital's streets would have been deserted as its citizens swarmed onto holiday trains taking them to the seaside at Brighton, Margate or Southend. But today, like a giant magnet, London had pulled in the crowds and the atmosphere was charged with electricity like the minutes preceding a thunder-storm. Inside the chamber the heat was pulverizing. For the first time in the century every MP was present, and the atmosphere, recalled the historian G. M. Trevelyan, was 'tense with dreadful doubt and expectation'. As the rows of sombrely clad MPs listened on the green-leather benches, Grey rose on the government front bench and quietly and calmly outlined the sequence of events before and since the Sarajevo shootings.

His face white and haggard with the strain of sleeplessness and nights broken by alarms and telegrams, Grey's opening sentence said it all: 'It has not been possible to secure the peace of Europe.' He then launched into an hour-long exposition of Britain's place in Europe, and its traditional policy of splendid isolation contrasted with the system of competing alliances that had come into being since 1900. He spoke of the vital necessity of an island nation guarding her home waters and the sea-routes of empire before coming to the point: it appeared that Germany was attacking Belgium, whose neutrality Britain had solemnly guaranteed. Quoting his great Liberal forebear Gladstone, Grey demanded to know whether 'Britain would stand quietly by and witness the perpetration of the direst crime that ever stained the pages of history and thus become participants in the sin'. And if Belgium fell, Grey warned, there would be a game of dominoes: France would follow, and then Denmark and Holland, and Germany would finally hold the entire Channel coast and have Britain at its mercy. The country had no choice, he concluded. 'If Britain stands aside, forfeiting her Belgian Treaty obligations, she would sacrifice her respect and good name and reputation before the entire world.' The foreign secretary sat down to thunderous applause from all sides of the House and the public galleries – another unprecedented breach of convention in a week of broken rules. The die was now cast – and the country had crossed the Rubicon.

'THE LIGHTS ARE GOING OUT': Foreign Secretary Sir Edward Grey who, despite travelling abroad (to Paris) just once in his eleven years in office, surprised his colleagues by the depth of his commitment to France in August 1914.

Grey returned to his room in the Foreign Office where he continued to work late as the long day faded and night drew near. Abstracted, as a visitor entered he rose from his desk and looked out of the long windows as a lamp-lighter went on his rounds in St James's Park. The famously acute sight in his piercing eyes was failing like the August day, and by the end of his life the statesman would be totally blind. 'The lamps are going out all over Europe,' he famously murmured. 'We shall not see them lit again in our lifetime.'

THE ELEVENTH HOUR CHIMES

Just after 8 a.m. on Tuesday 4 August, the first grey-clad German units crossed the frontier into Belgium. Acting according to long pre-arranged plans, the Belgian army, rather than rolling over and surrendering after a token show of resistance as the invaders had hoped, blew up the bridges over the River Meuse with prepared demolition charges, significantly hindering the early German advance. It was a spirited show of defiance, and enough to give credence to the first reports of 'gallant little Belgium's' brave stand against her ogreish neighbour that began to appear in the British press.

News of the German attack reached London within two hours – just in time for the daily cabinet meeting. According to Asquith, it 'simplified matters' enormously, enabling almost all members of the government to fall into line. It was the news, plus a strong personal appeal from Asquith, that was enough to persuade two members of the peace party – Sir John Simon and Lord Beauchamp – to withdraw the resignations they had submitted the previous day, though Morley and Burns remained resolute. At the cabinet meeting it was unanimously but grimly agreed to issue an ultimatum to Berlin in response to the invasion of Belgium. The ultimatum stated that, unless Britain heard by midnight that Germany was withdrawing her forces from Belgium, a state of war would exist between the British and German empires.

In the afternoon, the House of Commons again assembled, this time to hear the news from Asquith's lips. Walking the short distance from Downing Street to the House through crowds that swarmed around Whitehall like flies around a summer midden, Asquith noted with pained

distaste that he was being escorted by 'Cheering crowds of loafers and holiday-makers'. 'I have never been popular with the man-in-the-street,' he added with lofty disdain. 'And in all this dark and dangerous business it gives me scant pleasure.' By 4.30 p.m. MPs had learned that, barring miracles, they would be at war with Europe's most formidable military power within hours. They took the news, thought Asquith, 'very calmly and with a good deal of dignity'.

To dispel all doubt in Berlin, where eleventh-hour hopes were still entertained that even now Britain would not take matters beyond merely verbal protests for form's sake, Ambassador Goschen called on Foreign Minister Jagow at seven o'clock that evening. Unless Germany responded to the ultimatum and agreed to pull back from Belgium, he warned, he would ask for his passports, leave Berlin and the two nations would be at war. Jagow passed the envoy on to his boss, Chancellor Bethmann-Hollweg, whose policy of Anglo-German détente lay in ruins. Understandably agitated, the chancellor kept muttering '*Schrecklich, schrecklich*' ('terrible, terrible'). Then he rounded on the ambassador, beard bristling and eyes blazing: 'You mean you are going to war just for the word "neutrality",' he demanded in incredulity. 'A word which in wartime has often been disregarded – just for a scrap of paper Great Britain is going to make war on a kindred nation who desires nothing more than to be friends with her.' Both men were near tears, so to save further embarrassment, Goschen made his excuses and cut short the interview. Divided by the gulf of war, they would never meet again.

Bethmann-Hollweg's contemptuous phrase, 'a scrap of paper', skillfully exploited by British war propagandists after Goschen's report made it widely known, was used to illustrate Britain's case against Germany: that beneath her veneer of technological modernity, she was a barbarous state which had never known true civilization; a nation that valued its own *kultur* over the norms of civilized life. While the ambassador's fateful last meeting with the chancellor was still in progress, back in London Asquith went on a solitary motor-car ride, with only his chauffeur for company. He returned to Downing Street with his head clearer and adjourned to the cabinet room while the clock on the mantelpiece ticked away the final minutes of peace. Grey was with him, nervously chain-smoking.

Asquith's wife Margot witnessed the scene as the fateful hour struck – 11 p.m. in London, midnight in Berlin. 'We were at war. I left to go to bed, and as I was pausing at the foot of the staircase, I saw Winston Churchill with a happy face striding towards the double doors of the cabinet room.' Outside the summer night was split by the sound of mighty crowds, a sound heard simultaneously in every European capital. It was the roar of war.

HOW *THE TIMES* REPORTED THE STARK FACTS: 5 August 1914.

'NEVER SUCH INNOCENCE AGAIN': new recruits waiting to enlist, London, August 1914. Their headgear denotes class differences: straw boaters for the middle class, flat cloth caps for the workers.

11. NOW GOD BE THANKED

11. Now God be Thanked

A CLUTCH OF FIVE SONNETS entitled *1914* written by Rupert Brooke has become emblematic of the alleged national mood of exalted patriotism as Britain went to war. The most famous of them, with its iconic opening, 'The Soldier' speaks of a soldier's self-sacrifice in terms of mystic nationalism with an almost sensuous mix of blood and soil:

If I should die, think only this of me:
That there's some corner of a foreign field
That is forever England. There shall be
In that rich earth a richer dust concealed;
A dust whom England bore, shaped, made aware,
Gave, once, her flowers to love, her ways to roam…

But in this, and in the other sonnets, death is seen and welcomed as a clean release, a peaceful passing into a big sleep: there is none of the messy reality of how death would actually come to millions in a modern industrial war. Rather than being blown to atoms by heavy artillery, or rendered into screaming red jelly by shell splinters of razor-sharp steel, Brooke's soldiers pass smoothly, as the sonnet 'Peace' puts it, 'as swimmers into cleanness leaping'. There is no appreciation that the 'cleanness' of healing, purified spring water into which they dive would become the green and corpse-filled shell craters of Passchendaele.

'Peace' begins with a stirring invocation:

Now, God be thanked Who has matched us with His hour,
And caught our youth, and wakened us from sleeping

and it is this motif of the sleeper stirred from sottish slumber to become a willing participant in a collective and honourable sacrifice that pervades the whole sonnet sequence. For all its bathos and sentimentality, there is no doubt that Brooke caught a genuine – if passing – popular mood of elevated patriotism, coupled with a curiosity about what war would bring after a century in which the only conflicts involving Britain had been far-flung colonial wars fought by her small professional army.

HELL TO BE IN IT AND HELL TO BE OUT OF IT

The poet himself was in transit across eastern England on 4 August, the day that Britain declared war, travelling from his mother's home in Rugby, the small Midlands town where he had been born and educated, to stay with his friends Francis and Frances Cornford on the Norfolk coast at Cley-next-the-Sea. The day before he had celebrated his twenty-seventh – and last – birthday. In blatant contrast to the confident and serene public mood of the sonnets, Brooke privately greeted the prospect of war with conflicted, confused and downright depressive feelings, as his letters to friends reveal. To Lady Eileen Wellesley, daughter of the duke of Wellington and latest in a long line of lady loves, he mused aloud: 'If war comes, should one enlist? Or turn war correspondent? Or what?' The artist Stanley Spencer, meanwhile, was told:

> If fighting starts I shall have to enlist, or go as a correspondent.
> I don't know. It will be Hell to be in it and Hell to be out of it.
> At present I'm so depressed about the war, that I can't think,
> talk or write coherently.

On reaching the Cornfords and hearing the news of war the following morning, Brooke spent a fretful day on the windswept Norfolk beach. To distract himself, Brooke read aloud to soothe the couple's young daughter, Helena, who had swallowed a bead he had brought back from his South Seas expedition. In pale imitation of a Polynesian, he stuck a flower behind his ear. Ominously, the bloom he picked was a fast-fading poppy, soon to be the symbol of thousands of young men, scattered as dead petals over the torn fields of France and Flanders.

After a few days of troubled indecision – should he go to France to help the peasants gather in the harvest now that so many of their menfolk had been called to the colours? or try to get a newspaper to employ him to report on the war? – Brooke travelled to London and began knocking on government office doors and pulling strings with his influential friends in a bid to gain some useful war work. As he hurried between offices, he bumped into an acquaintance, the literary journalist J. C. Squire, who asked him what all the rush was about. 'Well, if Armageddon's *on*,' replied Brooke blithely, 'I suppose one should be there.'

It was Squire, like Brooke a protégé of the ubiquitous Eddie Marsh, who, observing the calls for divine backing made by the rival nations as the waves of war rippled across Europe, wrote the sardonic squib satirizing the competing God-bothering:

God heard the embattled nations sing and shout,
'Gott strafe England!' And 'God Save the King!'
God this, God that, and God the other thing –
'Good God!' said God, 'I've got my work cut out!'

ARTISTS AT WAR

Across the country from Brooke brooding in Norfolk, on Britain's western coasts two other men of letters weighed up their options as war began. At their summer holiday home near Harlech in North Wales, the Graves family from Wimbledon – an eccentric, scholarly clan with close German kin – were more troubled than most. Their eldest son Robert, an aspiring poet, had just left his public school at Charterhouse and expected to go up to Oxford in October when news of the war broke. Outraged at the stories of atrocities against civilians as the German armies marched across Belgium, and despite the fact that his German cousin Conrad would be on the other side, Graves decided to enlist almost at once:

> The nearest regimental depot was at Wrexham: the Royal Welch
> Fusiliers. The Harlech Golf Club secretary suggested my taking
> a commission instead of enlisting. He rang up the adjutant and
> said that I was a public schoolboy who had been in the Officers'
> Training Corps at Charterhouse. So the adjutant said 'Send
> him right along' and on 11th August I started my training.
> I immediately became a hero to my family.

On the coast of the Lake District D. H. Lawrence was taking a week's walking tour with a couple of friends. Although he had only recently married a German wife, Frieda von Richthofen – a cousin of the future air ace, the 'Red Baron' Manfred von Richthofen – the writer had fled to the mountains seeking shelter from the emotional storms engendered by Frieda's efforts to gain access to her three children by her first husband, Professor Ernest Weekley, the man she had deserted to elope with Lawrence. Both the law and outraged convention were on Weekley's side, and the fact that Frieda was German hardly helped her cause. Visiting the haunts of the Romantic Lake Poets, Lawrence – yet another of Marsh's discoveries – briefly escaped such domestic distress, little knowing that a greater disaster was about to swallow him, his country and the whole continent of Europe. He later recalled:

> We came down to Barrow-in-Furness, and saw that war was declared.
> And we all went mad. I can remember soldiers kissing on Barrow

station, and a woman shouting defiantly to her sweetheart 'When you get at 'em, Clem, let 'em have it' as the train drew off – and in all the tramcars, 'War'. Messrs Vickers-Maxim [manufacturers of machine-guns] call in their workmen – and the great notices on Vickers' gateways – and the thousands of men streaming over the bridge… and the electric suspense everywhere – and the amazing, vivid, visionary beauty of everything, heightened by the immense pain…

In Kent, the Garden of England, yet another Marsh protégé, Siegfried Sassoon, was also irresolute about the war. Desperate to be a poet, all he had to show for his literary efforts since leaving Cambridge without a degree was a profit of £5, and an expenditure of £100 on privately printed pamphlets of poems which had failed to sell. He had heard about the Sarajevo assassinations in July while staying alone at a hotel in Selsey, Sussex. Sunburned and irresolute, he had drifted back to Marsh's flat in London where he had had his single meeting with Brooke. He then returned to his mother's home, Weirleigh, in the village of Matfield in the smiling Kentish countryside – the landscape where since childhood he had delighted in the pastoral pastimes of cricket and hunting.

Here, Sassoon was somewhat shamed by the presence of Mab Anley, an old friend of his mother Theresa whose husband and two sons were professional soldiers. Mab spoke continually of the coming war 'like thunderstorms muttering beyond the Kentish horizon' and speculated about her sons' part in the coming conflict. Her musings led Sassoon to uncomfortable thoughts about his own enjoyable but slightly aimless existence, and to wonder whether he could match the manliness of the Anley boys.

Such musings were reinforced that weekend when, while taking part in a cricket match at Tunbridge Wells, he witnessed army officers at the game being summoned by telegram to join their regiments. On 31 July, with war now imminent, Sassoon cycled the thirty miles to Rye, took tea in the ancient town, and cycled back. Feeling his own youth and physical fitness, Sassoon's decision to enlist seems to have been crystallized by the trip: 'I'd got to go and be a soldier, [but] knew nothing about how to do it when I got there.' On 4 August, the day war was declared, Sassoon rode his favourite hunter, Cockbird, over to the neighbouring county and enlisted in the Sussex Yeomanry at Lewes Drill Hall. He spent the next two nights bedded down on the floor of Lewes Corn Exchange, and the rest of the summer under canvas on the South Downs.

Another lover of the English countryside whose literary career, though more advanced than that of Sassoon, was marking time – if not stagnating

– was Edward Thomas. At the end of June, when the shots at Sarajevo had still raised barely a ripple on the superficially placid waters of the English summer, Thomas and his wife Helen left a sweltering London, stifling in the midsummer heat, and gratefully caught a train at Paddington en route for Dymock in Herefordshire, that oasis for poets and their long-suffering spouses. En route, just north-west of Oxford, the train stopped 'Unwontedly' at an unremarkable halt named Adlestrop. The brief hiatus, recalled months later and reworked at leisure when Thomas had begun to write verse, gave birth to one of the best-loved poems in the language, as Thomas's contemporary notes jotted in the train record:

> Then we stopped at Adlestrop, thro the willows cd be heard a
> chain of blackbirds songs at 12.45 & one thrush & no man seen
> only a hiss of engine letting off steam… by banks of long grass
> willow herb & meadowsweet, extraordinary silence between the
> two periods of travel – looking out on grey dry stones between
> metals & the shiny metals & over it the elms willows & long grass
> – one man clears his throat – and a greater rustic silence. No
> house in view. Stop only for a minute till signal is up.

They reached their destination and strolled over the fields for a reunion with their friends Robert and Elinor Frost, who swept them up and took them over to the Old Nailshop, the cottage where Wilfrid and Geraldine Gibson had as their house-guest none other than the ubiquitous Rupert Brooke, looking, noted Thomas (who had not seen him since his return from the South Seas), 'Browner and older and better looking after his tour'. Joined by Lascelles and Catherine Abercrombie, this full complement of the Dymock poets spent the evening in laughter and conversation.

The summer heat burst in Herefordshire in July with torrential rain. The Thomases returned to their Hampshire home amidst the wooded hills known as 'hangers' in the aptly named village of Steep. Thomas occupied himself with completing his book *A Literary Pilgrim in England* and no fewer than three laudatory reviews, written for different publications, of his friend Frost's new book of poems *North of Boston*.

The hot weather had returned by August, a holiday month that Thomas had planned to spend back in Herefordshire. He had finished and delivered his book, but wondered what the future held for a freelance literary gent in a country engaged in the desperate business of war. He might as well, he told his friend Eleanor Farjeon, write some poetry. Cleverly combining the high temperatures of the returned summer heat with his own age, he punned 'Did anyone ever begin at 36 in the shade?' Answering that question in the affirmative led Thomas, in the less than two years of life that was left to him, to produce some of the most haunting and memorable poetry in the language.

On 3 August Thomas and his son Merfyn set off on bicycles bound for the Midlands. The weather had broken again and their nostrils pricked at the enticing smell of dry dust on roads suddenly wet with rain. They broke

THE POET SIEGFRIED SASSOON in 1914. Hungry for action, Sassoon would transfer from the horse-borne Sussex Yeomanry to the Royal Welch Fusiliers, but disillusion would soon follow.

THIN KHAKI LINE: Life Guards from Britain's small professional army parade without their horses, August 1914. They would get used to being foot soldiers: it would not be a war for the cavalry.

their journey for the night at Swindon. As they cycled through Wiltshire the next day, they learned that Britain was about to declare war.

A future writer who shared Thomas's love of the countryside and his upbringing in the suburbs of south-east London, which enabled both to explore the nearby countryside of Kent, was a nineteen-year-old City clerk named Henry Williamson. In January 1914, to escape his humdrum life as an employee of the Sun Life Insurance Company, and also to evade his fraught relationship with his straight-laced father, young Williamson joined the Territorial Force as a volunteer part-time soldier, enlisting in the 5th (City of London) Battalion of the London Rifle Brigade. Recruits were required to attend drill parades and shooting exercises three times a week, and were also expected for a fortnight at the Territorials summer camp, which in 1914 was due to be held in the South Downs near Eastbourne.

On 1 August the first contingent of Williamson's battalion set off for camp from Waterloo station, but they were recalled the very next day as the war clouds massed. Williamson and his comrades, who had joined the Territorials for larks rather than any sterner motivation, found themselves mobilizing:

Headquarters was all faces, movement, equipment, rifles, grey kit-bags… Hundreds of men in all sorts of suits, morning coats, tweed coats, blue serge, carters' jackets were waiting to join up… Later in the morning his bayonet was collected, without its sheath, and taken away with many others in a wheel-barrow. They were, said Lance-Corporal Mortimore, to be sharpened on the grindstone… After some drill by sections they paraded outside in the street for a route march. They were in drill order, wearing webbing belts… Rolled greatcoats, water-bottles, entrenching tools, ammunition in side-pouches were left in line in the company area. As they marched off, rifles at the slope, angles varying considerably, some people on the pavement cheered.

FOR KING AND COUNTRY

All over the country the scenes were the same. Men from a still rigidly class-divided Britain mingled in huge crowds waiting to enlist outside recruiting stations, their social status defined by their headgear: silk toppers for the upper crust; bowlers, trilbies or straw boaters for the middle-class men; and flat cloth caps for the workers. Such scenes were notably memorialized by Philip Larkin in his poem 'MCMXIV' when he wrote of 'The Crowns of hats, the sun/ On moustached archaic faces / Grinning as if it were all a Bank Holiday lark; …'

One such recruit was eighteen-year-old Gerard 'Ged' Garvin, whose Irish Unionist father J. L. Garvin was editor of the (then staunchly Tory) *Observer*, Britain's oldest national newspaper, and one of the country's most prominent political journalists. Ged Garvin, like Robert Graves, had just finished his public school education – in his case at Westminster School – and was about to go up to Oxford. A tall, popular youth, accomplished in sport as well as in his studies – he had been awarded a history scholarship to Christ Church – fluent in French and German but not above taking part in dangerous pranks like climbing over the roof of nearby Westminster Abbey, Ged was the apple of his parents' eye.

His father pulled strings to get Ged a commission, using the ubiquitous Eddie Marsh, the man who would reluctantly get his beloved Rupert Brooke an officer's place in his boss Winston Churchill's newly formed Royal Naval Division, as his go-between with government. Garvin's plan was to get Ged into the elite Irish Guards, but the young man, with the impatience of youth, was not prepared to wait. On Friday 28 August he joined the 7th Service Battalion of the South Lancashire Regiment – a regular regiment of the line. After a single weekend of reflection, by the beginning of September he and other dog-tired raw recruits found themselves marching around the 'horribly rowdy' town of Andover, looking in vain for billets. Two years later, in July 1916, Ged Garvin was killed by machine-gun fire on the Somme.

Public school-educated boys like Ged had several innate advantages over the mass of their less privileged countrymen when it came to instant promotion into the officer corps. Not only were they born into the ruling caste, with friends and influence to match; but most of them had received at least the rudiments of military training in the Officers' Training Corps at their schools, sharing summer camps with men of the Territorial Force who they would command in the field. But the vast majority of the hundreds of thousands who flocked to enlist were 'ordinary' members of the working and lower-middle classes: miners, dockers, shop-workers,

PATRIOTIC PALS: men of the Leeds Pals battalion in camp, Yorkshire Dales, September 1914. The government encouraged friends from the same towns to join up and serve together. Tragically, many died together too, leaving whole communities bereaved.

factory hands, clerks, agricultural labourers and the unemployed.

For some, the route into the army was an unorthodox one. The Tory MP the Honourable Aubrey Herbert, like Ged Garvin, wanted to get into the Irish Guards, but was rebuffed. Nothing daunted, he got his tailor to make a regimental uniform, and as they paraded past en route to France, he simply fell into step with the marching men. He bluffed his way into staying with his chosen unit by pretending he had joined as a French interpreter – a role which he filled with such exemplary efficiency that he was allowed to stay. Before August was out he had fought and been wounded and temporarily captured at the war's first battle – Mons – before being freed from captivity by the French.

YOUR COUNTRY NEEDS YOU!

The man who issued the call to arms that had them all flocking to the colours was Field Marshal Earl Horatio Herbert Kitchener of Khartoum, a towering titan with an enormous handlebar moustache who had gained his military reputation and huge public popularity by trouncing Mahdists at Omdurman in the Sudan in one of the British Army's last cavalry charges. He then ended the costly Boer War victoriously, if brutally, by a scorched-earth policy of covering the South African veld with barbed wire and blockhouses, and herding the civilian population who sustained the Boer guerillas into insanitary settlements known as 'concentration camps'.

Ironically, though himself an inarticulate autocrat who loathed journalists and had a poor grasp of public relations – 'Out of my way, you drunken swabs!' was his cheery greeting to the assembled press corps as he emerged from his tent in the Sudan – Kitchener's instantly recognizable features and foreshortened forearm became one of the twentieth century's most familiar images in a mass advertising campaign that helped to draw millions into the Great War. Asquith was painfully aware that he himself could not easily adopt the role of a belligerent war leader, so one of his first acts after the declaration of war was to relinquish the post of secretary for war which he had held along with the premiership since the inglorious episode of the Curragh Mutiny in Ireland. In a clever move to impress the public and add some much needed military know-how to his pacifically minded Liberal cabinet, he offered the portfolio to Kitchener – and the warlord accepted.

Kitchener's military mien and gruff public persona were misleading. A shrewd mind lurked behind the moustache, and – almost uniquely at a moment when men were falling over themselves to join up and see some fighting before the war ended, as they thought, by Christmas – he foresaw that the conflict would last a long time, and that fighting and winning it would require not only vast numbers of men but the mobilization of the huge resources of the entire British empire. He put these views forcefully at a meeting of his new cabinet colleagues on 5 August, and although sceptical, they accepted them and authorized an enormous recruiting drive.

Kitchener's initial estimate was that 100,000 new men aged between nineteen and thirty would be needed – equivalent to the size of the existing regular army. He got his men. Some 8,193 volunteers came forward in the first week of the war; 45,354 in the second; and 63,000 in the third. Within a month, the inevitable mission creep had taken place, and having secured his 100,000 with more to spare by September, he upped the ante and demanded another 100,000 – at the same time raising the recruiting age to thirty-five. By the middle of that month half a million men had enlisted, and the army was preparing to welcome in another half-million. Recruitment was aided by the infamous poster designed by the graphic artist Alfred Leete showing Kitchener's sternly hirsute features and his pointing finger with the slogan: 'Britons [Kitchener's picture] wants you. Join Your Country's Army. God Save the King.' Soon shortened to: 'Your country needs you!'

These raw recruits were not instantly bussed over to France and flung into the furnace of the war. A consummate professional soldier, Kitchener, somewhat unfairly, had a poor opinion of part-time weekend soldiers such as the Territorials and wanted to give the recruits rigorous and prolonged training before sending them off to war. He dubbed the influx the 'New Armies' – a third force distinct from the pre-war regulars who would fight the initial battles of 1914 (and would be largely used up by the end of the year), and the Territorials who would shoulder the burden in 1915. Only in 1916 would the jealously guarded New Armies – by that time some two million strong – be released to meet their tragic destiny on the Somme.

The motives behind the desire to join up were mixed. Patriotism, of course, was a major driver. But so was boredom. The ennui of dead-end, soul-destroying jobs inspired many to see fighting in an army as an attractive alternative. Even for those comfortably placed, with money in the bank and a leisured future stretching before them, the adventurous prospect of risking their necks for a great cause was not to be sniffed at. Another powerful motive – it had pushed Graves into the ranks – was the horror stories emerging of German atrocities as they marched through Belgium. By no means all of these were fabricated or even exaggerated by Allied propagandists. The Germans themselves were acting up to their stereotype as barbaric 'Huns'.

Hundreds of innocent Belgian civilians, including women, children and babies, were murdered in cold blood or executed in reprisal for alleged attacks on Germans. The library of Louvain University, with 230,000 rare volumes, was deliberately incinerated and 209 civilians killed, before the entire population

'REMEMBER BELGIUM': the propaganda may have been crude, but the German atrocities in the country on whose behalf Britain entered the war were all too real.

REMEMBER BELGIUM

ENLIST TO-DAY

of 42,000 people was forcibly evacuated. Such outrages – similar in spirit if not in scale to those carried out by the Germans in Poland and Russia in the Second World War – sparked justified horror in Britain, and the recruitment figures shot up exponentially with each such story of murder, torture, arson and rapine. Asking men to die for their own king and country had been thought a hard sell, asking them to die for a foreign king and country an impossible one; but accounts of babies butchered and women violated served as post facto justification for Britain's entry to the war in defence of 'gallant little Belgium' and her suffering people. The war had provided its own justification. Now it had to be decided how best to win it.

THE STRUGGLE FOR LIBERTIES: PATRIOT AND PACIFIST

Almost simultaneously with its despatch of the British Expeditionary Force to face the advancing German First Army in Belgium, Asquith's government took measures to tackle supposed enemies within. To cope with the social discontent that the government – wrongly – feared that the war might bring, and to counter the activities of German spies and saboteurs, within four days of the declaration of war the Defence of the Realm Act had been rushed through Parliament and into law. Soon known as DORA, the Act represented the biggest curtailment of civil liberties since the days of Oliver Cromwell's military dictatorship. Under it, the government armed itself with sweeping powers over the citizen that included prohibiting the spreading of false and demoralizing rumours, banning the promotion of pacifism and regulating the hours that pubs could open. (Not until 1988 were the regulations shutting pubs between lunchtime and 6.30 p.m. repealed.)

A minority had the courage – or the cussedness – to stand out against the patriotic tide. Those opposing the war on moral or religious grounds included the influential, such as the cabinet ministers John Morley, John Burns and Charles Trevelyan, who had all resigned from the government in protest at the declaration of war; intellectuals such as the aristocratic Cambridge philosopher and mathematician Bertrand Russell and the critic Lytton Strachey, a leading light in the Bloomsbury group of Bohemian writers and artists; the Labour leader – and future prime minister – Ramsay MacDonald and his future chancellor Philip Snowden; and the left- wing economists Norman Angell and J. R. Hobson.

The more militantly inclined pacifists formed a pressure group, the Union of Democratic Control (UDC), which was supported by several Liberal and Labour MPs and led by the crusading journalist E. D. Morel. Before the war, Morel had campaigned alongside the diplomat and Irish

'DORA': The Defence of the Realm Act at the outbreak of war gave the state sweeping powers to curb dissent and direct its citizens' lives. For free-born Englishmen and women it was a taste of big brothers to come.

nationalist Roger Casement against slavery and genocide in the Belgian-controlled Congo. Both Morel and Casement were openly pro-German, and it was easy to paint their activities as sedition or treason. The patriotic press encouraged their readers to break up the UDC's meetings, and their leaders Morel and Russell were eventually imprisoned under DORA. Although claiming up to half a million members by the war's end, the UDC remained a minority out of step with the overwhelming mood of the country at large.

Of the minority who opposed the war and all its works, a further minority – estimated to number about 1,500 and known as 'absolutists' – refused all alternatives to military service. They refused to work as agricultural labourers (an option chosen by some of the Bloomsbury group); or to take on non-combatant humanitarian roles within the armed forces, such as stretcher-bearing and driving ambulances (the route taken by many Quakers).

The Brocklesby brothers from Yorkshire provide a particularly piquant example of the division of family opinion on the war. The oldest brother, George, though medically unfit, joined his father in recruiting more than a thousand men for the army, while the two younger brothers, Phil and Harold, joined up and served at the front throughout the war. The second brother, however, the deeply religious Bert, after a prolonged tussle with his conscience – and tossing a coin to see what God wanted him to do – resolved to refuse any support for the war. When conscription was introduced, Bert and his fellow conscientious objectors – or 'conchies', as they soon became known – were imprisoned in a medieval castle dungeon at Richmond. Some ended the war sewing mail bags in prison while a few were even sentenced to death.

Popular hatred for conchies was one aspect of a widespread mood reflecting the darker side of the patriotic wave sweeping the nation as the first reports of the fighting in France and Flanders came home – along with the first British casualty figures and waves of Belgian refugees bearing tales of German atrocities. As a result, German shops were attacked and trashed, German residents rounded up and interned; there were even reports of German dog breeds such as dachshunds being kicked in the streets.

GERMANOPHOBIA GRIPS

There was also a lively fear of the activities of German spies – some of which were not wholly fabricated. At the outbreak of war Carl Hans Lody, an English-speaking German naval officer living in the US, received orders to sail to Britain and report on its navy. He arrived in Edinburgh under the American alias Charles Inglis and spent three weeks in the Scottish capital trying to pick up information about the Grand Fleet at its Scottish bases Rosyth and Scapa Flow. Sent to his spymasters in neutral Sweden, his coded reports – which even mentioned the widespread popular rumour that Russian troops had been seen in Britain with snow on their boots – were intercepted by the Post Office's efficient counter-espionage watchers and he was placed under surveillance.

Realizing that he was being followed, Lody panicked and fled to Ireland, where he

CARL LODY, the first German spy to die in the Tower. A naval officer, Lody was treated by his executioners with the honour due to a brave man – but they still shot him.

was arrested. Brought to trial by a court martial in London, Lody was condemned to death, and on the night before his execution on 5 November 1914 he was transferred from Wellington Barracks to the Tower of London. The following day he was shot in a rifle range erected in the Tower's moat by a firing squad from the Grenadier Guards – the first of a dozen German spies executed at the Tower during the war. Poignantly, Lody had said to the officer in charge of the firing squad, 'I suppose you will not shake the hand of a German spy?' To which the officer gallantly responded: 'No. But I will shake hands with a brave man.'

Germanophobia also forced the resignations of the First Sea Lord, the Austrian-born Prince Louis of Battenberg, who changed the family's name to Mountbatten in an effort to distance himself from his Teutonic roots; and, ironically enough, of the father of the Territorials, the Liberal statesman Lord Haldane, who was serving as Lord Chancellor when the war began. Neither connection to the royal family (in Battenberg's case) nor closeness to Prime Minister Asquith (in Haldane's) could save these two undoubted patriots, who had contributed so much to their country's readiness for war, from the fury of mob prejudice whipped up by the popular press, the *Daily Express* and Northcliffe's *Daily Mail*. Haldane was condemned for being an admirer of German philosophy – in an unguarded moment he was reported to have called Germany his 'spiritual home' – and Battenberg for his name alone.

Battenberg's son, the future Second World War military leader Louis Mountbatten, wrote home from the naval college at Osborne on the Isle of Wight:

What d'you think the latest rumour that got in here from outside is? That Papa has turned out to be a German spy & has rather discreetly been marched off to the tower where he is guarded by beefeaters… I got rather a rotten time of it for about three days as little fools… insisted on calling me German Spy & kept on heckling me & trying to make things unpleasant for me.

As women moved into offices and factories that their husbands, sons and sweethearts had left; as the state took unprecedented powers over people's lives; as sleepy towns and villages watched their menfolk marching off to war, Britain girded itself for the uncertainties that lay ahead. By the autumn of 1914, though, it was already clear that no one, pacifist or patriot, combatant or civilian, would be left untouched by what Winston Churchill called the 'hardest and the cruellest war ever fought by Man'.

READY FOR ACTION: men of the British Expeditionary Force disembark at Le Havre, 16 August 1914. Thanks largely to Sir Henry Wilson's forward planning, the BEF was rushed to France in record time, giving the enemy a nasty surprise.

12. First Blood

BRITAIN WAS NOT READY FOR WAR – let alone a modern, industrialized conflict involving the mobilization of millions of men. Not since Wellington's armies had returned victorious from the field of Waterloo a century before had the country deployed its soldiers in a continental conflict. True, there had been wars aplenty in the hundred years since. British redcoats – and, after the Boer War, Britons in the new half-mud, half-sand shade called khaki – had fought almost continuously in engagements in places as diverse as Canada, China, India, Sudan, Afghanistan, Zululand and South Africa itself. But these were contained colonial wars fought to hold, or expand, the far-flung dominions of the empire. They were different – none knew yet quite how different – from the war that the army would be called upon to fight against the comparable powers of Europe on fields within sight – and sound – of the garden of England itself.

While Kitchener husbanded and trained his masses of keen but green volunteers, fashioning them, he hoped, into a war-winning modern army, the initial fighting in France and Flanders would have to be done by the old sweats of the regular army – seasoned professionals who had mainly learned their trade in combat with the always restless tribal peoples of India's north-west frontier. That frontier was still restive in 1914 and would have to be guarded, and troops would also be needed to man the other outposts of empire: a total of four divisions in all would be left on these garrison duties overseas. Meanwhile, Field Marshal Sir John French, commander of the British Expeditionary Force (BEF) which would be going to France almost at once, marshalled the forces available to him.

The British Army's home establishment – regular soldiers based in Britain at any given time – mustered a total of around 150,000 men. The BEF would consist of six infantry divisions and one cavalry division, divided into two corps: the first commanded by General Sir Douglas Haig; the second by General Sir Horace Smith-Dorrien (replacing the original choice of Sir James Grierson, who died of a heart attack in a train almost as soon as he arrived in France). The BEF, then, would at first roughly equal the army fielded by tiny Serbia and was in no way comparable to the millions of men – chiefly conscripts – mustered by the other combatant nations of Germany, France, Russia and Austria-Hungary.

The man commanding this small force, Sir John French, was a peppery little bow-legged cavalryman, who preferred an old-fashioned cravat-style stock to wearing a collar and tie. French was an old school, walrus-moustached soldier with a penchant for liaisons with the ladies and

unwise financial investments, both of which had threatened his career (he had only narrowly survived the latter thanks to a timely loan from his future supplanter, Haig). Of Anglo-Irish descent and Unionist sympathies, French would be hampered in France, despite his surname, by his total lack of knowledge of the language. Having distinguished himself in colonial wars in Africa, French's career had been in the shadows for months since he had dramatically resigned during the Curragh Mutiny in protest at the proposal to coerce Ulster's Protestants. But on 30 July he had been summoned by the War Office and informed that he would command the BEF.

French spent the next few days in meetings with the cabinet, the French ambassador Paul Cambon, and France's army liaison officer, Major Victor Huguet; and not least with that grey eminence who had engineered Britain's military ties with France, his fellow Unionist General Sir Henry Wilson. It was only now that Wilson brought his civilian masters – the politicians he contemptuously nicknamed 'the frocks' – fully up to speed with the true extent of the commitment he had made to France during

Bᴿᴬᵛᴱ ᴬᴺᴰ ᴮᵁᴸᴸᴵˢᴴ: though a warrior in and out of the boudoir, the BEF's commander-in-chief, Sir John French, pictured with his new Field Marshal's baton in 1914, was utterly unfitted to command in a modern war.

the military 'conversations' he had been conducting with them since 1906.

Without the knowledge of the cabinet, Wilson had developed his well-honed plans for a rapid deployment of the BEF on the left flank of the French armies in the event of a German invasion. That event was now grim reality, with the French defending their homeland against the long grey columns of the Kaiser's army which were already streaming across Belgium. It was agreed that the BEF would concentrate around the small town of Maubeuge, and thus briefed, French and his staff crossed to France to join his troops on 12 August.

The foot soldiers of the British Army, its infantry units, were still organized in 1914 according to its traditional regimental system. Regiments of the line were based on their counties or cities of origin, where they had their bases and carried out their recruiting. Most regiments consisted of two battalions which rotated, one serving at home, the other in the empire, and it was the home battalions of these regiments that formed the bulk of the BEF. Though under strength, each of the BEF's six divisions fielded some 18,000 men, of whom 12,000 were infantry.

AN OLD ARMY AWAKES

The BEF's infantry was supported by cavalry, used chiefly as scouts and observers, and by the artillery arm, which manned each of the division's seventy-six field guns. These were mainly light eighteen-pounders, with a few heavier sixty-pounders and howitzers, and each division was allocated twenty-four machine-guns – still a rare and new-fangled weapon. In addition to the mounted troops and the gunners, each division was supported by engineering, communication, and supply units – the often despised cooks and bottle-washers – and was commanded by a divisional staff reporting to their corps commanders, who reported in turn to the general headquarters (GHQ) of the BEF. Last but by no means least, the BEF boasted four squadrons – fifty aircraft – of the infant Royal Flying Corps, which flew to Maubeuge airfield on 18 August.

In addition to the human 'tail' dragging behind the fighting forces, a vital component of the BEF was its horses. Mechanization in 1914 was in its infancy, and at the outset the BEF was equipped with just eighty lorries, twenty cars, and fifteen motorcycles – all attached to GHQ. Everything else – which included such tasks as pulling guns across rough country, along with carts carrying food and fodder, and advanced observation of the enemy – had to be carried out by horses. Since horses were expensive to keep and feed in peacetime, the army was forced to resort to the immediate impressment and requisition of horses from various branches of civilian life – horses that pulled trams in seaside resorts, racehorses, dray horses that drew heavy brewers' carts, shire horses that usually pulled ploughs on farms. By this revival of the press gang applied to horses, within ten days of mobilization, some 100,000 additional animals had been acquired by the army, bringing its equine establishment up to around 135,000.

Similar methods of forced requisition were required to transport the BEF across the Channel to France. The Royal Navy lent its warships to the job of escorting the troop-ships, but the merchant navy was also needed to do its bit. Destroyers, cross-Channel ferries, pleasure steamers and merchant ships were all drafted into service as carefully calculated trainloads of men – 1,800 trains travelled in the first five days of mobilization alone – funnelled south from the army's command areas to the ports from which they embarked for France. The principal port of embarkation for soldiers was Southampton, from where ships sailed across the Channel to Le Havre and thence down the River Seine to Rouen, where they disembarked. Others embarked from Glasgow, Folkestone, Liverpool, Avonmouth and Newhaven; and in Ireland from Dublin, Cork and Belfast. Portsmouth and Dover, meanwhile, were reserved for naval operations.

Upon arrival in France, the troops entrained for the areas where the BEF was mustering around Maubeuge, just inside the French frontier with Belgium. The area was a heavily industrialized coalfield, with terraced streets of mean houses, pitheads and slag heaps – not an ideal locale for soldiers trained to fight in open country with wide fields of fire. The BEF's depositions and their role in the campaign had been agreed at a meeting on 17 August at the HQ of the French 5th Army, the force holding the left flank of the French positions, commanded by General Charles Lanrezac.

A CLASH OF CULTURES

The British liaison officer with Lanrezac was a young Francophile lieutenant of the Hussars named Edward Louis Spears, later a bosom crony of Winston Churchill, who would play an important role in the often fraught Anglo-French relationship in both world wars. Spears's memoirs vividly describe the non-meeting of minds, characterized by mutual incomprehension and a fundamental clash of personality, between the diminutive, blue-eyed, white-moustached English field marshal and the tall, swarthy, sardonic, languid Lanrezac. When Sir John, in his fractured French, asked Lanrezac whether the Germans would cross the Meuse, Lanrezac replied sarcastically that they merely intended to go fishing in the river. Affronted, French departed in a huff after less than half an hour. The interview, in Spears's words, had 'resulted in a complete fiasco'.

Nonetheless, French determined to fulfil faithfully the terms of the alliance with France as determined by Wilson and the two governments, and accepted his subordinate role of guarding Lanrezac's left flank against the German 1st and 2nd Armies, which were now remorselessly bearing down upon him. The Germans, who had already captured the Belgian capital Brussels, were fast approaching the frontier and Lanrezac's fifteen divisions were outnumbered by more than two to one. Any British help would clearly be a forlorn hope, but it was gratefully grasped by the French nonetheless as a drowning man clutches at a straw. Obediently, French ordered

his two corps commanders, Haig and Smith-Dorrien, across the Belgian frontier with orders to stop – or at least delay – the German juggernaut by holding the Mons-Condé canal to the north of the little town.

On 21 August Britain sustained the first of almost a million fatal casualties that the mother country and its empire would suffer over the next four terrible years. Private John Parr was a sixteen-year-old member of the cyclists' reconnaissance unit of the 4th Battalion, the Middlesex Regiment. Born and bred in Finchley, north London, he had left school in his early teens and found work as a golf caddy before the lure of regular pay and meals – however meagre – tempted him into the army. Too young to enlist, he lied about his true age, adding four years. On the outbreak of war he was shipped from Folkestone to Boulogne and moved forward to Mons. Here, he was ordered with a fellow biker to cross the twenty-metre-wide industrial canal and report back on what they found. Parr and his comrade reached the village of Obourg, where they ran into a patrol of Uhlans.

The dreaded Uhlans, with their ten-foot steel lances, were the cavalry outriders belonging to General Alexander von Kluck's 1st Army, strongest of the six German armies scything through Belgium and France in fulfilment of the Schlieffen Plan. The 1st Army, with its 360,000 men, formed the crushing, swinging fist of the Schlieffen Plan's powerful right arm and it was bearing straight down on the oblivious BEF. Parr told his friend to pedal back with the news that they had found their first Germans, and as the boy rode off as fast as his young legs would carry him, Parr attempted to hold off the Uhlans, but was swiftly killed: the first Briton of the war to die.

A 'CONTEMPTIBLE LITTLE ARMY'? Troops of the 4th Battalion Royal Fusiliers resting in the Grand Place, Mons, 22 August 1914. In the next day's battle the BEF would belie their tiny size and refute the Kaiser's insult with the speed and accuracy of their rifle fire.

Reaching Mons on 22 August, the main body of the BEF only just had time to consolidate along the tree-shaded canal banks when the Germans appeared in front of them. They were blissfully unaware that they were alone. Lanrezac's 5th Army around Charleroi, to the BEF's right, was under heavy attack and was already falling back. Thanks in part to their mutual non-comprehension and dislike, French, newly established in his HQ at Le Cateau, was ignorant of his Gallic counterpart's decision to withdraw, opening up a yawning ten-mile gap on his right wing and leaving the BEF in acute danger of being surrounded and annihilated.

THE BATTLE FOR MONS

Fortunately, Kluck's 1st Army was in an equal state of ignorance about the strength, or even the presence, of the British. They fondly believed that the BEF was still in the process of embarking at the Channel ports, and when their cavalry patrols reported the presence of flat-capped troops in khaki, with a rapid rate of fire from their Lee-Enfield .303 rifles, they were not, at first, believed. As both sides fumbled for each other through the fog of war and an early morning summer mist at dawn on 23 August, they were each about to receive the rudest of surprises.

The forces immediately available to Kluck at Mons were immense, comprising some 160,000 men backed by 600 artillery pieces, attacking the BEF's 70,000 men with their 300 field guns. Around 6 a.m., as the church bells in Mons pealed out their Sunday morning call to worship and the black-clad faithful moved cautiously through the town's streets to church, the British opened fire on German cavalrymen cautiously approaching their positions. Such skirmishing continued through the early morning hours as the Germans brought up their infantry to prepare for a full-blooded assault on the canal, and the German guns, finding their range, started to plop shells on and around the British lines. (One narrowly missed General Smith-Dorrien's car as he inspected front-line positions.) For the first time since Waterloo, the British Army was engaging on a Belgian battlefield on the blood-soaked fields of Flanders, just a few miles from Malplaquet, where the Duke of Marlborough had gained his last, Pyrrhic victory.

Private Parr's Middlesex Regiment, known as 'the Diehards' from their stubborn refusal to surrender at the Battle of Albuhera in Wellington's Peninsular War, lived up to their proud tradition at Mons, where they formed the spearhead of the British line, manning a loop in the canal that stuck out defiantly like a sore thumb towards the advancing Germans. Moving in serried, parade-ground ranks, the Brandenburg Grenadiers led the German advance against the Middlesex Regiment, the Royal Fusiliers, the East Surreys, the Royal West Kents and the King's Own Scottish Borderers. Fast learners, the Germans would abandon sooner than their foes the tactic of such head-on, unprotected assaults, and Mons taught them the lesson.

The Germans were met with a stream of withering rifle fire from the British so intense that they reported back that the enemy must be equipped with machine-guns rather than rifles. Highly trained in musketry, the British infantryman was able to loose off twenty rounds a minute of rapid fire, and huge gaps were torn in the field-grey ranks as they came on in full view of the waiting 'Tommies'. 'As the enemy came through the wood about 200 yards in front they presented a magnificent target,' recalled Lieutenant George Roupell of the 1st East Surreys:

> We opened rapid fire. The men were very excited as this was their first 'shot in anger'. Despite the short range, a number of them were firing high, but I found it hard to control the fire as there was so much noise. Eventually I drew my sword and walked along the line beating the men on the backside and, as I got their attention, telling them to fire low. So much for all our beautiful fire orders taught in peacetime!

At Obourg, where Private Parr had met his end, his regimental comrade in the 4th Middlesex, Private Tom Bradley, sheltering in a shallow rifle pit that he had dug near a bridge over the canal, hardly had to take aim:

> They went down like ninepins until all we could see in front of us was a regular wall of dead and wounded. Above the noise of the rifle fire you could hear a strange wailing sound and they turned and ran for the cover of the fir trees.

But the Germans were quick learners. Realizing that parade-ground attacks were suicidal in the face of a sharp-shooting enemy firing from entrenched positions, they switched tactics and advanced again, this time in small formations running forward in short rushes, at the same time bringing up their heavy guns to pin down the British. By afternoon these looser tactics, heavy artillery fire and sheer weight of numbers were having their effect, and the British were under severe pressure.

The German attacks were heaviest at the Nimy bridge, where the canal looped into a salient. The Royal Fusiliers were holding this sector, and

OR VALOUR: Sidney Godley, 4th Battalion Royal Fusiliers, the first private soldier awarded the Victoria Cross in the First World War for his bravery at Mons. Taken prisoner, Godley survived the war.

one of their two allotted machine-guns was under the command of a young Irish officer, Lieutenant Maurice Dease. Despite being wounded no fewer than four times, Dease stuck to his post until he was hit a fifth time and, mortally wounded, carried away to die. His place manning the machine-gun was taken by Private Sidney Godley, who continued to fire, covering the withdrawal of his company's comrades across the bridge. When he saw that he was about to be overwhelmed by the advancing Germans, Godley deliberately destroyed the gun, throwing the pieces into the canal before he was captured – and spent the rest of the war in German hands. Both Dease and Godley were awarded the Victoria Cross, Britain's supreme award for valour, for their courage – the first VCs of the war. Two more VCs were awarded to sappers Captain Thomas Wright and Lance Corporal Charles Jarvis for destroying canal bridges under heavy fire to impede the enemy advance.

As the German infiltration of their positions continued, the British belatedly received news of Lanrezac's withdrawal. Realizing that they were in danger of being completely cut off, Smith-Dorrien ordered a withdrawal in the late afternoon. Six hours of heavy fighting had cost the BEF 1,600 casualties (killed, wounded and missing) in their first 'blooding'. But they had inflicted still greater losses – probably around 5,000 – on the enemy. Mons had taught both sides valuable lessons. The Germans had learned that their Kaiser's arrogant dismissal of the BEF as 'a contemptible little army' was very wide of the mark. The BEF was made up of trained professionals whose disciplined fire could inflict severe losses on troops advancing across open ground. The British, for their part, had been on the receiving end of the awesome power of artillery – destined, with the machine-gun, to be the major killer of the war. And they had learned that the 'Huns' facing them were magnificent soldiers: tough, disciplined and determined. It was going to be a long, hard war.

SAVED BY THE ANGELS

Smith-Dorrien, whose II Corps had fought the Battle of Mons, was a tough, experienced soldier with an independent mind. He did, however, have two problems which made it unlikely that his career as a front-line general would blossom. First, he shared Kitchener's foresight that the war would be a long, exhausting struggle. Unlike 'K', however, he foresaw that such a conflict would mean the extinction of Britain as a great power and, on the eve of war, had specifically warned officer cadets – thirsting for a pep talk – that Britain should on no account enter the war. Smith-Dorrien's second problem, besides this defeatism, was that his immediate superior, Sir John French, had taken against him, and once such a prejudice had formed in French's limited mind, it was impossible to shift. French distrusted his II Corps commander and had opposed his appointment, and although he had been obliged to give way by 'K', a festering distrust remained between the two men which boded ill for the conduct of the campaign.

For the moment, Smith-Dorrien pulled his exhausted men back to new positions three miles south of Mons while he awaited French's orders. Those orders, when they came just before midnight on 23 August, were for a further retreat. With Lanrezac withdrawing his 5th Army to his right, French was not prepared to risk his army being cut off and annihilated. In the early hours of 24 August, therefore, the weary foot-soldiers of the BEF were roused and told to continue their retreat southwards. Haig's I Corps moved first, covered by the already blooded men of Smith-Dorrien's II Corps. As dawn broke, the Germans resumed the attack they had started at Mons, and once again, despite their advance being preceded by an artillery barrage, they were met with the BEF's characteristic rifle fire, which they again mistook for machine-guns. Checked, the Germans paused to lick their wounds, but when their advance resumed, they found that the British had taken advantage of the lull to slip away.

Just as their right flank was in danger because of the disappearance of Lanrezac's 5th Army, so the BEF was in constant danger of being out-flanked on their left. This was countered by the BEF's only cavalry division, led by General Sir Edmund Allenby – later to command British forces in the Middle East. In an exploit lifted straight from the pages of a previous era in warfare, Allenby's 2nd Cavalry Brigade charged and lanced those Germans whom they caught in the open advancing on the British posi-tions. The cavalry made a magnificent sight as they swept across the British front, but unfortunately they were in full view of the Germans too, who took full advantage. A storm of fire hit the charging cavalrymen – one of the final examples of a cavalry charge in the history of western warfare –

RIDING THE WRONG WAY: beaten back by sheer weight of German numbers, horsemen of the BEF's Cavalry Division retreat from Mons, late August 1914.

mowing down both horses and their riders. One of the 250 casualties was Captain Francis Grenfell, who won a VC for extricating and withdrawing a battery of guns in spite of severe wounds from heavy enemy fire. (Grenfell would die the following year in the Second Battle of Ypres.)

As the shadows lengthened across another scorching summer's day on the evening of 24 August, the retreat continued. The BEF had successfully avoided Kluck's attempts to outflank it and cut it off, and the Germans had received a bruised, if not a bloody, nose, but the two days of fighting had caused considerable attrition in terms both of battle casualties and of stragglers getting lost or falling by the wayside. Even though these gaps in the ranks would be compensated for by the arrival of a fresh division – General Thomas D'Oyly Snow's 4th Division – from England on the 25th, it was clear that if the retreat continued for long, there was a danger that the BEF would lose its coherence as a fighting force. Sleep, food and water were all in short supply, and the men were dog-tired after three days of continual marching and fighting in the blistering heat of high summer. Even when they were not engaged in battle, the sheer pain of feet rubbed raw in new boots pounding the cobbled pave of the long, straight French roads – agony compared by some veterans to hot pins being thrust into the soles of their feet – was hitting morale, as were the sight and sound of weeping

Belgian refugees crowding the same roads with their pathetic salvaged belongings piled onto farm carts.

It was during the early days of the retreat from Mons that the legend sprang up that the weary and footsore soldiers had been inspired by the sight in the skies of the spectres of English archers from the Battle of Agincourt in the Hundred Years' War, or, in an alternative version, by angels clad in shimmering white. The origin of these stories was later traced to a fictional story, 'The Bowmen', by the journalist Arthur Machen, which appeared in a London evening newspaper in September 1914. Although Machen repeatedly protested that his story was pure fiction, the myth gathered momentum when it was taken up by credulous clergymen, who repeated and elaborated the 'Angels of Mons' as a genuine heavenly visitation, and may even have been propagated by intelligence sources at the BEF's HQ at a low point in Allied fortunes.

On 25 August the BEF was obliged to split in two as it retreated. The division was forced by the dense Mormal Forest which lay directly across the route of the army's retirement. Therefore Smith-Dorrien's II Corps took the road south on the eastern side of the forest, while Haig's I Corps took the road on the western side. French, who was in the process of moving his headquarters south from the town of Le Cateau to Saint-Quentin, visited and kept in touch with Haig, but, probably because of his distaste for Smith-Dorrien, failed to do so with the commander of II Corps, who was obliged to go in person to French on the evening of 24 August and seek further orders. French apparently told Smith-Dorrien brusquely to act on his own initiative. During the course of the following day, as his men plodded wearily down the road along the Mormal Forest's edge, con-tinually pausing to return fire as they were harassed by Kluck's outriders, Smith-Dorrien decided that it was essential, if he were to prevent his force from becoming a disorganized rabble, to stop and make a stand.

BEWARE THE CORNERED FOE

Reaching the small town of Le Cateau, Smith-Dorrien was expecting to reunite with Haig's I Corps, but two facts prevented this. First, Haig's Corps had become hopelessly entangled with elements of Lanrezac's 5th Army, flying south along the same road. Secondly, upon reaching the village of Landrecies where he was billeted on the night of 24–25 August, Haig too was harassed by German forward units – an incident which, in an uncharacteristic panic, he misinterpreted as a full-blown assault by an entire German army. Smith-Dorrien was therefore on his own. As his men, marching asleep, weary and soaking wet from a sudden summer storm,

WALKING WOUNDED: British and Belgian troops retreat after the Battle of Mons.

trailed in dribs and drabs into Le Cateau, he concluded that they were in no state to continue their retreat on the next day without a respite. And with the Germans snapping hard at his heels, he knew that such a respite meant giving battle.

After consulting Allenby, who agreed to place the cavalry at his disposal, and the chiefs of the two divisions in his corps, Smith-Dorrien announced: 'Very well, gentlemen, we will stand and fight and I will ask General Snow to act under me as well.' Smith-Dorrien's battle plan was simple: he intended a hit-and-run action. He aimed to deal a sudden smashing 'stopping blow' at the enemy, who would not expect such an aggressive attack from a retreating, outnumbered and presumably demoralized enemy; and then, before they had fully recovered, to slip away with his scattered forces now concentrated and intact. After sending a message to French outlining his intentions – and receiving an ambiguous reply allowing him freedom of action but encouraging him nonetheless to continue the retreat – Smith-Dorrien prepared for action.

The story of Mons was repeated at Le Cateau but on a greater scale. Once again British defenders thinly holding a long front faced masses of German infantry. The Germans, however, had neglected to make a preparatory artillery bombardment and, once again, British rifles took a heavy toll of their infantry, with the 2nd Suffolk Regiment and the King's Own Yorkshire Light Infantry bearing the brunt of the action. The British infantry was supported by units of the Royal Field Artillery, with their light guns firing at the oncoming Germans at virtually point-blank range over open sights. As at Mons, however, the longer the fighting went on, the more the sheer superiority in German numbers began to tell, and the greater the danger of the British being outflanked both on their left wing, held by Snow's newly arrived troops, and on their right, where there was a yawning gap between II Corps and Haig's I Corps. At midday, therefore, satisfied that he had successfully delivered his stopping blow, Smith-Dorrien ordered a general withdrawal.

Thanks to the courage of the gunners and the spirit of their horses, who galloped up, gathered their guns and rode away under a hurricane of shot and shell, most of the artillery was retrieved and withdrawn intact under the very noses of the Germans. Twenty-five guns, however, had to be left on the field, their gun crews disabling them by removing the breech-blocks so that the enemy could not use them. Three gunners received VCs for their part in saving the weapons.

The guns and gunners were followed by the infantry, who withdrew in good order, section by section, pausing to give covering fire to their comrades as they left the field. Watching the retreat from his HQ, Smith-Dorrien even compared his troops' behaviour to that of a victorious crowd heading home after a sports meeting: 'The men smoking their pipes and chatting away discussing the events of the day, apparently completely unconcerned.' Losses, however, had been grievous, more than three times those at Mons, with almost 8,000 casualties compared to the enemy's 3,000–5,000. In no way can Le Cateau be compared to Crécy, on the anniversary of which the engagement had been fought, as a glorious victory against superior numbers. It had, however, achieved its primary purpose – that of keeping Smith-Dorrien's corps together and delaying the German advance.

THE TIDE SLOWLY TURNS

Le Cateau had bought time for the BEF, but it had not turned the tide of war. Remorselessly, the retreat continued. The following fortnight was characterized by confusion, indecision and increasing ill-temper among the Allied commanders as they fell back. The French worried that the British had been too badly mauled at Mons and Le Cateau to fight any further; while the British wondered whether they had been forgotten in the midst of a French desire to 'sauve qui peut'. The initial hostility between French and Lanrezac deepened, while French snarlingly blamed Smith-Dorrien for disobeying orders to make his stand at Le Cateau. Finally, wiser, cooler heads were called in to impose order on the increasing chaos.

The imperturbable if uninspired French commander-in-chief Joseph Joffre sacked Lanrezac, appointing in his place to command the 5th Army Louis Franchet d'Espèrey, a stocky dynamo who immediately proposed a plan to stand and fight along the Marne – the last river line between the Germans and Paris. Meanwhile, no less a figure than the towering war secretary Lord Kitchener arrived in his field marshal's uniform to knock heads together and pull rank over French, telling him to co-operate with the Allied plans or face dismissal.

A total Allied defeat was prevented not only by this stiffening of resolve, but also by the innate imperfections of the Schlieffen Plan, which depended on the German war machine continuing to move according to a rigid timetable – ignoring the fact that a month of marching and fighting in the broiling heat of a burning summer had taken its toll of German troops too. Worn shoe-leather, blisters, sunburn, total exhaustion, the morale-sapping loss of comrades, failure to decisively defeat their elusive enemy – all had conspired to put several spokes in the smooth unrolling of the plan. The invaders – particularly Kluck's 1st Army, which had to march furthest and

F IELD OF BATTLE: a dead German soldier after the Battle of the Marne, September 1914. Aided by the BEF, the French counter-attacked outside Paris and forced the Germans to retreat north-east, thereby scuppering the carefully worked-out Schlieffen Plan and ushering in four years of attritional trench warfare.

fastest and fight hardest – were not the same men who had so confidently advanced just a month before.

Moreover, the mechanics of the invasion plan were beginning to go badly awry. On the distant Eastern Front, contrary to expectations, the Russians had mobilized relatively rapidly, and their vast peasant armies were swarming in to invade East Prussia. Troops were already being detached from the five German armies marching through France and rushed east to meet the threat. On the ground in France, meanwhile, a dangerous gap had opened up between Kluck's 1st Army and Karl von Bülow's 2nd, obliging Kluck to sidestep to his left to keep in touch with his colleague. Not only did this mean that Kluck would – contrary to Schlieffen – pass inside the French capital to its east, rather than cutting it off by going around it to the west, but by swerving east to keep contact with Bülow, Kluck exposed his right flank to a surprise counter-attack by the still undefeated Allies.

To its credit, the French high command grasped the opportunity and responded at once. The French government had already left Paris, fearing that the capital would fall to the Germans, as it had in 1871. When a French aviator reported that Kluck's columns were streaming in a south-easterly direction towards Bülow, delighted officers exulted: 'They are presenting us with their flank!' Franchet d'Espèrey's plan to counter-attack along the Marne was hastily adopted by Joffre, and a grumpy Sir John French agreed to lend the BEF to take part in the offensive. The long retreat was over.

On 5 September the Allies attacked along the whole line of the Marne. The Germans reeled back in confusion, and the 'miracle of the Marne' – aided by the rushing of thousands of French soldiers from Paris in the city's taxi-cabs – was accomplished. Now it was the Germans who were in full retreat, withdrawing to the line of the River Aisne, where they dug in to make a stand. By mid-September, the broken German commander-in-chief, Helmuth von Moltke, was telling the Kaiser that the war was irretrievably lost. He was right: but it would take four more years of slaughter and stalemate to prove it.

EPILOGUE:
CHRISTMAS 1914

PEACE AND WAR: laden with Christmas gifts in December 1914, two soldiers at Victoria station, London, leave for the front. Victoria was a main departure point for France – and was also where the wounded came home.

Epilogue: Christmas 1914

AS THE TWILIGHT OF THE SHORT WINTER DAY faded away on Christmas Eve, 24 December 1914, Lieutenant Charles Bruce Bairnsfather felt 'a sense of strangeness' pervading the air in the sector of the trenches at Saint-Yvon, south of Ypres, which had been constructed that autumn and which his unit, the 1st Battalion of the Warwickshire Regiment, was now holding. Recalling the momentous day later, Bairnsfather remembered:

'I came out of my dugout and sloshed along the trench to a dry lump, stood on it and gazed at all the scene around: the stillness, the stars, and the now dark blue sky… From where I stood I could see our long line of zigzagging trenches and those of the Germans as well. Songs began to float up from various parts of our line.'

One of them, 'not far away', closed:

If old Jerry shells the trench
Never mind!
Though the blasted sandbags fly
You have only once to die.
If old Jerry shells the trench
Never mind!
If you get stuck on the wire
Never mind!
Though the light's as broad as day
When you die they stop your pay.
If you get stuck on the wire
Never mind!

As the strains of the song faded, Bairnsfather thought he heard it succeeded by the mournful sound of a distant harmonica. It was, as the saying goes, 'Quiet, too quiet'. Bairnsfather took advantage of the lull to visit a forward dug-out closer to the German lines, where the music of the mouth organ could be heard more clearly. He found a group of his men daringly peering over the trench parapet towards where the music was coming from. 'What's up?' Bairnsfather demanded.

'The Boche, sir,' a Tommy replied. 'You can 'ear 'em quite plain. There's a feller over there shouting in English and one of 'em's got a concertina or something.' Bairnsfather listened. Sure enough, and quite distinctly, he then heard the anthem 'Deutschland über Alles', accompanied by an accordion and sung by gruff Teutonic voices. When the song ended, shouts floated across the strangely still air of No Man's Land, the barren stretch of mud – pockmarked by shell-holes, festooned with barbed wire, littered with metal debris and, here and there, the rotting remains of body parts – that divided the British and German front-line trenches.

'Come over here, Tommy! We won't shoot,' came a voice from the German lines, followed by the riposte, 'Come over yourself, nor will we.'

As the evening sky darkened and the glowing red winter sun was replaced by a silver moon, the mood turned sentimental and the patriotic songs were replaced by Christmas carols – especially 'Stille Nacht, Heilige Nacht'. From the British trenches, voices chimed in with the English translation: 'Silent Night, Holy Night'. Then, extraordinarily, one or two more daring spirits on either side of the lines heaved themselves on top of the parapet, gingerly picked their way across the tangles of barbed wire and ventured into the darkness of No Man's Land.

Later in the war Bruce Bairnsfather was to become one of the most ubiquitous recorders of trench life. He was a talented cartoonist, through the creation of his moustachioed character 'Old Bill', an everyman figure who stoically witnesses and withstands the suffering, and Bairnsfather's humour went some way towards humanizing and rendering endurable the inhuman and unendurable. Some said that Old Bill was based on photos of Sidney Godley, the winner of one of the war's first VCs at Mons, and certainly Godley bore a marked facial resemblance to the cartoon image – and he even played Old Bill on stage to raise money for the British Legion on his release from German captivity at the end of the war.

What Bairnsfather was witnessing at the war's outset was the beginnings of one of the most remarkable events in the history of conflict: an all too brief moment when the soldiers of two hostile armies, against the explicit orders of their high commands, forgot their deadly enmities for a few hours, stopped shooting at and killing each other, and celebrated the Christian festival of peace and life in the midst of a barren wasteland of death and desolation.

The Christmas truce that ended 1914 followed four months of bitter fighting after the failure of the Schlieffen Plan and the thwarting of the German drive to capture Paris and end the war in the west within six weeks. Retreating from the Marne, the Germans halted after a week of unaccustomed flight along the line of the River Aisne, a naturally strong defensive position, with high ground north of the river strengthened by natural caves and caverns dug into the hillside over the centuries by the local population.

From this redoubt, the Germans withstood all attempts by the French army and the BEF to dislodge them. Sergeant Thomas Painting of the 1st King's Royal Rifle Corps remembered:

> We got over the river and into the high ground over a mile in front of the Aisne. We knew there was about a brigade of Jerries in front of us and we were only seven platoons. During the fight we got pushed back about 300 yards and had to leave our dead and wounded. The Highland Light Infantry and Worcesters came up. Private Wilson of the HLI and one of our men attacked a machine gun. Our man got killed but Private Wilson killed the machine-gunner, captured the position and got the Victoria Cross. Our man got a wooden cross. That's the difference, you see. One killed – one a Victoria Cross.

In fact George Wilson had shot the machine-gun's whole crew of six and bayoneted the officer in charge. He survived the war to die of tuberculosis in his native Edinburgh in 1926.

In mid-September, after the failure to break through on the Aisne, the British commander-in-chief Sir John French gave the fateful order to entrench. Using whatever tools they could steal or scrounge, the surviving men of the BEF dug in where they happened to be standing – usually on lower ground than their German opposite numbers. They did not yet know it, but these early trenches would form the first tentative scrapings of what would become a vast labyrinth of underground warfare – a complex spider's web of trenches, tunnels, fire-bays, traverses, dug-outs, front lines, support lines, reserve lines and communication trenches: a city of the living and the dead extending some 400 miles from the Belgian coast at Nieuport to the Swiss frontier near Belfort.

The geography of the trench lines, the system that soon became known as the Western Front, was dictated by the positions reached by the rival armies after the three-week period of manoeuvring and fighting following the Battle of the Aisne that became known as the 'Race to the Sea'. Both armies – Allies and Germans – had experienced the futility and folly of direct frontal assaults on fixed, well-defended positions. Now they attempted repeatedly to outflank each other, the Allies trying to get around the German left, the Germans attempting the same with the Allied left.

TAKE COVER: troops
from the Oxfordshire
and Buckinghamshire
Light Infantry sheltering
from shrapnel, Ypres,
October 1914; Britain's old
professional army would
be decimated in the first
months of war.

This 'race' ended, for the British, around Ypres, an ancient Flemish
town that stood at the epicentre of a low 'saucer' of slight hills and ridges
in the north-western corner of Belgium. It was the sole slice of the country
that remained unconquered by the German steamroller after the fall of
the port of Antwerp – despite a last-minute attempt to hold it by Winston
Churchill's Royal Naval Division (an episode in which Rupert Brooke
experienced his only brief taste of real warfare). Britain had entered the
war in defence of Belgium and it was on Belgian soil – or rather Belgian
mud – where it would make a stand.

A town with fortified ramparts that had grown rich on the medieval
cloth trade, Ypres was the last remaining citadel between the Germans and
the Channel ports of Dunkirk, Calais and Boulogne. The British, therefore,
were desperate to hold it – and the Germans equally determined to take
it. Battle was joined in October after the remnants of the Belgian army,
clinging to the fragment of their country that remained unconquered,
undammed the dykes and locks along the River Yser between Nieuport

and Diksmuide, flooding the surrounding polders and literally damming the German advance behind a wall of water.

The inundation merely added to the naturally watery state of the low-lying Flanders plain surrounding Ypres. Four years of almost constant artillery fire from both sides added the finishing touches by destroying the intricate irrigation of the area's farmland, so reducing the area to one stinking sea of clinging, glutinous mud. The mud became the terror of all who fought in and around Ypres, as a letter home from Private Warwick Squire of the 1/13th London Regiment, written as early as 19 November, makes all too clear:

> The mud is awful. Everything is mud and we are just lumps of mud. In parts of the trenches the mud just comes up to one's thighs, soft, slushy mud and in others sticky clingy mud over one's knees. I've had quite enough of mud. With mud, love and best wishes for the New Year to you all.

The high water table around Ypres made the digging of trenches there all but impossible. Instead, the British built gun-pits with walls of sandbags, loosely connected with strands of barbed wire. But the first clash of arms in the shallow saucer of mud that finally comprised the Ypres salient – a bulge sticking into the enemy lines – at the end of October and beginning of November was, like the actions at Mons and Le Cateau, still relatively open warfare.

On 20 October the new German commander-in-chief, Erich von Falkenhayn, appointed after the broken von Moltke had been sacked in mid-September, ordered a full-scale assault on Ypres. Captain Harry Dillon of the 2nd Oxfordshire and Buckinghamshire Light Infantry watched in horror:

> A great grey mass of humanity was charging, running for all God would let them, straight on to us not 50 yards off. Everybody's nerves were pretty well on edge as I had warned them what to expect, and as I fired my rifle the rest all went off almost simultaneously. One saw the great mass of Germans quiver. In reality some fell, some fell over them, and others came on. I have never shot so much in such a short time, could not have been more than a few seconds, and they were down. Then the whole lot came on again and it was the most critical moment of my life.
>
> Twenty yards more and they would have been over us in thousands, but our fire must have been fearful, and at the very last

Digging in: as the autumn rains begin, men of the 2nd Battalion Scots Guards dig a muddy trench; 19 November 1914. It was going to be a long war.

moment they did the most foolish thing they possibly could have done. Some of their leading people turned to the left for some reason, and they all just followed like a great flock of sheep. I don't think one could have missed at the distance and just for one short minute or two we poured the ammunition into them in boxfuls. My rifles were red hot at the finish.

The firing died down and out of the darkness a great moan came. People with their arms and legs off trying to crawl away; others who could not move gasping out their last moments with the cold night wind biting into their broken bodies and the lurid red glare of a burning farmhouse showing up clumps of grey devils killed by the men on my left further down. A weird awful scene; some of them would raise themselves on one arm or crawl a little distance, silhouetted as black as ink against the red glow of the fire.

At Langemarck, north of Ypres, the Germans – many of them young students freshly arrived at the front – were mown down in serried ranks as they attacked, with 'Deutschland über Alles' on their lips. The slaughter was so severe that the battle – enshrined in German military myth – became known as the *Kindermord*, or the 'Slaughter of the Innocents'.

West of Ypres, the fighting was concentrated around the village of

Gheluvelt, which saw the blooding of the Bavarian List regiment, containing a newly enlisted young Austrian who had been living in Munich when war broke out: Adolf Hitler. The future Führer was one of just 600 survivors out of an original 3,500 members of the regiment who had fought in the battle. The dead included its commander, Colonel List.

The BEF, however, suffered almost as grievously. It is not too much to say that the First Battle of Ypres was the graveyard of the old British Army. They may have clung on by the skin of their teeth – aided by reinforcements, in an echo of the taxis of the Marne, rushed to the town on red open-topped London double-decker buses – and, with the aid of the French army, they continued to hold an ever-shrinking perimeter front around Ypres. The original regular professionals, however, were decimated, to be replaced by the reservists of the Territorial Force. Private Clifford Lane of the 1st Hertfordshire Regiment recalled:

> We moved to the front in 30 or 40 London omnibuses… everybody wanted to get on top because it was a nice, bright day for November. But we had not been going very long before it started to rain, so we got thoroughly soaked. On the road into Ypres there was the sound of heavy gunfire, and, after a few seconds, three violent explosions. When the smoke had cleared we saw this group of French soldiers picking up one of their number and immediately start to dig a grave for him, so the shell had killed him. That was the first time we realised what the war was about – what the Germans could do.

One of the raw reservists who arrived at the front in November, serving with the 1st London Regiment, was the future writer Henry Williamson, author of *Tarka the Otter* and many autobiographical novels about the war:

> It is true to say that we enjoyed our first visit to the trenches. The weather was dry [and] we went through a wood under Messines Hill. We were brigaded with regulars who wore Balaclava helmets. The whole feeling was one of tremendous comradeship, and these old sweats who were survivors of Mons and the Aisne, they had no fear at all, and any apprehension we had of going in under fire was soon got rid of. We could also go into estaminets and have omelettes and café rum for about a halfpenny. It was great fun.

The fun, of course, would not survive Williamson's first taste of action. As Christmas approached, the weather grew colder, and rain and snow made

conditions in the trenches even grimmer. Even before the festive season, there were occasional truces, local and unofficial, caused by the need of both sides to drain their flooded trenches or – more grimly – to bury the dead left lying, stinking and rotting in No Man's Land. Despite this 'live and let live' modus vivendi between the front-line troops, artillery shells – fired from well behind the front lines – and snipers continued to do their deadly work.

The troops in the trenches were uppermost in the thoughts of loved ones left at home, and such feelings were reciprocated. This was especially so among men from the east coast after the towns of Whitby, Scarborough and Hartlepool were bombarded in a surprise raid by a marauding squadron of the High Seas Fleet's battle cruisers on 16 December. The attack killed 137 people, including seventy-eight women and children – the first casualties of the war on the home front – and caused enormous outrage. The German guns fed patriotic propaganda showing pictures of the devastation and orphaned children with the slogan: 'Men of Britain! Will you stand this? Enlist Now!' The result was another rush of volunteers to enter the army.

Along with individual Christmas presents from home, each man at the front received an embossed brass box known as 'Princess Mary's Gift Box' after the eldest child of King George and Queen Mary. The royal gift, sent to more than two-and-a-half million men serving in the forces, contained an ounce of tobacco, a packet of twenty cigarettes, a pipe, a bar of chocolate, a Christmas card from the royal family and a photograph of the princess. In an age when smoking was virtually universal, it was both a welcome present and an adroit piece of royal PR from a family only too painfully conscious of its German roots. To make the message more explicit, the Prince of Wales, the future Edward VIII, joined the army and would join the staff on the Western Front, while his shy and stammering younger brother, the future George VI, was already a naval cadet and would serve in the main naval clash of the war at Jutland.

The scale of the Christmas truce surprised and alarmed the high command on both sides. Centred around Ploegsteert Wood – the sector on the Franco-Belgian frontier south of Ypres where both Churchill and Hitler would fight (and paint) later in the war – the truce began in the same spontaneous way that Bruce Bairnsfather had witnessed.

'Everything was covered in snow. Everything was white,' recalled Private Frank Sumpter of the London Rifle Brigade. 'The devastated landscape looked terrible in its true colours – clay and mud and broken brick – but when it was covered in snow it was beautiful. Then we heard the Germans singing "Silent Night" and they put up a notice saying "Merry Christmas" so we put one up too.'

After some tentative joint carol singing, bolder spirits stood up and waved at the Germans, who waved back. The next step was to shake hands across the barbed wire; and then the wire was crossed and real intermingling and fraternization began, as Princess Mary's pipe tobacco was exchanged for German Turkish tobacco (Turkey had entered the war on Germany's side a few weeks previously). Pipes were smoked, cameras produced and photographs taken: 'We found our enemies to be Saxons,' recalled Rifleman J. Selby Grigg of the London Regiment. 'I raked up my rusty German and chatted with some of them. None of them seemed to have any personal animosity against England and they all said they would be fully glad when the war was over.'

'All Christmas Day we were walking about in front of our trenches,' remembered Private Warwick Squire of the 1/13th London Regiment. 'The Germans came out of theirs and we met halfway and talked and exchanged souvenirs – our bullets for theirs. They also gave some of our fellows cigars of which they had plenty, and we gave them tins of bully beef as they said they had very little food.'

The truce continued over Christmas and up to the New Year. In one sector there was an impromptu football match between the two warring enemies. (The Germans reportedly won.) Then Prussian units replaced the less warlike Saxons, and the brief cessation of hostilities drew to a close. The following day the war would resume on schedule and continue for four more terrible years. Peace, it seemed, was not part of the plan of those who had plunged the world into war.

'I AM THE ENEMY YOU KILLED, MY FRIEND': British and German soldiers fraternizing during the 1914 Christmas truce at Ploegsteert ('Plug Street'), Belgium.

SMOKING

'Goodbyee-ee, don't sigh-ee': a soldier on the way to the front says goodbye to a loved one; Victoria Station, London, December 1914.

Further Reading

1. THE DARKENING SKY

Recommended biographies of the era's leading politicians include Roy Jenkins's *Asquith* (1966). A patrician radical's elegant life of his hero is restrained on the racier aspects of the prime minister's private life. Stephen Koss's *Asquith* (1985) is a rather more acerbic account. Asquith's own *Letters to Venetia Stanley*, edited by Michael and Eleanor Brock (1985), reveals the still shocking vulnerability and indiscretion of the nation's leader as he pours out his heart (and much else) to his mistress. Those who still doubt the depths of Asquith's intimacy with Venetia should read Bobbie Neate's *Conspiracy of Secrets* (2012), a memoir of the couple's secret love child, Louis T. Stanley. Stephen Bates's concise *Asquith* (2006) is an admirable summary of the premier's life.

Asquith's great rival and eventual supplanter Lloyd George has been faithfully served by a great multi-volume life by John Grigg. The relevant volume for this book is *Lloyd George: From Peace to War, 1912–1916* (1985). Earlier, fellow Welsh radical Kenneth O. Morgan wrote an admiring and briefer illustrated life – *Lloyd George* (1974) – while more recently the Labour politician Roy Hattersley produced *David Lloyd George: The Great Outsider* (2010). We still await a more objective critical account of this great but controversial figure.

Lloyd George's younger friend and rival, Winston Churchill, has of course been over-covered, biographically speaking, particularly in the eight tombstone volumes of the official life by Martin Gilbert – *Winston S. Churchill* (1966–88). More manageable are Henry Pelling's *Winston Churchill* (1974) and Roy Jenkins's *Churchill* (2001). Perhaps best of all, and more concise and less reverential than any of them, is Piers Brendon's *Winston Churchill: A Brief Life* (1984, 2001). Churchill's own multi-volume history of the years up to and including the Great War, *The World Crisis, 1911–1918* (1923–31), penned in his own incomparable prose, still repays reading, even if, as Arthur Balfour jibed, 'Winston has written a book about himself and called it The World Crisis'.

Balfour himself has found excellent modern biographers in Max Egremont's *Balfour* (1980) and R. J. Quince Adams's *Balfour: The Last Grandee* (2007). Quince Adams also wrote the life of Balfour's successor as Tory leader, the much harder-nosed *Bonar Law* (2004), which superseded Law's memorial life by the Tory historian Robert Blake, *The Unknown Prime Minister* (1955).

For Richard Haldane, architect of the Territorials, see *Lord Haldane: Scapegoat for Liberalism* by Stephen Koss (1969). Sadly, another senior statesman of the epoch, Foreign Secretary Sir Edward Grey, still lacks an adequate biography, though he wrote his own memoirs. The recent *Edwardian Requiem: A Life of Sir Edward Grey* by Michael Waterhouse (2013) is excellent on Grey's life as a countryman, angler and ornithologist but uninformative on the events of 1914 in which he played such a crucial role.

Fortunately, the Anglo-German naval race has attracted the attention of a superb historian, Robert Massie, whose two narrative volumes *Dreadnought* (1991) and *Castles of Steel* (2004) cover the subject in depth and with thrilling verve. For the central figure of Jacky Fisher, see the conventional authorized biography *First Sea Lord* by Richard Hough (1969), and the distinctly original and unconventional but fascinating *Fisher's Face* by Jan Morris (1995).

The craze for invasion literature is covered in the essays edited by I. F. Clarke in *The Great War with Germany* (1997) and in the same author's *Voices Prophesying War, 1763–1984* (1966).

The astonishing career of the press baron who epitomized the era, Alfred Harmsworth, and that of his brother Esmond are related by S. J. Taylor in *The Great Outsiders: Northcliffe, Rothermere and the Daily Mail* (1996).

Britain's once ultra-secret services have become something of an open book in recent years, and guarded, cryptic works like Richard Deacon's *A History of the British Secret Service* (1969) have blossomed into a fascinating literary subgenre all of its own. The most authoritative and best-informed academic historian of the secret world is Professor Christopher Andrew, whose pioneering *Secret Service: The Making of the British Intelligence Community* (1985) is informative, seminal and immensely readable. Andrew followed up with *The Defence of the Realm* (2009), the authorized history of MI5.

There have been three equally excellent histories of MI5's overseas counterpart MI6/SIS: Nigel West's *MI6: British Secret Intelligence Operations, 1909–1949* (1983); Michael Smith's *Six: A History of Britain's Secret Intelligence Service – Part 1: Murder and Mayhem, 1909–1939* (2010); and Keith Jeffery's *MI6: The History of the Secret Intelligence Service, 1909–1949* (2010). Jeffery also wrote the best biography of the man most responsible for preparing Britain's army to go to war along with France against Germany: *Field Marshal Sir Henry Wilson: A Political Soldier* (2006). The founder of MI6 found an excellent biographer in Alan Judd, who wrote *The Quest for C: Mansfield Cumming and the Founding of the Secret Service* (1999).

2. ULSTER WILL FIGHT
The best general account of the Ulster crisis before the Great War is still A. T. Q. Stewart's *The Ulster Crisis* (1967). Stewart also wrote *Edward Carson* (1981) on Ulster Unionism's most pugnacious prophet. Carson found a loyal Unionist biographer in H. Montgomery Hyde (*Carson* (1974), who was answered by a rather more sceptical Geoffrey Lewis in *Carson: The Man who Divided Ireland* (2005).

Two other useful books on Ireland's troubles in these years, both broadly sympathetic to the cause of Home Rule, are Robert Kee's three-volume *The Green Flag* (1972) and George Dangerfield's *The Damnable Question* (1979).

The strange, contradictory career of Erskine Childers is told in the official life by Andrew Boyle, *The Riddle of Erskine Childers* (1977), and by Jim Ring in *Erskine Childers: A Biography* (1996). Childers's own classic thriller *The Riddle of the Sands* (1903) has never been out of print and is a rattling good yarn.

3. VOTES FOR WOMEN
There are numerous accounts of the suffragettes, of which I have found most useful *Votes for Women* by Roger Fulford (1957), a sympathetic traditional narrative; *Votes for Women: The Virago Book of Suffragettes* edited by Joyce Marlow (2000); and the more critical *The Ascent of Woman* by Melanie Phillips (2003). Jad Adams's plain-speaking *Pankhurst* (2003) pulls no punches in its critique of the authoritarian Emmeline and Christabel. Julie Gottlieb's *Feminine Fascism* (2003) details the post-war Blackshirt career of Mary Richardson and other erstwhile suffragettes.

4. HOME FIRES
Among many excellent general studies of Britain immediately before the war, I have found especially useful *The Perfect Summer: England 1911, Just before the Storm* by Juliet Nicolson (2007) and *The Last Summer: May to September 1914* by Kirsty McLeod (1983), although both

deal chiefly with the upper reaches of society. Standish Meacham's *A Life Apart: The English Working Class, 1890–1914* (1977) is a thorough study of its subject.

The classic *The Strange Death of Liberal England* by George Dangerfield (1935), though dated, is still seminal and indispensable – as well as very readable. Barbara Tuchman's *The Proud Tower: A Portrait of the World before The War* (1966) is also dated, but has all the ambition, narrative sweep and exhilarating readability to be expected from the author of the classic account of the opening weeks of the Great War, *The Guns of August* (1962) (a.k.a. *August 1914*). G. R. Searle's *A New England? Peace and War 1886–1918* (2005) is a massive and authoritative narrative history of the vast social and political changes from the Victorian age to the end of the Great War.

The following, which all have the word 'Edwardian' in their titles, in fact stretch the term beyond the reign of the eponymous King Edward VII, which ended in 1910, and cover the country up to and sometimes beyond 1914. *The Edwardian Crisis: Britain 1901–1914* by David Powell (1996) and *The Last Years of Liberal England, 1900–1914* by K. W. W. Aikin (1972) both follow Dangerfield in seeing the Edwardian era as a time of ferment and crisis rather than stable serenity. *Life in Edwardian England* by Robert Cecil (1969) shows the gross social disparities of the age, along with beguiling images of life as lived by the leisured classes.

The novelist J. B. Priestley's *The Edwardians* (1970) is a typically acerbic and opinionated review by an astute observer who experienced the era in person. *Edwardian England: Society and Politics, 1901–1915* by Donald Read (1972) is a wide-ranging survey. Read also edited *Edwardian England* (1982), a stimulating collection of essays on such subjects as Edwardian socialism, the Edwardian Empire and the coming of the Great War. Brian Dobbs's *Edwardians at Play: Sport, 1890–1914* (1973) surveys the explosion in organized sport in the era.

The Edwardian Turn of Mind by Samuel Hynes (1968) is a classic American academic consideration of an age which 'began as a garden party and ended in unparalleled slaughter'.

Another American view, John Paterson's *Edwardians: London Life and Letters, 1901–1914* (1996) concentrates on the capital's artistic and literary scene and its leading personalities, while George L. Bernstein's *Liberalism and Liberal Politics in Edwardian England* (1986) argues that the Liberal party was doomed by the rise of the working class, despite efforts to reinvent itself as a neo-socialist 'New Liberalism'. Kenneth O. Morgan's *The Age of Lloyd George: The Liberal Party and British Politics, 1890–1929* (1971, 1978) examines the decline of the party in the context of the career of its last star.

5. LINERS

Robin Gardiner's *History of the White Star Line* (2002) tells the story of the line that operated the tragic *Titanic* and *Britannic*. The *Empress of Ireland* disaster is recounted in several books, including Logan Marshall, *The Tragic Story of the Empress of Ireland* (1914, 1972); James Croall, *Fourteen Minutes: The Sinking of the Empress of Ireland* (1980); H. P. Wood, *Till We Meet Again: The Sinking of the Empress of Ireland* (1982); and David Zeni, *Forgotten Empress: An Edwardian Liner* (1998).

6. POETS

For the Dymock poets see *The Muse Colony: Rupert Brooke, Edward Thomas, Robert Frost and Friends – Dymock 1914* by Keith Clark (1992); and *Now All Roads Lead to France: The Last Years of Edward Thomas* by Matthew Hollis (2011) – an especially sympathetic and sensitive treatment. For Rupert Brooke see my own *Rupert Brooke: Life, Death and Myth* (1999; 2004; revised re-issue forthcoming from Head of Zeus, 2014); and the more adulatory *Rupert Brooke* by Christopher Hassall (1964), who also wrote the unrevealing official life of Eddie Marsh – *Edward Marsh: Patron of the Arts* (1959). Eddie surely awaits a livelier and more daring Boswell.

Siegfried Sassoon has three modern biographies: *Siegfried Sassoon: The Making of a War Poet* by Jean Moorcroft Wilson (1998); *Siegfried Sassoon* by John Stuart Roberts (1999); and *Siegfried Sassoon: A Biography* by Max

Egremont (2005). For Julian Grenfell see *Julian Grenfell* by Nicholas Mosley (1976).

For the tiresome, over-hyped and really quite poisonous Bloomsbury Set, see Peter Stansky's over-admiring *On or About December 1910: Early Bloomsbury and its Intimate World* (1996); or the more objective *Lytton Strachey: A Biography* by Michael Holroyd (1968). Holroyd also wrote another essential life – *Augustus John* (1975). Though enormous, they are lively and unmissable portraits of two very different but key figures of the arts in the Edwardian age.

7. PAINTERS

David Boyd Haycock's *A Crisis of Brilliance: Five Young British Artists and the Great War* (2009) is itself a brilliant group biography and critical study of the quintet of young artists who studied at the Slade School and whose lives were made or marred by the war: Stanley Spencer, Paul Nash, Mark Gertler, Christopher Nevinson and Dora Carrington.

Percy Wyndham Lewis, wayward ringmaster of the avant-garde revels and rebels in pre-war artistic and literary London, has in recent years begun to attract the serious attention his erratic genius deserves. *The Enemy* by Jeffrey Meyers (1980) and *Some Sort of Genius* by Paul O'Keeffe (2000) are both valuable biographies, while Lewis's own memoir, *Blasting and Bombardiering* (reprinted 1992), though unreliable, is as lively and original as its author. Lewis's contemporary, rival and sometime disciple Christopher Nevinson wrote an equally unreliable but interesting autobiography: *Paint and Prejudice* (1938).

The intellectual powerhouse behind the new art, the philosopher T. E. Hulme, was honoured by an excellent modern life – *The Short Sharp Life of T. E. Hulme* by Robert Ferguson (2002).

Three books which examine the culture spawned by London's pre-war revolution in the arts are *Rites of Spring: The Great War and the Birth of the Modern Age* by Modris Eksteins (1989); *A War Imagined: The First World War and English Culture* by Samuel Hynes (1990); and *A Terrible Beauty: British Artists in the First World War* by Paul Gough (2010).

8. CLUBS AND COTERIES

For pre-war social sets, see Nicolson, *The Perfect Summer* and McLeod, *The Last Summer*, both cited above, and *Unquiet Souls: The Indian Summer of the British Aristocracy, 1880–1918* by Angela Lambert (1984). *Raymond Asquith: Life and Letters*, edited by John Jolliffe (1980), gives a picture of the brilliant but cynical eldest son of the prime minister, who led the Corrupt Coterie. For a fuller portrayal of the Asquiths and their set, read *The Asquiths* by Colin Clifford (2002), an indiscreet and gossipy account of a privileged but troubled first family.

For the Cave of the Golden Calf and similar pre-war 'decadence', see *Cruel Banquet: The Life and Loves of Frida Strindberg* by Monica Strauss (2000) and *Wilde's Last Stand* by Philip Hoare (1997).

9. THE LAST SEASON,
10. DESCENT INTO THE DARK

There are innumerable studies of the lead-up to the Great War on both a European and a local London level. Recent additions to the literature include the much-acclaimed *The Sleepwalkers: How Europe Went to War in 1914* by Christopher Clark (2012), a well-written but not entirely convincing revisionist account that seeks to shift the main weight of guilt for the war's outbreak from Germany to Serbia. Sean McMeekin's *July 1914: Countdown to War* (2013) agrees, though is less blatantly Teutonophile than Clark.

Europe's Last Summer: Why the World Went to War in 1914 by David Fromkin (2004), in complete contrast, lays the blame for the conflict squarely on the aggression of the Kaiser's Germany. *The War that Ended Peace: How Europe Abandoned Peace for the First World War* by Margaret Macmillan (2013) widens the focus to seek causes in social discontent and technological change as well as in political, military and diplomatic decisions.

Dance of the Furies: Europe and the Outbreak of World War One by Michael S. Neiberg (2011) seeks to prove that the common picture of Europe's masses seething with nationalist and patriotic passion on the eve of war is a myth:

loyalties, argues Neiberg, were by no means so clear cut, and the descent into war was largely the fault of European elites. A similar argument is advanced by Clive Ponting in *Thirteen Days: Diplomacy and Disaster – The Countdown to the Great War* (2002); Ponting, like Clark, acquits Germany of war guilt and blames the war on events in the Balkans and diplomatic non-communication.

The Origins of the First World War, edited by H. W. Koch (1972, 1977), represents German historians' reaction to the explosive findings of Fritz Fischer in his *Griff nach der Weltmacht* ('Bid for World Power' (1961); published in Britain in 1967 under the title *Germany's Aims in the First World War*) that the war had been caused primarily by a deliberate German decision to risk catastrophe in its drive for world power.

The Origins of the First World War, edited by by Annika Mombauer (2002), is another essay collection representing current historiography on the war, and broadly accepts Fischer's thesis that the main blame rests with Germany.

11. NOW GOD BE THANKED...

For D.H. Lawrence see *D.H. Lawrence's Nightmare: the writer and his circle in Years of the Great War* by Paul Delany (1978).

Apart from his widow Helen's memoirs of their marriage *As It Was* (1926) and *World Without End* (1931) which are moving but, since they were written as therapy for her grief, idolatory and unrevealing about the tensions between them; and his platonic friend Eleanor Farjeon's similarly hero-worshipping *Edward Thomas: the last four years* (1958); there are several biographies of Edward Thomas, notably by John Moore (1939); William Cooke (1970); Jan Marsh (1978); and R. George Thomas (1965), but all have been superseded by Matthew Hollis's superb *Now All Roads Lead to France* (2011) a sensitive and honest biography which shows Thomas as a depressive, tortured genius.

For 'Ged' Garvin, see *We Hope to Get Word Tomorrow: The Garvin Family Letters, 1914–16* edited by Mark Pottle and John Ledingham (2006).

For German atrocities in Belgium in the Great War, see *German Atrocities 1914–18: A History of Denial* by John Horne and Alan Kramer (2001); *The Rape of Belgium: The Untold Story of World War One* by Larry Zuckerman (2004); and *Rehearsals: the German Army in Belgium, August 1914* by Jeff Lipkes (2007). All three meticulously documented modern books make it abundantly clear that the German Army's atrocious behaviour during its invasion of Belgium was similar in spirit if not in scale to their genocide in Poland in 1939, and that Allied propaganda on the subject was, to a large extent, true.

12. FIRST BLOOD

The actual fighting in 1914, like the war's outbreak, is covered in manifold accounts, of which Barbara Tuchman's *The Guns of August* (1962) is probably the most widely known. Edward Spears's *Liaison 1914* (1930, 1999) tells the story of the BEF's retreat from the viewpoint of a man with a ringside seat: Spears was the French-speaking British liaison officer with Lanrezac's army and witnessed the fraught meetings between Sir John French and the French command. Correlli Barnett's *The Swordbearers* (1963, 2000) is an iconoclastic military historian's caustic view of how the Schlieffen Plan failed and the errors of the German command cost them the quick victory they had counted on. *The Old Contemptibles: The British Expeditionary Force, 1914* by Robin Neillands (2004) is a solid, reliable account of the BEF's 1914 campaign, from Mons and Le Cateau to the Marne and Ypres.

EPILOGUE: CHRISTMAS 1914

This quartet of books covers similar ground and they can all be recommended: *Christmas Truce: The Western Front, December 1914* by Malcolm Brown and Shirley Seaton (1999); *Silent Night: The Remarkable 1914 Christmas Truce* by Stanley Weintraub (2001); *Christmas in the Trenches* by Alan Wakefield (2006); and *Meetings in No Man's Land: Christmas 1914 and Fraternization in the Great War* by Marc Ferro, Malcolm Brown, Rémy Cazals and Olaf Mueller (2007).

Acknowledgements

I am grateful to my agent Georgina Capel, my publisher Anthony Cheetham and my incomparable editor Richard Milbank for their help in bringing this book to fruition. My family and friends have also assisted in a too protracted birth. My thanks to them all.

SOURCES OF QUOTED MATERIAL

Page 20
Osbert Sitwell: from *Great Morning* (1948).
Philip Larkin: from his poem 'Wants', which first appeared in the collection *The Less Deceived* (1955).
J. B. Priestley: from *The Edwardians* (1970).

Page 22
Rudyard Kipling: from 'Recessional', composed on the occasion of Queen Victoria's Diamond Jubilee (1897).

Page 122
Frances Cornford: from her poem 'Youth', in *Poems* (1910).

Page 127
John Wain: in *Georgian Poetry 1911–22, The Critical Heritage* (1997), edited by Timothy Rogers.

Page 129
Robert Frost: quoted in *Now All Roads Lead to France* (2011), by Matthew Hollis.

Page 135
W. W. Gibson: from his poem 'The Golden Room', published in his collection *The Golden Room and Other Poems* (1927).

Page 137
Robert Frost: from his poem 'The Road Not Taken', published in his collection *Mountain Interval* (1916).

Page 140
Filippo Marinetti: Futurist Manifesto quoted in *Some Sort of Genius: A Life of Wyndham Lewis* (2000), by Paul O'Keeffe.

Page 149
Wyndham Lewis: quoted in *Some Sort of Genius: A Life of Wyndham Lewis* (2000), by Paul O'Keeffe.

Page 163
Osbert Sitwell: quoted in *The Edwardians* (1970), by J. B. Priestley.

Page 175
Raymond Asquith: letter to his wife.

Page 182
J. B. Priestley: from *The Edwardians* (1970).

Page 201
Winston Churchill: from *The World Crisis, vol. 1, 1911–1914* (1923).

Page 212
Rupert Brooke: from his poems 'The Soldier' and 'Peace', published in the collection *1914 & Other Poems* (1915).

Page 213
Rupert Brooke: from a letter to Stanley Spencer, June 1914.

Page 214
Robert Graves: from *Goodbye to All That* (1929).
D. H. Lawrence: quoted in *D. H. Lawrence's Nightmare: The Writer and his Circle in the Years of the Great War* (1978), by Paul Delany.

Page 216
Edward Thomas: from Thomas's notebook, quoted in *Now All Roads Lead to France* (2011), by Matthew Hollis.

Page 219
Henry Williamson: quoted in *Henry Williamson and the First World War* (2004), by Anne Williamson.

Page 220
Philip Larkin: from his poem 'MCMXIV', published in the collection *The Whitsun Weddings* (1964).

Page 236
George Roupell: quoted in *The Great War: 1914–1918* (2013) by Peter Hart.
Tom Bradley: quoted in *The Great War: 1914–1918* (2013) by Peter Hart.

Page 248
Bruce Bairnsfather: from *Carry on, Sergeant!* (1927).

Page 250
Thomas Painting: quoted in *Forgotten Voices of the Great War* (2002) by Max Arthur.

Page 252
Warwick Squire: quoted in *Christmas in the Trenches* (2006) by Alan Wakefield.
Harry Dillon: quoted in *Christmas in the Trenches* (2006) by Alan Wakefield.

Page 254
Clifford Lane: quoted in *Forgotten Voices of the Great War* (2002) by Max Arthur.
Henry Williamson: quoted in *Christmas in the Trenches* (2006) by Alan Wakefield.

PICTURE CREDITS

The Publishers wish to thank the following for permission to reproduce images in this book:

British Library: page 32.

Corbis: pages 70–71, 77, 79, 104–5, 109, 114–15, 206–7.

Getty Images: pages 6–7, 8–9, 11, 13, 14–15, 17, 18, 22–3, 26, 29, 30–31, 37, 41, 44–5, 47, 51, 53, 54–5, 60–61, 65, 67, 69, 86–7, 90–91, 93, 95, 98, 101, 103, 107, 113, 117, 131, 133, 143, 147, 153, 169, 172–3, 174–5, 176–7, 178–9, 181, 185, 187, 192–3, 194–5, 197, 200, 205, 217, 225, 226, 241, 245, 246–7, 258–9.

Imperial War Museum: pages 2, 209, 210–11, 218–19, 221, 223, 228–9, 231, 234, 237, 239, 251, 253, 255, 257.

Museum of London: pages 74–5, 83.

Museum of London/Wyndham Lewis Memorial Trust: page 162.

The National Portrait Gallery: pages 120–121, 123, 155.

Tate London: pages 138–9, 144–5, 158–9.

Wikimedia Commons: pages 126, 157.